Introduction to LISP and Symbol Manipulation

Sharam Hekmatpour
The Open University, UK

PRENTICE HALL
New York   London   Toronto   Sydney   Tokyo

First published 1988 by
Prentice Hall International (UK) Ltd,
66 Wood Lane End, Hemel Hempstead,
Hertfordshire, HP2 4RG
A division of
Simon & Schuster Internatioal Group

© 1988 Prentice Hall International (UK) Ltd

All rights reserved. No part of this publication may be
reproduced, stored in a retrieval system, or transmitted,
in any form or by any means, electronic, mechanical,
photocopying, recording or otherwise, without prior
permission, in writing, from the publisher.
For permission within the United States of America
contact Prentice Hall Inc., Englewood Cliffs, NJ 07632.

Printed and bound in Great Britain at the
University Press, Cambridge.

Library of Congress Cataloging-in-Publication Data

Hekmatpour, S. (Sharam), 1961-
   An introduction to Lisp and symbol manipulation/
     S. Hekmatpour   p.   cm.
   Bibliography: p.
   Includes index.
   ISBN 0-13-486192-2
   1. LISP (Computer program language)   I. Title.
QA76.73.L23H46 1988
005.13'3–dc 19   87-30862

British Library Cataloguing in Publication Data

Hekmatpour, S.
   An introduction to Lisp and symbol
   manipulation.
   1. LISP (Computer program language)
   I. Title
   005.13'3   QA76.73.L23

ISBN 0-13-486192-2

1 2 3 4 5   92 91 90 89 88

ISBN 0-13-486192-2

To my parents

Contents

Preface — xiii
    History — xiii
    Organisation of this book — xiv

1 Introduction — 1
  1.1 Why LISP? — 1
  1.2 The LISP interpreter — 4
  1.3 Symbolic expressions — 5
  1.4 Evaluation — 7
      Binding symbols — 9
      Suppressing evaluation — 11
      Enforcing evaluation — 12
  1.5 Indentation and comments — 14
  1.6 Special symbols — 14
  1.7 Errors and termination — 15
  1.8 Summary — 16
      Projects — 17

2 Primitives — 18
  2.1 List manipulation — 18
      Decomposing lists — 18
      Composing lists — 21
      Transforming lists — 23
      Extracting from lists — 24
  2.2 *Set* versus *setq* — 26
  2.3 Predicates — 26
      Conjunctions and disjunctions — 29
      Identity — 30
  2.4 Summary — 32
      Projects — 33

3 User-defined Functions — 34
  3.1 Defining functions using *defun* — 34
      Arguments and parameters — 37
      Structure of defun — 37
      Free and bound variables — 38
      Dynamic and static scoping — 39

	3.2	Use of conditionals	40
		Structure of cond	42
		Super brackets	42
		Other conditionals	43
	3.3	Anonymous functions	46
		The let *construct*	47
	3.4	Other ways of calling functions	49
		Functions as arguments	50
		Argument lists as arguments	51
	3.5	Summary	52
		Projects	53
4	**Storage Principles**		**55**
	4.1	Representation of s-expressions	55
		Cons-cell allocation	57
		Eq *revisited*	59
	4.2	Destructive primitives	60
		Destructive composition and transformation	60
		Changing head and tail	62
		Circular lists	63
	4.3	Storage management	65
		Garbage collection	66
	4.4	Dotted pairs	67
	4.5	Summary	68
		Project	68
5	**Recursion and Iteration**		**69**
	5.1	Recursion	69
		Tail recursion	71
		Multi-arm recursion	72
		Mutual recursion	74
	5.2	Iteration	76
		Prog-*based iteration*	77
		Do-*based iteration*	79
	5.3	Mapping functions	81
		Mapcar	81
		Mapc	83
		Mapcan	84
	5.4	Recursion versus iteration	84
	5.5	Summary	85
		Projects	86

Contents

6	**Input and Output**		**87**
	6.1	Ordinary I/O	87
		Strange atoms and strings	88
	6.2	External I/O	91
	6.3	Pretty printing	92
		Saving and loading LISP programs	93
	6.4	The LISP top level	94
	6.5	Summary	95
		Projects	96

7	**Macros and Other Functions**		**97**
	7.1	Defining fexprs	97
	7.2	Defining macros	99
		Data manipulation	100
		Use of defmacro	101
		Use of backquote	102
		The let *and* do *macros*	102
	7.3	Name clashes	104
	7.4	Defining lexprs	107
	7.5	General structure of definitions	108
	7.6	Summary	109
		Project	110

8	**Further Topics**		**111**
	8.1	Property lists	111
	8.2	Association lists	114
	8.3	Array structures	115
		Hunk structures	117
	8.4	String and symbol manipulation	118
	8.5	Error handling	121
	8.6	*Catch* and *throw*	123
	8.7	Summary	125
		Project	125

9	**Advanced Topics**		**127**
	9.1	Debugging and tracing	127
		Interrogating the stack	128
		Using a debugger	129
		Using a tracer	132
		Code instrumentation	133
	9.2	Compilation	135
		Compiler options	136

		Compiler declarations	137
	9.3	Use of foreign functions	139
	9.4	Autorun and snapshot	141
	9.5	Summary	143
		Projects	144

10 Programming Style — 145

	10.1	Software design	145
		Design iteration	146
		On decomposition	148
		Design criteria	149
	10.2	Documentation	151
	10.3	Functional programming	153
	10.4	Object-oriented programming	155
	10.5	Summary	156
		Project	156

11 Pattern Matching — 157

	11.1	Introduction	157
	11.2	Pattern symbols	159
	11.3	Pattern variables	162
	11.4	Summary	165
		Projects	166

12 Data Structures for Searching — 167

	12.1	Tree structures	167
		Depth-first search	168
		Breadth-first search	169
		Binary trees	171
	12.2	Table structures	173
		Binary search	173
		Hash-and-link (HAL) structures	175
	12.3	Graph structures	178
		Notation	179
		Graph search	179
		And-or *graphs*	184
	12.4	Summary	189
		Projects	189

13 Symbolic Differentiation — 192

	13.1	Introduction	192

	13.2	A differentiation program	193
	13.3	Notation conversion	196
	13.4	Notation reversion	201
	13.5	Symbolic reduction	202
	13.6	Summary	206
		Projects	207
14	**Functional Extensions**		**208**
	14.1	Finite sets	208
		Set operators	209
		Implicit sets	213
	14.2	Finite sequences	215
		Sequence operators	216
		Implicit sequences	218
	14.3	Finite mappings	220
		Mapping operators	220
		Implicit mappings	223
	14.4	Relations	225
	14.5	Equality operators	229
	14.6	Logic	231
	14.7	Pretty printing objects	235
	14.8	Summary of notation	239
	14.9	Examples of functional programs	241
		Quick sort	242
		Relation types	242
		A cross-usage program	244
	14.10	Summary	248
		Projects	248
	Appendix 1	**Summary of LISP Functions**	**251**
	Appendix 2	**Answers to Exercises**	**268**
	Bibliography		**295**
	Index		**299**

Preface

Certain programming tasks involve the manipulation of symbols rather than numbers. Take algebraic equations for instance. They are composed of various symbols such as variables, constants, and operators. A program which is supposed to solve such equations analytically, clearly needs to be able to do symbol manipulation. Being heavily geared towards number crunching, traditional programming languages such as FORTRAN and Pascal are inadequate for such purposes; LISP is the answer.

The material in this book is organized as a tutorial which, step by step, introduces the reader to the LISP language and its applications. The book is therefore suitable for undergraduates/postgraduates in computing, and computing professionals who have had little or no past experience of LISP programming. No knowledge of other programming languages is assumed. However, readers who have had some exposure to programming and are familiar with the fundamental concepts (e.g. variables) are likely to be able to go through the material in a shorter period of time. Readers who are already proficient in another programming language should have no difficulty reading and fully absorbing the book in a few weeks. Care has been taken to ensure that each concept is introduced before it is actually used. Consequently, the book should also be useful as a teach-yourself guide to those who are learning LISP out of personal interest, and who have no access to formal lectures.

History

LISP was invented in the late 1950s by John McCarthy and is in fact one of the oldest programming languages still in active existence. Having gone through three decades of evolution, it has now matured into a serious and widely-acknowledged language. The success of LISP is marked by a large and rapidly expanding user community, and by numerous international interest groups and conferences which are devoted to the subject. LISP is best known for its high productivity, its potential for the modern parallel hardware architectures, and its long-established links with research into artificial intelligence.

Probably no other programming language has had as colorful a history as LISP. The wide interest in the language over the past two decades has resulted in its development in a number of directions. This has lead to numerous LISP dialects, some even fairly remote from the once regarded standard LISP (i.e., LISP 1.5 [McCarthy 1962]) which is now practically obsolete.

A number of LISP dialects have evolved successfully over the past few years and now coexist. Amongst these, MacLISP [Moon 1974], InterLISP [Teitelman 1974], Franz LISP [Foderaro 1983], Common LISP [Steele 1984], and Scheme [Abelson ans Sussman 1985] appear to be most popular and widely used. Although attempts have been made to standardize the language (e.g., the proposed standard for Common LISP), no credible agreement has yet been reached by the software community. Indeed, the current trends suggest that, far from being standardized, LISP dialects are only likely to increase in number and variety in the future.

LISP is now available on numerous computer systems, ranging from mainframes and minis to workstations and even microcomputers. Much of the shortcomings of the earlier versions of LISP have been overcome by recent advances in hardware and software technology. As a result, earlier criticisms of the language, such as slowness and high memory consumption, are no longer valid. Modern LISP systems, especially those based on dedicated hardware, compete extremely well in terms of performance with other programming languages. Also, some very powerful programming environments have been built around LISP. The technology has improved to such an extent that some LISP environments are now used in the capacity of a complete operating system.

Organization of this book

The organization of this book is as follows. Chapter 1 introduces the basics of LISP. It describes symbolic expressions as the main medium for creating LISP programs and data structures, and evaluation – the process through which LISP executes programs. Chapter 2 describes the fundamental primitives of LISP for manipulating symbolic expressions. User-defined functions are discussed in Chapter 3, which also describes the use of conditionals and anonymous functions. Chapter 4 looks at the storage principles of LISP and describes how symbolic expressions are internally represented, manipulated, and managed. The objective of this chapter is to provide the reader with a conceptual view of the storage mechanisms in order to clarify the way some of the LISP functions (especially the destructive ones) work. Chapter 5 deals with recursion and iteration – two important and useful techniques for formulating repeated computations. LISP facilities for performing explicit input and output operations are described in Chapter 6. Three additional categories of functions are described in Chapter 7. The main focus of this chapter is on macros – a facility which allows the user to extend LISP by defining new constructs. Any remaining topics which do not naturally fit into the earlier chapters are discussed in Chapter 8. These include a number of data structures (e.g., property lists and arrays), and some issues concerning error handling and unconventional styles of control flow. Chapter 9 looks at a number of advanced topics, such as debugging, tracing, and compilation of LISP programs. Chapter 10 focuses on the issue of programming style: how to write clear programs.

The last four chapters describe some applications of LISP through actual case studies, and also illustrate the issues covered in Chapter 10. Chapter 11 introduces pattern matching – a technique commonly used in artificial intelligence – and illustrates how a practical pattern matcher can be developed in LISP. Chapter 12 describes a number of useful data structures, and uses these to illustrate various search strategies. Chapter 13 guides the reader through the development of a symbolic differentiation program which can work out the derivative of some nontrivial functions analytically. The final chapter introduces a number of new data types and shows how these may be used to support an elegant, purely functional style of programming in LISP.

Each chapter is divided into a number of sections; some sections are further divided into subsections. Most sections are followed by one or more exercises which are intended to familiarize the reader with the topics covered in those sections. Sample solutions to all such exercises are provided in Appendix 2. All chapters begin with an overview and end with a summary of the main points, followed by a set of projects. The projects are larger undertakings than normal exercises, and may be skipped during a first reading. A summary of the LISP functions used in this book is provided in Appendix 1, which the reader may consult as he reads through. The summary also furnishes some additional, useful information such as whether a function is pure or destructive, and how universal a function is (i.e., whether it is likely to be different in different LISP dialects).

Needless to say, the best way to learn LISP, and indeed any other programming language, is by actual practice involving the use of a computer. Consequently, each description of a LISP facility or feature in this book is followed by one or more examples in the form of a small function or program together with the results of its execution. The reader is strongly advised to both read and try these examples for himself, and to try to devise a few of his own. The end-of-section exercises should also be treated similarly.

As far as concrete examples are concerned, the dialect used in this book will be Franz LISP – the standard LISP dialect for the widely available UNIX[1] system. Throughout the book, however, emphasis will be on principles rather than very dialect-specific information. In this way, we hope, the book will be useful to a larger audience, including those who have access to other LISP dialects. Of course, certain topics (e.g., compilation) cannot be taught in general terms, as these vary considerably from one LISP system to another. Such discussions are nevertheless included to give at least a taste of the kind of facilities that are offered by LISP systems. The idea is that once you know what is available for use, you can easily obtain the exact details from the user manual of your system.

S. Hekmatpour
Milton Keynes, November 1987

---

1 UNIX is a trademark of AT&T Bell Laboratories.

Chapter 1

Introduction

The purpose of this chapter is two-fold: firstly, to provide some motivation as to why LISP is an important language for symbol manipulation, and secondly, to introduce you to some of the elementary concepts of LISP. We shall describe symbolic expressions and their constituents, that is, lists and atoms, as the primary medium for writing LISP programs and creating data. We shall also describe evaluation, the process by which LISP executes programs. Different categories of atoms will be described during the course of our discussion. In particular, we shall see how symbolic atoms can play the dual role of functions and variables. The use of functions will be illustrated with some simple examples involving the arithmetic functions of LISP.

1.1 Why LISP?

Imagine yourself walking into a university library, looking for a book. You find out that the library has just installed a computerized system to assist readers in locating publications. Excited by this news, you sit down behind a terminal and start a dialog, which goes something like this:

Computer	What can I do for you?
You	I am looking for a book.
Computer	Do you know the name of the author, or the title?
You	No, but I know it's about Ada.
Computer	Do you know the publisher, or the year of publication?
You	I think it's Prentice Hall, probably around 1985.
Computer	The closest book to these descriptions that I know of is: Watt, D. A., *et al.* 1987, *Ada Language and Methodology*, Prentice Hall, London. Is this any good?
You	Yes, where is it located?

1

Computer   Second floor, shelf 21, under class 001.642.
You   Do you know of any other book on Ada?
Computer   Yes, 16 others. Do you want me to list them out?
             ...

Though intelligent and formidably complex such systems may appear at first sight, the principles behind them are relatively straightforward, and sometimes even trivial. The apparent complexities untangle once we start thinking in terms of a medium that frees our mind from unnecessary, low-level detail, and allows us to concentrate on the real issues. LISP is one such medium.

Through the years, LISP has gradually become a synonym for symbol processing – programming with symbols. But programming in other languages such as FORTRAN and Pascal also involves the use of symbols: variables, functions, and the like. So what is so special about LISP?

Well, many things, but most important of all is this: symbols in LISP are not just convenient names for numeric values; they are real symbols, they are stored as symbols, and can represent symbols. Furthermore, they can be grouped easily, using list structures which may be arbitrarily long and complex, but are conveniently manipulated: taken apart, put together, transformed, and so on.

A more convincing argument is obtained by comparing the facilities offered by a conventional programming language to those of LISP for developing a symbol manipulation-oriented program, such as the library example above. Let us assume that we all know a bit about Pascal – the wonderful language of orthodox programmers – or some other similar programming language. Now, take the second sentence in the dialog above and think how we can analyze it. To analyze the sentence, we need to represent it. A string is the obvious choice:

```
"I am looking for a book"
```

To analyze this, we need to know what words it contains, so we have to break it down into words. To do so, we probably write a procedure that extracts individual words from the sentence. But we still do not know what each word is, so we need a way of comparing words against those that we already know about, i.e., words that constitute our dictionary. This requires another procedure. The next problem is that of organizing the dictionary. Where do we store it? How do we store the attributes of each word (e.g., whether it is a verb, noun, pronoun, etc.)? What about different tenses? What about ...?

It is obvious that before addressing the real issues – how to 'understand' a sentence and how to respond 'intelligently' to it – we are already lost in endless detail. LISP gets us out of this mess.

First of all, representing a sentence is trivial; a simple list will do the job (Do not worry what exactly these LISP fragments mean yet, you will learn them later; for the moment, just observe the simplicity):

1.1 Why LISP?

```
(I am looking for a book)
```

Now, if we call this list `sentence`, we can readily extract individual words:

(nthelem 1 sentence)	gives	I
(nthelem 2 sentence)	gives	am
(nthelem 3 sentence)	gives	looking
...	...	...

Making a dictionary is just as easy. Take a word, `look`, say; we can load it with as many attributes as we like:

```
(putprop 'look 'verb 'class)      ; look is a verb
(putprop 'look 'present 'tense)   ; look is present tense
(putprop 'look 'looked 'past)     ; its past tense is looked
...                               ; ...
```

To find out whether a word is `look`, all that we have to do is this:

```
(eq word 'look)
```

To find out the past tense of a verb, we just say,

```
(get verb 'past)
```

and so on.

Note that without actually writing any program yet, we have got rid of much of the nitty gritty, all because LISP has just the right facilities which are essential for working with symbols, and which we would otherwise have had to create ourselves.

The above example is typical of the kind of problems LISP is exceptionally good at: *symbol manipulation*. When working with LISP, one always works with symbolic expressions. The sentence,

```
(I am looking for a book)
```

for example, is a symbolic expression. The words in this sentence are also symbolic expressions. One may refer to this sentence as data. However, LISP does not distinguish between data and programs, programs are themselves symbolic expressions. This remarkable feature of LISP leads to much simplicity and flexibility. For example, one can write programs that compose other programs as easily as data.

Add to all these an interactive programming environment (as all LISP systems are) and you have a highly productive tool which is capable of doing very complex and novel computations in often a few lines of code. You might think that given so many powerful features, LISP must be a complex language and very difficult to learn. On the contrary, it turns out to be one of the easiest programming languages in existence.

In the rest of this chapter you will be introduced to some of the fundamental and elementary concepts of LISP. Before starting our discussion, however, it is necessary to take a brief look at the LISP interpreter. This is the main computer-based tool that you will be using for writing your LISP programs.

1.2 The LISP interpreter

A LISP interpreter is an interactive program which takes your LISP definitions (typed interactively at a terminal say), executes them immediately, and displays the endresults. Access to a LISP interpreter is a must if you want to learn LISP, so make sure you have one available for use during the course of reading this book.

To start the interpreter you should type the appropriate command (this will depend on your machine and the particular LISP system you are using). For example, in UNIX the command `lisp` will load and run the Franz LISP interpreter as shown below:

```
$ lisp
Franz Lisp, Opus 38.79
->
```

The interpreter usually comes up with a prompt (-> in this case), indicating that it is ready for your commands. What happens next is very much like a dialog. You send your requests to LISP by typing appropriate commands, which LISP interprets by doing the necessary calculations. If your request is a valid one LISP will display the result; otherwise, it will come up with an error message, telling you what has gone wrong. For example, to add the numbers 10 and 20 you may type (user input is printed in italics):

```
-> (plus 10 20)
30
->
```

LISP does the calculation and comes up with the answer 30, followed by another prompt indicating that it is ready for your next request. Throughout the rest of this book we shall use this style of dialog for our examples.

1.3 Symbolic expressions

Central to LISP is the notion of symbolic expressions, commonly referred to as *s-expressions*. These are the main medium for creating programs and data. An s-expression is either an *atom* or a *list*. We saw an example of an s-expression in the previous section

    (plus 10 20)

which is itself a list, consisting of three atoms: plus, 10, and 20. Lists are written using brackets and always start with a left bracket and end with a right bracket. Each object inside a list is said to be an *element* of that list. For example, plus and 10 are two elements of the list above. List elements are themselves s-expressions. As a result, lists may be nested. For example,

    (plus (plus 10 20) (plus 22 18))
    (plus (plus 10 (plus 1 2)) 90)

are both valid lists. Note that the number of left and right brackets in a list must always match. So,

    (plus 10 (plus 1 4)
    plus (plus 2 5))

are not valid lists.

A list can always be conveniently regarded as a tree, where the elements of the list correspond to the nodes of the tree, and the atoms in the list correspond to the leaves of the tree. For example, the list

    (plus 5 (plus 8 12))

can be represented by the following tree.

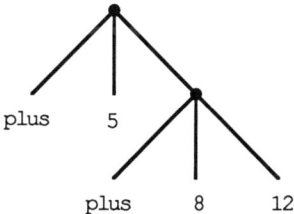

Note that a list does not necessarily have to contain elements. So, () is a perfectly valid list, and is usually called the *empty list* or *nil*.

An atom is either a *symbolic atom* (e.g., plus) or a *numeric atom* (e.g., 10).

Symbolic atoms consist of a sequence of characters and roughly correspond to identifiers in other programming languages. However, almost any character may be used in an atom. For example,

```
man   r2d2   6men   %%   &@x   1$s+
```

are all valid symbolic atoms. A numeric atom is simply a number which may be an integer or a real. The former is usually called a *fixed* number; the latter is called a *float* number. For example,

```
100   23   0   1   566
```

are all fixed numbers, while

```
1.045   0.998   188.665   1.0
```

are all float numbers. Symbolic and numeric atoms are often referred to as *symbols* and *numbers* for short respectively.

The general structure of an s-expression may be specified hierarchically and recursively as shown in Figure 1.1.

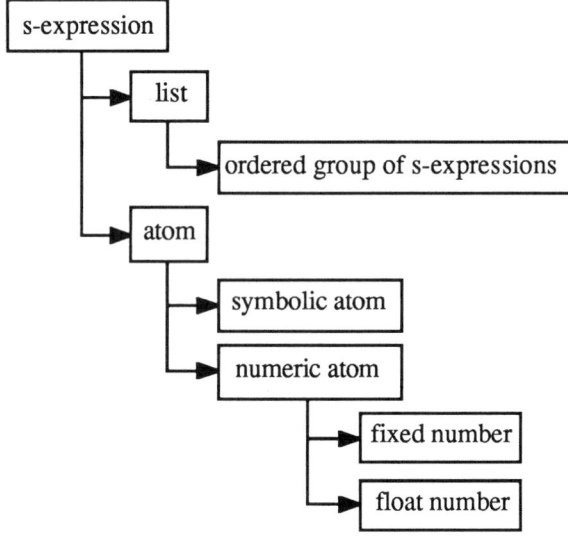

Figure 1.1 The general structure of an s-expression.

1.4 Evaluation

EXERCISE 1.1
State which of the following is an s-expression, and if so, whether it is a list or an atom.

```
10                    (10 20)
(5 ())                plus (2 5)
'plus                 '(list of atoms)
Jack                  atom
list                  10-20*6
*s*t*a*r*             $%s=k
5=10                  -+-+
```

1.4 Evaluation

Programs in LISP are written as s-expressions and computation progresses by a process of evaluating these expressions. For example, when given

(plus 10 20)

LISP will evaluate this s-expression by treating plus as a *function* and applying it to the remaining elements of the list. So when evaluating a list, the first element will always be treated as a function and subsequent elements as *arguments* to that function. Of course, to be intelligible to LISP, a function must have already been defined. The function plus, for example, is a predefined function in LISP. There are many other such functions. Here are a few for doing arithmetic:

```
-> (difference 108 22)
86
-> (times 8 10)
80
-> (quotient 9 3)
3
->
```

Two points need further explanation. The first point concerns the number of arguments of a function; this may be fixed or variable. For example, all arithmetic functions described above can take any number of arguments:

```
-> (plus 12 3 2)
17
-> (plus 12)
12
```

```
-> (times 1 2 3 4 5)
120
-> (quotient 200.0 20.0 3.0)
3.333333333333333
-> (quotient)
1
->
```

Some other functions require a fixed number of arguments. For example, the remainder (`remainder`) and the exponent (`expt`) functions require exactly two arguments, while the absolute value (`abs`) and minus (`minus`) functions require exactly one argument:

```
-> (remainder 10 3)
1
-> (expt 3 2)
9
-> (abs -99)
99
-> (minus 10)
-10
->
```

The second point concerns the way function arguments are treated. Most functions (including all those discussed so far) evaluate their arguments. For example in

```
(times 10 20)
```

the function `times` evaluates 10 and 20. By convention, numbers evaluate to themselves, so, in this case, the evaluation is not visible. The following example illustrates the point more clearly:

```
-> (times (plus 2 4) 20)
120
->
```

Here, the evaluation of the first argument of `times` produces the result 6 which is then multiplied by 20 to produce 120.

The use of function applications as arguments to other functions is called *nested application* and is a very common practice in LISP. Functions can be nested to any required depth, as illustrated by the following examples:

1.4 Evaluation

```
-> (plus (times (times 2 3) 3 2) (expt 3 3))
63
-> (minus (minus (minus 1)))
-1
-> (add1 (add1 (sub1 (sub1 0))))
0
-> (expt (expt (expt (plus 1 1) 2) 2) 2)
256
->
```

Binding symbols

So far we have only seen the use of symbols as function names. As one would expect, symbols have other uses too. One such use reflects the similarity of symbols to identifiers in most other programming languages. Symbols may be used to store arbitrary values. This process is known as *symbol binding* and is facilitated by certain LISP functions, most commonly `setq`:

```
-> (setq a 10)
10
->
```

Here, `setq` takes two arguments, the first of which must be a symbol. It first evaluates the second argument and then stores the resulting value in the first argument, and returns this value as its final result. After this function is performed, a is said to be bound to 10. This means that from now on every time we evaluate a we will get 10:

```
-> a
10
->
```

Note that a symbol has no value unless it is explicitly bound to one. For example, if we ask LISP about a new symbol, `six` say, that has not been bound to any value previously, it will produce an error message:

```
-> six
Error: Unbound Variable: six
```

Also note that every time we bind a symbol to a new value the old value will be lost:

```
-> (setq myatom (plus 10 15))
25
```

```
-> myatom
25
-> (setq myatom 99)
99
-> myatom
99
->
```

This phenomenon is known as a *side-effect*. Functions such as setq which cause side-effects are called *impure*, since their effects can not be naturally reversed. The following example shows a more general use of setq:

```
-> (setq x 10 y 20)
20
-> x
10
-> y
20
->
```

This shows that setq can take any even number of arguments and binds the arguments pairwise from left to right. So the above call is equivalent to:

```
(setq x 10)
(setq y 20)
```

Once a symbol is bound it may be used in any subsequent computation (as long as it remains bound to some value) so that we may have:

```
-> (add (times 3 x) (times 2 y))
70
->
```

It is worth mentioning that a symbol may be a function name and, at the same time, be bound to a value.[1] For example, the function times, discussed earlier, may be bound to a value and yet remain a function:

```
-> (setq times 99)
99
```

---

[1] This is the case in most LISP systems (including Franz), but not all.

1.4 Evaluation

```
-> times
99
-> (times 2 times)
198
->
```

LISP distinguishes between these two according to the context within which a symbol is used. The value of a symbol is called its *value binding*. The function identified by a symbol is called its *function binding*. A symbol which has a value binding is often called a (bound) *variable*. A symbol with no value binding, on the other hand, is called an *unbound* symbol (variable).

This dual role of symbols is a useful feature of LISP. As we shall see later on, symbols can be overloaded with yet extra information (e.g., property lists).

Suppressing evaluation

As we have seen so far, LISP attempts to evaluate every s-expression it is given. Often it is desirable to avoid this. This usually arises when we want to represent some data using s-expressions. For example, suppose we want to store a list of prime numbers in *x*:

```
-> (setq x (2 3 5 7))
Error: eval: Undefined function 2
```

Here, LISP tries to evaluate the list (2 3 5 7) and assumes that 2 is a function, since it always assumes that the first item in a list is a function. This obviously fails. The problem can be avoided by the use of a special function called quote. When applied, quote does not evaluate its argument; it simply returns the argument as it is:

```
-> (quote (2 3 5 7))
(2 3 5 7)
-> (setq x (quote (2 3 5 7)))
(2 3 5 7)
-> x
(2 3 5 7)
->
```

The single quote character provides a shorthand for quote. For example,

```
(quote (1 2))
```

may be written as:

```
-> '(1 2)
(1 2)
->
```

The LISP system will in fact, upon reading `'(1 2)`, transform it to `(quote (1 2))`. Any valid LISP object can be quoted to avoid evaluation. So, regardless of whether the symbols `atom1` and `atom2` are bound or not, the following will work:

```
-> 'atom1
atom1
-> (setq atom1 'atom2)
atom2
-> atom1
atom2
->
```

Enforcing evaluation

LISP offers a function called `eval` which does just the reverse of `quote`; it causes an extra evaluation of its argument. `Eval` takes exactly one argument and evaluates it twice: once when `eval` is called and once by `eval` itself. It then returns the final outcome of the evaluation as its result. Here is an example:

```
-> (setq x '(setq y 10))
(setq y 10)
-> x
(setq y 10)
-> (eval x)
10
-> y
10
->
```

This example works as follows. First x is set to the s-expression `(setq y 10)`, which since quoted is not evaluated. Evaluating x confirms this. The call `(eval x)` then evaluates x twice successively. The first evaluation produces `(setq y 10)`, which when evaluated again produces 10, and at the same time binds y to 10.

One must ensure that the argument to `eval`, when evaluated twice, will produce a meaningful result. Otherwise, an error should be expected:

1.4 Evaluation

```
-> (setq x '(disaster))
(disaster)
-> (eval x)
Error: eval: Undefined function disaster
```

Eval is one of the most useful functions of LISP. The LISP interpreter in fact makes constant use of this function; whenever an s-expression is given to LISP, it applies eval to it and prints the result. Hence the common remark that 'LISP evaluates everything'.

EXERCISE 1.2
Write down s-expressions, using the LISP arithmetic functions, to calculate the following:

```
10*(9+61-20)
(52-16/3)*(2+8^5)
(99-√18)/(√99-18)
1*2*3*4*5/55+81*81-17^3
```

EXERCISE 1.3
Try the following function applications and write down two of your own for each function (see Appendix 1 for a summary of these functions). Note that 1+ and 1- work for fixed numbers only.

```
(add1 10.5)                        (sub1 10.5)
(1+ 10)                            (1- 10)
(exp 2.5)                          (fix 2.56)
(float 5)                          (log 1.62)
(min 5 9 11.2 0 14 8.9)            (max 5 9 11.2 0 14 8.9)
(sine 0.42)                        (cos 0.42)
(+ 10.6 21.3)                      (- 10.11 2.65)
(* 1.62 2)                         (/ 19 4.2)
(fix (* (/ 22 3) (log 12.3)))
(max (fix (log 1.66)) (exp 4.6) (sine (/ 5.8 9.23)))
```

EXERCISE 1.4
Work out the values of x, y and z after each of the following forms is evaluated, in the order given.

```
(setq x 10)
(setq y (times 5 x))
(setq z (setq y (plus x y)))
(setq x y y z z x)
```

EXERCISE 1.5
Work out the result of evaluating each of the following forms, in the order given.

```
(quote quote)                      (quote (quote LISP))
''LISP                             (eval (quote (times 5 10)))
(eval (eval (eval 5)))
(setq x '(plus 5 6) y '(difference 10 8))
(eval x)                           (times (eval x) (eval y))
```

1.5 Indentation and comments

In general, s-expressions can extend beyond one line and occupy as many lines as necessary. An example is shown below:

```
-> (setq sentence1 '(this is the first sentence)
         sentence2 '(this is the second sentence))
(this is the second sentence)
->
```

Here, the second line has been indented so that the symbol `sentence2` appears exactly beneath `sentence1`. This style of indentation is a common practice in LISP and can significantly enhance the readability of programs.

Readability is also enhanced by the use of comments. A comment is an arbitrary sentence appearing after a semicolon character on the same line:

```
-> (setq x 10        ; store 10 in x
         y 20)       ; store 20 in y
20
->
```

Comments are included only for the information of LISP programmers and are altogether ignored by LISP. They are useful in explaining those parts of a program which are not immediately obvious, and for documenting any other information relevant to the program (see Section 10.2).

1.6 Special symbols

Two symbols are special and predefined in LISP; these are `t` and `nil`. They are special in that they evaluate to themselves, although they are not numbers:

```
-> t
t
-> nil
nil
->
```

In most LISP systems you cannot change the value of these symbols, and even if you can, you must *not* attempt to do so, as this may have rather adverse effects. The symbol `nil` is the only s-expression which is an atom and a list at the same time. It is in fact an

1.7 Errors and termination 15

abbreviation of the empty list:

```
-> ()
nil
-> '(())
(nil)
->
```

Note that (nil) is not an empty list. It is a list of one element: nil.

The main role of t and nil is that they are the simplest forms of *predicates* in LISP. They roughly (but not exactly) correspond to *true* and *false* in most other programming languages. In LISP, false is represented by nil, while true can be represented by any nonnil object (e.g., 1, (1), 'true, t), the simplest of which is t. We shall explain the role of t and nil further in the next chapter when describing the predicate functions of LISP.

1.7 Errors and termination

We noticed earlier that when we ask LISP to do something illegal (e.g., to evaluate an unbound variable, or to apply an undefined function) it comes up with an error message. Upon registering an error, most LISP systems change their prompt and enter a so called *debug loop*. For example, in

```
-> peter
Error: Unbound Variable peter
<1>:
```

the symbol <1> signifies that LISP has entered a debug loop. This means that you can use the debugging facilities of LISP to investigate what has gone wrong. On the other hand, you can carry on as if nothing has happened. The prompt, however, will remain as it is.

It is not advisable to worry about debugging at this early stage. (These will be described in Section 9.1.) For the moment, you can ignore any debug prompt and return back to where you were by typing (reset)

```
<1>: (reset)
[Return to top level]
->
```

which causes LISP to clear up the mess and return back to the original prompt. This is called the *top level*. LISP maintains track of what it does on an internal stack (the details of which you need not know about, but will be explained in Section 9.1). Whenever LISP successfully completes your request it clears the stack, and this is essentially what top level is about. If in the middle of the calculation an error occurs then LISP will not clear the stack and will leave it as it is for your examination. This is known as a different level. `Reset` simply clears the stack and terminates the debug loop, thereby taking you back to the top level.

Obviously, at some stage of your interaction with LISP, you would like to leave the system. This may be done by calling `exit`,

```
-> (exit)
$
```

which simply terminates the LISP system and takes you back to the operating system. You may exit at any stage in your dialog with LISP, including levels other than the top level.

1.8 Summary

In this chapter we have been through some of the basic features and facilities of LISP, and have observed the following points.

- Certain programming problems involve *symbol manipulation*.
- LISP is the right language for symbol manipulation.
- LISP programs are made up of *s-expressions*.
- An s-expression is either a *list* or an *atom*.
- A list is an ordered group of zero or more s-expressions.
- An atom is either *numeric* or *symbolic*.
- An atom can have a *value binding* as well as a *function binding*.
- `Setq` binds atoms to values.
- A *function* application is written as a list, where the first element of the list is the function name and the subsequent elements are its *arguments*.
- LISP evaluates every s-expression it is given.
- `Quote` suppresses evaluation.
- `Eval` enforces extra evaluation.
- The symbols `t` and `nil` are special atoms and evaluate to themselves.
- A list containing no elements is called an *empty list* and is equivalent to `nil`.
- `Reset` takes you back to the top level, and `exit` gets you out of LISP.

Projects

1.1 Choose a traditional programming language that you are familiar with (e.g., FORTRAN, ALGOL, Pascal, C, etc.) and compare it to LISP. You should specifically cover the following points.

- A comparison between symbols and variables.
- A comparison between s-expressions and the data structures of the language you have chosen.
- A comparison of the way computation is performed in either language.
- A comparison of the complexity of the syntax of either language.

Summarize your results by constructing a table which highlights the strengths and weaknesses of each language.

1.2 Choose a number of complex hierarchical data structures and write them down, once using s-expressions, and once using the data structures of the language you chose above. You will notice that in the latter case you will need some auxiliary functions or procedures to create the data structures. Compare these two representations using the following criteria.

- The time spent to create each data structure.
- The size of the code used for creating each data structure.
- The ease with which each data structure may be changed.
- The ease with which each data structure may be understood by a second party.

Chapter 2

Primitives

The LISP language is simply made up of a good number of useful functions which enable us to manipulate s-expressions in a variety of ways. Such functions are called primitives,[1] since they are predefined and directly supported by the LISP system. In this chapter we will examine some of the LISP primitives for the composition of, decomposition of, transformation of and extraction from lists. We will also introduce a number of logic-oriented primitives. In the next chapter we will describe how you can define your own functions and add them to the LISP system.

2.1 List manipulation

Lists are useful data structures for storing information. But programming is not only concerned with storing information; it also involves the manipulation of the stored data. So a need arises in LISP for facilities that would allow us to manipulate lists by breaking them apart, sticking them back together, transforming them, and extracting useful information from them. Such facilities are provided as primitive functions as described below.

Decomposing lists

Earlier we defined a list as an ordered group of s-expressions. It is now about time to define two further subparts of a list. These are called *head* and *tail*. The head of a list is simply its first element. The tail of a list is the same as the list itself excluding its first element. This is shown graphically below.

---

[1] Here we have used the term 'primitive' in a rather broad sense: any function which is predefined in LISP. The alternative is to restrict the term to a much smaller set of functions, in terms of which all other functions can be defined.

2.1 List manipulation

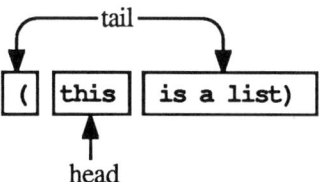

So, for example, the head of (1 10 20 30) is 1 while its tail is (10 20 30).

The head of a list is extracted by the function car. The tail of a list is extracted by cdr. Each of these is a function which expects or takes exactly one argument, which must be a list:

```
-> (car '(7 2 1))
7
-> (cdr '(7 2 1))
(2 1)
->
```

Note that the tail of a list is always a list, whereas its head may or may not be a list:

```
-> (car '((5 4) (3 2) 1))
(5 4)
-> (cdr '((5 4) (3 2) 1))
((3 2) 1)
-> (car '(5 4))
5
->
```

So, remember, car returns the first *element* of a list but not necessarily the first *atom*.

Compositions of car and cdr allow us to extract any part of a list. For example, let x be a nested list of cities

```
-> (setq x '(Rome London (Munich Tokyo)))
(Rome London (Munich Tokyo))
->
```

then to extract London from x, we may write

```
-> (car (cdr x))
London
->
```

This works as follows: `(cdr x)` returns

    (London (Munich Tokyo))

to which we apply `car` to get London. Other cities in x can be extracted similarly:

    -> (car x)
    Rome
    -> (car (car (cdr (cdr x))))
    Munich
    -> (car (cdr (car (cdr (cdr x)))))
    Tokyo
    ->

By now, you are probably wondering why head and tail have been given such obscure names in LISP. Historically, these names were used as abbreviations for 'content address register' and 'content decrement register' in very early LISP implementations, probably because they facilitate a shorthand for their compositions. Any composition of `car` and `cdr` can be abbreviated to one function name which starts with the letter c and ends in r, with as and ds in the middle representing `car` and `cdr`, respectively. So, `(car (cdr x))` is equivalent to `(cadr x)`, and so on:

    -> (cadr x)
    London
    -> (caaddr x)
    Munich
    -> (cadaddr x)
    Tokyo
    ->

A graphical representation makes the convention more clear:

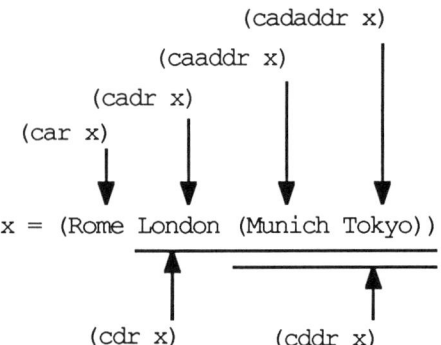

2.1 List manipulation

The names and the convention may seem rather uncomfortable at this stage, but once you get used to them you will appreciate their brevity. Throughout the rest of this book we will use the terms head and `car`, and tail and `cdr` interchangeably, however, you should remember to use only `car` and `cdr` in your programs; the other two are just convenient names which convey the same meanings.

An important point that needs to be mentioned is the effect of `car` and `cdr` on the empty list. Depending on your LISP system, this may or may not work. In most systems, it works and the result is always `nil`:

```
-> (car nil)
nil
-> (cdr nil)
nil
->
```

In certain other systems it is considered as an error and will fail. In this book we will assume the former convention.

Composing lists

Having seen how we can break lists apart, let us see how we can put them back together. LISP provides three primary primitives for this purpose, the simplest of which is `cons`. This is a function of two arguments and does just the reverse of `car` and `cdr`. It constructs a list whose head is the first argument to `cons` and whose tail is the second argument:

```
-> (cons 5 '(6 7))
(5 6 7)
-> (car (cons 5 '(6 7)))
5
-> (cdr (cons 5 '(6 7)))
(6 7)
->
```

Looking at this the other way round, we have

```
-> (setq x '(5 6 7))
(5 6 7)
-> (cons (car x) (cdr x))
(5 6 7)
->
```

which in turn explains the effect of `cons` when its second argument is an empty list:

```
-> (cons 5 '())
(5)
->
```

The last example suggests that using cons we can in fact compose entire lists:

```
-> (cons 5 (cons 6 (cons 7 '()))) 
(5 6 7)
-> (cons '(5 6) '(7 8))
((5 6) 7 8)
-> (cons '(5 6) (cons '(7) '(8 9)))
((5 6) (7) 8 9)
->
```

Another function, list, makes composing long lists easier. It takes zero or more arguments and returns a list so that the given arguments are elements of this list in that order:

```
-> (list 5)
(5)
-> (list 5 6 7)
(5 6 7)
-> (list '(5 6) '(7) 8 9)
((5 6) (7) 8 9)
-> (list (list 5 6) (list 7) 8 9)
((5 6) (7) 8 9)
-> (list)
nil
->
```

It is easy to see that any list form can be written as an equivalent cons form, and this is in fact what the LISP system does internally:

```
-> (list 2 3 (list 4 5))
(2 3 (4 5))
-> (cons 2 (cons 3 (cons (cons 4 (cons 5 '())) '())))
(2 3 (4 5))
->
```

The last function to be described here is append which simply sticks lists together. It takes two or more arguments, all of which must be lists, and appends them in that order:

2.1 List manipulation

```
-> (append '(2 4) '(7 8))
(2 4 7 8)
-> (append '(2) '(3 5 6) '(9 11))
(2 3 5 6 9 11)
-> (append '(2) '() '(11 12) '())
(2 11 12)
->
```

Note that list and append are quite different. The former returns a list whose elements are the arguments of the function. The latter returns a list whose elements are those of the arguments of the function:

```
-> (list '(1 2) '(3))
((1 2) (3))
-> (append '(1 2) '(3))
(1 2 3)
->
```

Transforming lists

Certain LISP primitives are suitable for transforming a list from one form to another. Remove, for example, removes from a list those elements which are identical to a given s-expression. It takes two arguments and removes the first argument from the second argument (which must be a list):

```
-> (remove 5 '(2 6 5 9 5))
(2 6 9)
-> (remove '(2 3) '((11) 9 (2 3) 6 (2 3 4)))
((11) 9 6 (2 3 4))
-> (remove 9 '(5 (9) 2))
(5 (9) 2)
->
```

The last example illustrates the fact that remove does not remove all occurrences of an s-expression from a list, but only those *elements* which match the s-expression (i.e., s-expressions in the top level of the list). So, although 9 appears in the list, it is not an element of the list. The corresponding element is (9) which is not the same as 9.

A different kind of transformation is done by subst, which substitutes one s-expression for another in a list. It substitutes its first argument for all occurrences of its second argument in the third argument:

```
-> (subst 50 5 '(9 5 11 5))
(9 50 11 50)
-> (subst 50 5 '((5 9 (5)) 2))
((50 9 (50)) 2)
->
```

As shown by the last example, unlike remove, subst does the substitution at all levels of a list and not just the top level.

Another transformation function, reverse, rearranges a list so that its elements appear in the reverse order. Like remove, it only operates on the top level of a list:

```
-> (reverse '(2 6 9))
(9 6 2)
-> (reverse '(2 (11 16 2) 9 (6 5)))
((6 5) 9 (11 16 2) 2)
->
```

Extracting from lists

Earlier, we saw two simple list extracting primitives (i.e., car and cdr) which extract the head and tail of a list respectively. Three others will be described here. The first function is length and simply returns the length of a list, where the length of a list is defined to be the number of elements of that list:

```
-> (length '(5 2 11))
3
-> (length '())
0
-> (length '((2) (9 11 6) 1 4))
4
->
```

The end of a list, i.e., a list containing the last element (if any), is extracted by last:

```
-> (last '(5 2 9))
(9)
-> (last '(5 (2 6) (2)))
((2))
-> (last '())
nil
```

2.1 List manipulation

```
-> (last (last '(2))
(2)
->
```

Note that `last` does not return just the last element, but a list of that element.

Finally, `member` returns the longest portion of a list whose head is identical to a given s-expression. It returns `nil` if its first argument is not a member of its second argument:

```
-> (member 2 '(3 4 2 9 2 1))
(2 9 2 1)
-> (member '(5 11) '(6 9 (5 11) 16))
((5 11) 16)
-> (member '(5 11) '(2 5 11 9))
nil
->
```

EXERCISE 2.1

For each of the following lists, write down expressions, using `car` and `cdr`, which extract each individual atom.

```
(LISP is fun)
(lists (have) brackets)
(like ((this)) or (even (this)))
((((trapped))))
```

EXERCISE 2.2

Write down expressions, using `cons` only, to produce the following lists:

```
(one two three)
(two and (four times two) is (ten))
(a list can be as ((deep)) as you like)
((()))
```

Now do the same, using `list` only.

EXERCISE 2.3

Work out the result of evaluating the following lists, in the order given:

```
(append (list) (cons (list) '(2)))
(append (append () (cons () ())) (list (list)))
(setq x (list 'append (list 'quote (list 2)) nil))
(eval x)
(remove (list 5) (cons (10 (list 2 11 5)))
(subst (list (list)) nil (list 2 nil nil 5 nil))
(subst 'good 'hard (list 'LISP '(is hard)))
(reverse '(2 (3 (4) 5) 6))
```

```
(reverse '(((list))))
(reverse nil)
(length '(((list))))
(length '(()))
(last (reverse (cons 6 (list 5 10))))
(member 'member '(I am a member of IEEE))
```

2.2 *Set* versus *setq*

As you should have noticed by now, the first argument of `setq` is always a symbol. This is because `setq` does not evaluate its first argument. There is a more general form of `setq` called `set`. The only difference is that `set` does evaluate its first argument. The overall effect of `set` is that it evaluates its first arguments (which should obviously evaluate to a symbol) and then binds the resulting symbol to the value of its second argument:

```
-> (set 'x '(value of x))
(value of x)
-> (set 'y 'x)
x
-> y
x
-> (set y '(value of y))
(value of y)
-> x
(value of y)
->
```

`Set` is rarely used in programs, as its role, in most cases, can be accomplished by `setq`. Nevertheless, we shall see a few interesting uses of `set` towards the end of this book.

2.3 Predicates

Occasionally, we may require to find out whether an object is a list or an atom. Two LISP primitives, called `atom` and `listp`, enable us to do just that:

```
-> (atom 'x)
t
-> (atom '(x))
nil
```

2.3 Predicates

```
-> (listp 'x)
nil
-> (listp '(x))
t
->
```

Atom returns t if its first argument is an atom, otherwise it returns nil. Similarly, listp returns t if its argument is a list, and nil otherwise. Functions like these are called *predicates*. Note that the empty list, being an atom and a list at the same time, satisfies both atom and listp:

```
-> (atom '())
t
-> (listp '())
t
->
```

The predicate null detects empty lists. It returns t if and only if its argument evaluates to an empty list:

```
-> (null '())
t
-> (null '(x))
nil
->
```

LISP provides many other similar predicates, most of which operate on numbers:

```
-> (lessp 2 5 11.6 66.9)          ;; less than.
t
-> (greaterp 5.6 5.2 1 -6.11)     ;; greater than.
t
-> (fixp 11)                      ;; fixed number.
t
-> (floatp 11.6)                  ;; float number.
t
-> (evenp 12)                     ;; even number.
t
-> (oddp 13)                      ;; odd number.
t
```

```
-> (numberp 20.36)                    ;; number.
t
-> (numberp 'x)
nil
```

The predicate `equal` returns `t` if its arguments are equal s-expressions. Two s-expressions are defined to be equal if they are identical atoms or if they are lists of equal length with equal elements in the same order:

```
-> (equal 5219.2 5219.2)
t
-> (equal 'x 'x)
t
-> (equal '(x y z) '(x y z))
t
-> (equal '(a (b (c)) (d)) '(a (b (c)) (d)))
t
-> (equal '(a b) '(b a))
nil
->
```

A predicate can be negated using the `not` operator which returns `t` if its argument evaluates to `nil`, otherwise it returns `nil`. The operators `not` and `null` are in effect identical and may be used interchangeably:

```
-> (equal 'x 'y)
nil
-> (not (equal 'x 'y))
t
-> (null (equal 'x 'y))
t
->
```

The last two forms can be abbreviated using `nequal`:

```
-> (nequal 'x 'y)
t
->
```

2.3 Predicates

Conjunctions and disjunctions

A number of predicates can be combined into one predicate using the conjunction and disjunction operators `and` and `or`. The operator `and` takes zero or more arguments and evaluates them from left to right. If an argument evaluates to `nil` then evaluation will cease and `nil` will be returned. Otherwise, `and` returns the value of its last argument:

```
-> (and (equal 5 5) (listp '()))
t
-> (and (atom '(x y)) (listp '(z)))
nil
-> (and (atom x))
t
-> (and)
t
->
```

Similarly, `or` evaluates its arguments from left to right. It stops the evaluation as soon as an argument evaluates to a non`nil` object, and returns that object. Otherwise, `or` returns `nil`:[2]

```
-> (or (numberp nil) (equal 'x 'x))
t
-> (or (nequal 'x 'x) (equal 'x 'y))
nil
-> (or)
nil
->
```

Note that when given no arguments, `and` returns `t` while `or` returns `nil`. Also note that some of the arguments to `and` and `or` may not be evaluated at all since evaluation may cease at any point depending on the outcome of the evaluation of the previous argument:

```
-> (setq x 10)
10
-> (and (equal x 10) (setq x 20))
20
-> x
20
```

---

[2] In some LISP systems `and` and `or` are boolean operators which only return `t` or `nil`.

```
-> (and (equal x 10) (setq x 30))
nil
-> x
20
->
```

Later in the book we will see how this property may be exploited in writing conditional expressions.

The three primitives `and`, `or` and `not` provide a powerful tool for writing logical expressions, and are usually referred to as the *logic operators*.

Identity

We have already seen how we can test whether two s-expressions are equal using `equal`. LISP provides a further equality function called `eq` which, although at first sight equivalent to `equal`, is rather different:

```
-> (eq 'x 'x)
t
-> (eq '(arbitrary list) '(arbitrary list))
nil
-> (setq y '(arbitrary list) z y)
(arbitrary list)
-> y
(arbitrary list)
-> z
(arbitrary list)
-> (eq y z)
t
->
```

The behavior of `eq` may seem rather strange but is easy to explain. Unlike `equal`, `eq` returns `t` only when its arguments are *identical* objects. This means that they must both refer to the same memory location. With symbols this creates no difficulty since symbols are stored only once and every reference to a symbol refers to the same location. With lists, however, the outcome may be different. For example, in

```
(setq m '(a) n '(a))
```

the first `(a)` and the second `(a)` may appear to be the same but are in fact slightly different

2.3 Predicates

in that they occupy different memory locations. In other words, they are two copies of the same thing. So,

(eq m n)

will produce `nil`, whereas

(equal m n)

will produce `t`, since `equal` checks the equality of two lists element by element.

The effect of `eq` on numbers is less obvious; it usually works for small fixed numbers only (-1024 – 1024, say). Most LISP systems provide an internal table for small fixed numbers so that whenever you refer to such a number it is the same number and not a copy. The main objective here is to make `eq` much faster than `equal`. However, you need not be concerned about these measures yet. All you should remember is that `eq` is a special case of `equal` and that it returns `t` if and only if it is applied to two perfectly identical objects. In any case, if you are in doubt just use `equal`. The difference becomes much more clear in Chapter 4, when we describe the way objects are internally stored in LISP. Incidentally, `eq` has also a negated form which is similar to `nequal`:

```
-> (neq 'x 'y)
t
->
```

Some of the primitives described earlier have additional versions based on `eq` rather than `equal`. For example, `remq` is the `eq` versions of `remove` and removes those elements of a list which are `eq` to a given s-expression:

```
-> (remq 5 '(2 6 5 10))
(2 6 10)
-> (remq '(2) '(2 (2) 6))
(2 (2) 6)
->
```

Similarly, `memq` is the `eq` version of `member`:

```
-> (memq 5 '(2 6 5 10))
(5 10)
->
```

EXERCISE 2.4
> Evaluate the following forms and write a few of your own (see Appendix 1 for a summary of the new functions).

```
(greaterp 100 10.5 0)
(greaterp 0 10.5 100)
(lessp 0 10.5 100)
(< 100 100.2)
(< 100.5 100.5)
(> 10.16 10.15)
(= 2.555 2.555)
(onep 1)
(zerop 0)
```

EXERCISE 2.5
> Which of the following lists will evaluate to t?

```
(equal (setq x 'a y '(a) z 'a) 'a)
(equal y '(a))
(eq y '(a))
(and (eq y (list x)) (eq (set z 'b) x))
(eq a 'b)
```

2.4 Summary

In this chapter we have been through a number of the primitives of LISP for manipulating list structures. We have also examined some useful predicates for doing logic. To summarize, we have observed the following points.

- The first element of a list is called its *head*; the rest of the list is called its *tail*.
- Car extracts the head of a list; cdr extracts its tail.
- Combinations of car and cdr may be abbreviated to c...r, where ... can be any sequence of as (for car) and ds (for cdr).
- Cons, list and append compose lists out of s-expressions.
- Remove, subst and reverse transform lists.
- Useful information is extracted from lists using the functions length, last and member.
- Set is just like setq but evaluates its first argument.
- Atom and listp tell us whether an s-expression is an atom or a list.
- A predicate is negated by not; this is equivalent to null.
- Predicates are combined using the functions and and or.
- Equal tells us whether two s-expressions are equal.
- Eq is a special, weaker form of equal, which tells us whether two s-expressions are identical.

Projects

2.1 Consider the problem of substituting a word for another word in a piece of text, where the text may be a piece of program or English prose. Write a program in a procedural language that you know in order to do this. Then use `subst` to implement the same program in LISP. (Obviously to do so, you will have to represent the text as a long list.) Compare these two approaches by commenting on issues such as the simplicity, length, and complexity of the programs. Which approach do you consider more flexible? Which approach do you consider more general?

2.2 Write a program, in a procedural language that you are familiar with, to compare two tree structures for equality. (See Section 12.1 for a description of what a tree is.) Then use list structures to represent trees in LISP, and the function `equal` for comparing such trees. Compare these two approaches by commenting on the same issues as suggested by the previous project. Also, compare `equal` with the equality operator of the procedural language you have chosen, by commenting on their generality.

Chapter 3

User-defined Functions

In this chapter we will explore some of the facilities of LISP for defining functions. The main purpose of defining such functions is to achieve *functional abstraction* – an indispensable tool in any serious programming activity. Functional abstraction serves two purposes. Firstly, it enables us to break a program down into smaller, more manageable units and secondly, it aids us in making our programs shorter. Using functions, we can package a chunk of code and give it a name, thereby avoiding the rewriting of the code every time it is required.

We will also introduce some ingredients which assist us in writing more general and useful functions. These will include functions for conditional evaluation of s-expressions, a facility for defining local variables, and some exotic ways of calling functions.

3.1 Defining functions using *defun*

Let us begin our discussion of functions by going through a few simple examples of actual function definitions. Our first example concerns the definition of a function called is-0-1 which returns t if and only if its argument is 0 or 1. It is defined as follows:

```
-> (defun is-0-1 (num)
         (or (eq num 0)
             (eq num 1)))
is-0-1
->
```

Defun enables us to define other functions. The first argument to defun is a symbol – the name of the function being defined (is-0-1 here). The second argument is a *parameter list*. This is a list of zero or more symbols which are bound to the function's arguments when it is called. The above function has only one parameter, namely num. The remaining

3.1 Defining functions using defun

arguments to defun are one or more s-expressions. These form the so called *body* of the function. The body of the above function consists of one s-expression only:

```
(or (eq num 0)
    (eq num 1))
```

Note that a function's parameter can be used freely in its body.

Defun does not evaluate any of its arguments; it just processes them and establishes a new function accordingly. As its result, defun returns the name of the function being defined (is-0-1 in the above example). Once a function is defined, it may be used just like any other LISP function:

```
-> (is-0-1 0)
t
->
```

The effect of this call is that the parameter num is first bound to the value of the argument 0. The body of is-0-1 is then evaluated, which in this case is equivalent to:

```
(or (eq 0 0)
    (eq 0 1))
```

The resulting value (i.e., t) is then returned by is-0-1.

We can also define functions which take more than one parameter. For example,

```
(defun is-longer (list1 list2)
    (greaterp (length list1) (length list2)))
```

defines a function called is-longer which takes two lists as arguments and returns t if and only if the length of the first list is greater than the length of the second list:

```
-> (is-longer '(a b c) '(a b))
t
->
```

Here, list1 is bound to (a b c) and list2 is bound to (a b). The body of is-longer is then evaluated which will be equivalent to:

```
(greaterp (length '(a b c)) (length '(a b)))
```

which obviously evaluates to t.

It is worth noting that a function defined using defun always evaluates its arguments.

For example, `is-0-1` and `is-longer` both evaluate all their arguments:

```
-> (is-0-1 (plus 1 0))
t
-> (is-0-1 (difference (plus 2 3) (plus 2 1)))
nil
-> (is-longer (append '(a b) '()) (append '(a b) '(a b)))
nil
->
```

Also worth noting is that a currently defined function (e.g., `is-0-1`, or any LISP primitive) can be redefined, in which case the new definition will replace the old definition.

The body of a function can consist of more than one s-expression. As a general rule, when a function is called, the s-expressions in the body are evaluated in the order they occur and the value of the *last* s-expression is returned as the final result. Consider the following function

```
(defun heads (list1 list2)
       (setq x (car list1)
             y (car list2))
       (list x y))
```

which returns a list consisting of the heads of its two arguments (which must, of course, be lists). The body of `heads` consists of two s-expressions. The first s-expression stores the `car` of `list1` and `list2` in `x` and `y` respectively. The last expression simply returns a list of `x` and `y`:

```
-> (heads '(a b c) '(d e f))
(a d)
-> x
a
-> y
d
->
```

The role of the first s-expression, therefore, is to cause side-effects which are then used by the second s-expression. Needless to say, the above function could have been defined more elegantly as

```
(defun heads (list1 list2)
       (list (car list1) (car list2)))
```

which does not involve any side-effects, and whose body consists of one s-expression only. In later chapters we will come across examples which illustrate that, in certain cases, multiple s-expressions are genuinely needed in order to define useful functions.

Arguments and parameters

It is rather easy to confuse the role of arguments and parameters in relation to functions. The following points will aid you in understanding the differences between these two more easily.

- An argument is what you supply to a function when you call it. Depending on the type of the function, an argument may or may not be evaluated.
- A parameter is a symbol in a function's parameter list and is used as a place holder. It facilitates the communication between the function and its outside world.
- When a function is called, there must be a one-to-one correspondence between the arguments and the parameters. The first parameter is bound to the value of the first argument, the second parameter to the value of the second argument, etc.
- A function parameter is bound to an argument temporarily. The binding lasts for the duration of the call to the function only. As soon as the evaluation of the function is completed, all its parameters are restored to their previous values (if any).

Structure of defun

We are now in a position to give the overall structure of a function definition using defun. This is shown in Figure 3.1.

```
(defun  function-name  (par1 par2 ... parn)
        s-expression-1
        s-expression-2
            :
        s-expression-k )
```

Figure 3.1 The structure of defun.

The effect of the general call

```
(function-name arg1 arg2 ... argn)
```

is as follows.

1. Save the values of par1, par2, ..., parn in a safe place which can be retrieved later on (usually the LISP system stack).
2. Evaluate arg1, arg2, ..., argn and bind par1, par2, ..., parn to these values respectively.
3. Evaluate s-expression-1, s-expression-2, ..., s-expression-k in that order and save the value of the last s-expression.
4. Restore the values of par1, par2, ..., parn to whatever they were before the call (as saved in Step 1).
5. Return the value of the last s-expression (as saved in Step 3).

Free and bound variables

The fact that the body of a function can alter variables raises the interesting question of what the effect of these changes would be once the function is terminated. Let us formulate an example around which we can discuss this issue:

```
(defun strange (x y)
        (setq x 'intermediate-x
              z 'intermediate-z))
```

The body of this function refers to three variable. Two of these variables (i.e., x and y) are parameters of the function; these are called *bound variables*. The other variable (i.e., z) is called a *free variable*. The changes that a function makes to a bound variable (e.g., x) are temporary and are forgotten once a call to the function is completed. The changes that a function makes to a free variable (e.g., z) are permanent; they last even after a call to the function has been completed:

```
-> (setq x 'old-x y 'old-y z 'old-z)
old-z
-> (strange 'new-x 'new-y)
intermediate-z
-> x
old-x
-> y
old-y
-> z
intermediate-z
->
```

The effect of the above calls is as follows. First, x, y, and z are bound to old-x, old-y, and old-z respectively. Next, strange is called which causes x and y to be bound to new-

3.1 Defining functions using defun

x and new-y respectively. The value of x is changed by the function to `intermediate-x`. Similarly, the value of z is changed to `intermediate-z`. Examining the values of the variables after the call reveals that x is restored to its original value, while z has retained the value it was given in the body of `strange`. We may therefore reach the following conclusions.

- If a variable appears in a function's parameter list it is a bound variable; otherwise, it is a free variable.
- If a variable is a bound variable with respect to a function, then any changes to the variable during a call to that function are forgotten once the call is completed.
- If a variable is a free variable with respect to a function, then any changes to the variable during a call to that function are remembered even after the function has been completed.

Evidently, a function can refer to and make changes to bound as well as free variables. However, care should be taken to ensure that a free variable is bound to some value before it is referred to.

Dynamic and static scoping

The *scope* of a variable is the largest section of code within which that variable can be referred to, and any changes to that variable will be remembered. Referring back to `strange`, for example, the scope of x and y is confined to the body of `strange` since any changes to x or y will not be remembered outside `strange`. The scope of z is less clear. If we call `strange` directly at the top level then the scope of z will be the top level. However, if we call `strange` via `strange1`

```
(defun strange1 (z)
    (strange 'new-x 'new-y))
```

then the scope of z will be the body of `strange1` and the body of `strange`.

As you can see, the scope of a variable is very much dependent on where, when, and how it is reached. In other word, it is not possible to decide what the scope of a variable is by just looking at a LISP program's text, simply because the scope may vary during the execution of the program. This style of scoping is referred to as *dynamic* scoping, in virtue of the fact that it is decided at run-time.

The opposite of dynamic scoping is *static* (or *lexical*) scoping, where one can always determine the scope of a variable by studying a program's text. In static scoping the scope of variables always remains the same. For example, in a LISP system which employs static scoping, the scope of z in `strange` will always be the top level, regardless of whether `strange` is called directly from the top level or via `strange1`.

Most LISP systems are based on the dynamic scoping discipline. Some well-known exceptions are Common LISP [Steele 1984], Scheme [Abelson and Sussman 1985], and ExperLISP [ExperTelligence 1986]. Readers who are familiar with procedural languages (e.g., Pascal) are probably more familiar with static scoping. Virtually all such languages use the static scoping discipline.

EXERCISE 3.1
Define head and tail, two functions which are identical to car and cdr respectively.

EXERCISE 3.2
Define last-elem, a function which returns the last element of a list. (Note that last-elem is not equivalent to the LISP primitive last.)

EXERCISE 3.3
Define circumference and area, two functions which when given the radius of a circle return the circumference and the area of the circle respectively.

3.2 Use of conditionals

One of the most basic facilities provided by every programming language is that which enables one to make a selection between two or more alternatives. LISP is no exception. As we all know by now, LISP is all about evaluation, so selection boils down to deciding which s-expressions to evaluate amongst a number of s-expressions. The primary function for this style of selection is cond (standing for conditional) and supports the conditional evaluation of s-expressions. Let us look at a few examples.

Suppose we want to define a function which returns positive when its argument is greater than or equal to zero, and negative otherwise. Here is how it may be defined:

```
(defun sign (num)
        (cond ((minusp num) 'negative)
              (t 'positive)))
```

Each argument to cond is a list of s-expressions and is called a *clause*. Cond processes its clauses in the order they occur as follows. It first evaluates the head of a clause; this is called the *clause predicate*. If it evaluates to a nonnil object, it then evaluates subsequent s-expressions in the clause and returns the value of the last s-expression. If the clause predicate evaluates to nil then cond will move on to the next clause and proceed as before. If no clause is satisfied (i.e., no clause predicate evaluates to nonnil) then cond will return nil.

In the above example, cond first evaluates (minusp num) and if this returns t then cond will return negative. Otherwise cond moves to the next clause and evaluates t (which obviously produces t) and returns positive:

3.2 Use of conditionals

```
-> (sign 2)
positive
-> (sign -5)
negative
-> (sign 0)
positive
->
```

Cond can take any number of clauses. The next example shows a version of sign which also treats the special case when the argument is zero, using a cond of three clauses:

```
(defun sign1 (num)
       (cond ((minusp num) 'negative)
             ((plusp num) 'positive)
             ( t 'zero)))
```

Note that, in general, a clause can consist of any number of s-expressions. The following rules apply.

- If a clause is simply nil then that clause will never be satisfied. Indeed, it is difficult to see if such a clause could have any use at all!
- If a clause contains only one s-expression then cond will return the value of that s-expression if and only if it evaluates to nonnil.
- If a clause consists of two or more s-expressions then cond will evaluate the first s-expression, and if it evaluates to nonnil it will evaluate all subsequent s-expressions in that order and return the value of the last s-expression.

The last case is illustrated by the next example which takes an s-expression and returns is-list if it is a list, and is-atom otherwise. It also binds the value of the free variable list or atom to the argument depending on whether the argument is a list or atom:

```
(defun list-or-atom (exp)
       (cond ((listp exp) (setq list exp) 'is-list)
             ((atom exp) (setq atom exp) 'is-atom)))
```

Evaluating list-or-atom reveals its effect:

```
-> (list-or-atom '(a b c))
is-list
-> list
(a b c)
```

As suggested by the first two examples above, the predicate of the last clause of `cond` is often simply `t`. This ensures that the last clause will be satisfied if no other clause does. Such a clause is usually called the *default clause*. The defined function `list-or-atom` does not require a default clause since at least one of the clause predicates will always be satisfied.

Structure of `cond`

The general structure of `cond` is shown in Figure 3.2. A `cond` expression consists of zero or more clauses, where each clause is a list of zero or more s-expressions.

```
(cond   (s-expression-1 ... )
        (s-expression-2 ... )
              :
        (s-expression-n ... ) )
```

Figure 3.2 The general structure of `cond`.

Evaluation progresses as follows. Starting at 1, suppose the current clause is the `i`th clause, `(s-expression-i ...)`, then the following steps will take place:

1. If there are no more clauses left to be considered return `nil`.
2. Evaluate s-expression-i.
3. If it evaluates to non`nil`:
   3.1 if `s-expression-i` is the only s-expression in this clause then return its value,
   3.2 otherwise evaluate the remaining s-expressions in the clause, in the order they occur, and return the value of the last s-expression.
4. If it evaluates to `nil` then increment `i` and go to Step 1.

Super brackets

Most LISP systems allow the use of square brackets as well as round brackets for representing lists. However, these two are not exactly equivalent. The use of square brackets, also called *super brackets*, is governed by two rules.

- A right super bracket will close as many open left brackets as there are.
- A right super bracket will close only one matching open left super bracket.

For example,

3.2 Use of conditionals

```
(list (list '(a b c) (list '(e f))))
```

may be written as

```
(list (list '(a b c) (list '(e f])
```

using the first rule, to save brackets. On the other hand,

```
(cond ((eq x 0) 'zero)
      ((eq x 1) 'one)
      (t 'other))
```

may be written as

```
(cond [(eq x 0) 'zero]
      [(eq x 1) 'one]
      [t 'other])
```

using the second rule, to enhance readability.

You should be warned that it is rather easy to over use super brackets, in which case they lose their beneficial effect. Throughout the rest of this book we will develop a consistent style of using super brackets which is based on the use of the second rule only. You are strongly encouraged to follow this style, and avoid the use of the first rule.

Other conditionals

Certain conditionals may also be expressed using the logical operators and and or. For example,

```
(cond [(numberp n) (exp n)])
```

may be written equivalently as:

```
(and (numberp n) (exp n))
```

Similarly,

```
(cond [(numberp n)]
      [(listp n)])
```

may be written as :

```
(or (numberp n) (listp n))
```

In general,

```
(and s-expression-1 s-expression-2 ... s-expression-n)
```

is equivalent to

```
(cond [s-expression-1
       (cond [s-expression-2
              ...
              (cond [... s-expression-n]) ...])])
```

and

```
(or s-expression-1 s-expression-2 ... s-expression-n)
```

is equivalent to:

```
(cond [s-expression-1]
      [s-expression-2]
      ...
      [s-expression-n])
```

More complicated cond structures may be represented by combinations of and and or. For instance,

```
(cond [(listp l) (set m (car l))]
      [(numberp l) (setq n l)])
```

may be written as:

```
(or (and (listp l) (setq m (car l)))
    (and (numberp l) (setq n l)))
```

The only excuse for using and/or instead of cond is that they are generally more efficient. However, care should be taken to ensure that these operators are not overused in this capacity. Deeply nested and/or expression can be especially difficult to understand. So it is best to use them only when the conditional involved is simple and short. Otherwise, cond should be used.

3.2 Use of conditionals

EXERCISE 3.4
Suppose that in your LISP system `car` and `cdr` are undefined for `nil`. Define `head` and `tail`, two functions which are identical to `car` and `cdr` respectively, but return `nil` when given `nil`.

EXERCISE 3.5
Define `divisible`, a function which takes two numbers m and n as arguments and returns t if and only if m is divisible by n. `Divisible` should return `nil` when m or n is a real number, or when n is zero.

EXERCISE 3.6
Use super brackets to make the following expressions more readable:

```
(cond ((member x y) (list x))
      (t (last y)))

(cond ((is-employee name)
         (cond ((does-overtime name) (extra-earning name))
               (t (normal-earning name))))
      ((is-retired name) (pension name))
      (t (report-unknown name)))

(let ((token (get-token)) (context (get-context)))
    (cond ((is-variable token context)
             (add-table token 'var))
          ((is-function token context)
             (add-table token 'fun))
          (t (error token 'unknown))))
```

EXERCISE 3.7
Rewrite the following conditionals using `and` and `or` instead of `cond`. (Note: the intention of this exercise is to familiarize you with the properties of `and` and `or`, not to suggest that they are superior for writing the following conditionals.)

```
(cond [(plusp n) (sqrt n)])

(cond [(plusp n) (sqrt n)]
      [t (sqrt (abs n))])

(cond [(atom x) x]
      [t (car x)])

(cond [(null x) 'empty]
      [(atom x) 'atom]
      [t 'list])
```

3.3 Anonymous functions

Consider the following function:

```
(defun size (list)
       (cond [(lessp (length list) 10) 'short]
             [(lessp (length list) 100) 'medium]
             [t 'long]))
```

which returns a symbol, giving an indication of the length of its argument. We note that (length list) appears twice in the function, so we may be tempted to avoid the overhead by using a free variable to hold the length of the list:

```
(defun size (list)
       (cond [(lessp (setq n (length list)) 10) 'short]
             [(lessp n 100) 'medium]
             [t 'long]))
```

This will work as required. Unfortunately, however, by introducing a free variable, we have turned size into an impure function. Ideally, we would like to keep size pure and yet avoid the overhead of evaluating the length of list twice.

One way to do this is to break size into two functions, both of which are pure:

```
(defun size (list)
       (size-aux (length list)))

(defun size-aux (n)
       (cond [(lessp n 10) 'short]
             [(lessp n 100) 'medium]
             [t 'long]))
```

Here, the first function supplies the length of list to the second function, thereby avoiding the use of a free variable. However, it seems unlikely that we will have any use for size-aux other than that made by size. So, although this solution is better than the previous one, it is rather wasteful in that it employs two functions whereas one would be quite adequate.

An improved solution is based on using a so called *anonymous function*. These are just like other LISP functions except that, because they are used only once, they take no name. Anonymous functions are defined by the function lambda. Using lambda, we can define size-aux anonymously within the body of size, where it actually belongs:

3.3 Anonymous functions

```
(defun size (list)
    ((lambda (n)
        (cond [(lessp n 10) 'short]
              [(lessp n 100) 'medium]
              [t 'long]))
     (length list)))
```

Note that the lambda definition (printed in bold here) appears in exactly the place of size-aux in the previous definition of size. It defines a nameless function of one parameter (n) which is then called with (length list) as its argument.

The general structure of a lambda form is exactly the same as defun and follows the same principles, except that it needs no function name. A lambda form can appear anywhere that a function name may appear. In general,

```
(fun-name arg1 ... argn)
```

may be written as

```
((lambda (par1 ... parn) ...) arg1 ... argn)
```

where the body of lambda is identical to the body of fun-name in every respect except (possibly) the name of the parameters.

It should be obvious that lambda forms are useful when we want to avoid the definition of a new function which is not going to be used more than once. If such a function is small and straightforward then the use of lambda is well justified. However, if the function is long and/or complicated then we will probably be better off defining it as a new function anyway.

The let *construct*

The problem that we have discussed above may in fact be very easily overcome by a function called let:

```
(defun size (list)
    (let [(n (length list))]
        (cond [(lessp n 10) 'small]
              [(lessp n 100) 'medium]
              [t 'large])))
```

Let simply names one or more s-expressions within other s-expressions. In the above function, for instance, it binds n to the value of (length list) within the subsequent cond expression. The general structure of a `let` expression is shown in Figure 3.3.

```
(let    [(var1 init1)  ...  (varn initn)]
        s-expression-1
              :
        s-expression-k )
```

Figure 3.3 The general structure of `let`.

Here, `var1 ... varn` are all symbols and `init1 ... initn` are all s-expressions. Let first binds `var1 ... varn` to the values of `init1 ... initn`, respectively. It then evaluates `s-expression-1 ... s-expression-n` in that order and returns the values of `s-expression-k`. Note that the binding of the variables is local, i.e., `var1 ... varn` will retain their values only for the duration of a call to `let` (analogous to a function's parameters). For this reason, they are usually called *bound* or *local variables*. Also, `init1... initn` are all optional and if they are not present the corresponding variable will be bound to `nil`.

Interestingly enough, LISP translates a call to `let` to an equivalent `lambda` form. For example, the definition of the function `size` above is translated automatically by LISP to the `lambda` version of `size` given earlier. The main reason for having `let` is that it is more readable than its equivalent `lambda` form. This is especially the case for long and complicated functions.

As a final point, you should be aware that `let` binds its local variables in *parallel* and not *sequentially*. The following example illustrates this:

```
-> (setq x 20)
20
-> (let [(x 10) (y (plus x 1))]
        (list x y))
(10 21)
->
```

There is also a variant of `let`, called `let*`, which may be used to obtain the sequential effect. This function is identical to `let` except that it binds its variables sequentially from left to right:

```
-> (setq x 20)
20
-> (let* [(x 10) (y (plus x 1))]
         (list x y))
(10 11)
```

3.4 Other ways of calling functions

EXERCISE 3.8
Redefine the following function using `lambda` to avoid the use of `setq`:

```
(defun pronoun (subject)
    (setq sex (sex-of subject))
    (cond [(eq sex 'female) 'she]
          [(eq sex 'male)   'he]
          [(eq sex 'neutral) 'it]
          [t                '??]))
```

EXERCISE 3.9
The following function solves a quadratic equation of the form a*x^2+b*x+c=0 where the coefficients a, b and c are supplied as arguments to the function. It returns the roots of the equation as a list, if any. Otherwise, it returns `no-solution`. Redefine `quad-equation` as a pure function, once using `lambda` and once using `let`.

```
(defun quad-equation (a b c)
   (setq delta (difference (times b b) (times 4 a c)))    ;; Δ = b^2 - 4ac.
   (cond [(plusp delta)                                   ;; Δ > 0?
            (setq left (quotient b (times 2 a))
                  right (quotient (sqrt delta) (times 2 a)))
            (list (plus left right) (difference left right))]
         [(minusp delta) 'no-solution]                    ;; Δ < 0?
         [t (list (minus (quotient b (times 2 a))))]))    ;; Δ = 0.
```

3.4 Other ways of calling functions

LISP provides two primitives, called `funcall` and `apply`, for calling functions in exotic ways. `Funcall` takes one or more arguments, all of which are evaluated. The first argument should evaluate to a function which `funcall` calls with subsequent arguments as arguments to this function:

```
-> (funcall 'plus 10 20 30)         ;; (plus 10 20 30).
60
-> (funcall 'append '(a b) '(c))    ;; (append '(a b) '(c))
(a b c)
->
```

In general,

```
(funcall fun arg1 arg2 ... argn)
```

is equivalent to:

```
((eval fun) arg1 arg2 ... argn)
```

`Apply` is rather similar to `funcall`. It takes two arguments, both of which are evaluated. Again, the first argument should evaluate to a function. The second argument should evaluate to a list. `Apply` calls the function (depicted by its first argument) with the elements in the list (depicted by its second argument) as arguments to this function:

```
-> (apply 'plus '(10 20 30))           ;; (plus 10 20 30)
60
-> (apply 'append '((a b) (c)))        ;; (append '(a b) '(c))
(a b c)
->
```

In general,

```
(apply fun '(arg1 arg2 ... argn))
```

is equivalent to:

```
((eval fun) 'arg1 'arg2 ... 'argn)
```

The functions `funcall` and `apply` might seem rather spurious. However, they have some genuine uses, as shown below.

Functions as arguments

Consider the problem of writing a function which takes two measures and calculates the ratio of the error between the measures with respect to the average of the measures:

```
(defun error-ratio (measure1 measure2)
       (quotient (error measure1 measure2)
                 (quotient (plus measure1 measure2) 2)))

(defun error (measure1 measure2)
       (abs (difference measure1 measure2)))
```

Now, suppose we had a number of error functions, similar to `error`, and we could not decide in advance which one of these we would be using at any occasion. For example, we may happen to be interested in defining the error as the square of the difference between the two measures:

3.4 Other ways of calling functions

```
(defun error1 (measure1 measure2)
        (expt (difference measure1 measure2) 2))
```

Unfortunately, every time we change the error formula, we have to change either the definition of `error` or the name of the error function in `error-ratio`. Both approaches are clumsy. A much neater solution can be obtained by passing the error function as an argument to `error-ratio` so that its actual form need not be known in advance. Funcall enables us to do this easily:

```
(defun error-ratio (err-fun measure1 measure2)
        (quotient (funcall err-fun measure1 measure2)
                  (quotient (plus measure1 measure2) 2)))
```

Now we can call `error-ratio` using any error function we like:

```
-> (error-ratio 'error 99.0 101.0)
0.02
-> (error-ratio 'error1 99.0 101.0)
0.04
-> (error-ratio '(lambda (m1 m2)
                          (sqrt (abs (difference m1 m2))))
                99.0 101.0)
0.01414213562373095
->
```

Argument lists as arguments

We note that `funcall` is adequate for calling functions (passed as arguments) as long as the number of arguments to such functions is fixed and known in advance. Difficulties may arise when a function takes a variable number of arguments (e.g., `plus`). These difficulties are overcome by using `apply` which assumes that the arguments to a function are provided in a list. To give an example, suppose we want to define `sorted`, a function which returns t if and only if a list of numbers (of arbitrary length) is sorted. Here is how it may be defined:

```
(defun sorted (order num-list)
        (cond [(eq order 'ascending) (apply 'lessp num-list)]
              [t (apply 'greaterp num-list)]))
```

The first argument to `sorted` indicates which order of sorting should be assumed (i.e., ascending or descending). The second argument is a list of numbers. The function checks whether the list is sorted by applying `lessp` or `greaterp` to the list:

```
-> (sorted 'ascending '(10 20 21 36 100))
t
-> (sorted 'descending '(40 11 -1))
t
->
```

Alternatively, `sorted` may be defined as

```
(defun sorted (order num-list)
        (apply (cond [(eq order 'ascending) 'lessp]
                     [t 'greaterp])
               num-list))
```

to get exactly the same effect.

EXERCISE 3.10
Redefine the last version of `error-ratio` (in Section 3.4) so that the average of two measures is also calculated by a function passed as an argument to `error-ratio`.

EXERCISE 3.11
Redefine `error-ratio` again so that it accepts a list of measures rather than two measures. The error will be assumed to be the error between the first and the last measure in the list. Extend the function so that it caters for the cases when the measure list is empty, and when it contains one measure only.

3.5 Summary

In this chapter we have described some of the facilities of LISP for defining our own functions. The main points of the chapter may be summarized as follows.

- New functions may be defined using `defun`.
- A function definition consists of a function name, a *parameter* list, and a function *body*.
- Parameters and arguments are different things; the former appears in a function definition, the latter appears in a function call.
- A symbol appearing in a function's parameter list is a *bound variable* with respect to that function, otherwise, it is a *free variable*.
- Changes to a bound variable are forgotten after a call to the corresponding function is completed.
- Changes to a free variable persist after a call to a corresponding function has been completed.
- `Cond` enables selective evaluation of s-expressions.

- And and or may be used in certain cases as conditionals.
- Disciplined use of *super brackets* makes programs more readable.
- Lambda defines anonymous functions.
- Anonymous functions are useful for expressing simple functions which are used only once.
- Bound variables are defined by let.
- Functions can be called in exotic ways using funcall and apply.
- Funcall is useful for calling a function (with a fixed number of parameters) passed as argument to another function.
- Apply is useful for calling a function (with a fixed/variable number of parameters) passed as argument to another function.

Projects

3.1 Compare the cond function of LISP to the conditional constructs of a procedural language that you are familiar with. Using examples, show that all such conditionals can be expressed using cond. Now consider the reverse: are there any cond forms that cannot be equivalently represented using the conditional constructs of the procedural language you have chosen? (Hint: consider nested applications of cond, where one or more cond expressions appear inside another.)

3.2 Define perform, a function which takes one argument only. This argument will be a quoted list of one of the following forms, and the function will have an effect as specified below each form:

>(**if** s-expr1 **then** s-expr2)
>S-expr1 will be evaluated first and if it evaluates to nonnil then s-expr2 will be evaluated and its result will be returned, otherwise, nil will be returned.

>(**if** s-expr1 **then** s-expr2 **else** s-expr3)
>As above, except that s-expr3 will be evaluated and its result returned when s-expr1 evaluates to nil.

>(**unless** s-expr1 **then** s-expr2)
>The reverse of the first case above.

>(**unless** s-expr1 **then** s-expr2 **else** s-expr3)
>The reverse of the second case above.

>(**case** num **of** s-expr1 ... s-exprk)
>Num is evaluated first and must evaluate to a fixed number. If it evaluates to i then s-expri will be evaluated and its result returned, provided 1≤i≤k, otherwise, nil will be returned.

The following examples illustrate:

```
(perform '(if (listp x) then (setq x (cdr x))))

(perform '(if (eq (car x) 'ascending)
          then (cdr x)
          else (reverse (cdr x))))

(perform '(case page of (process page1)
                       (process page2)
                       (process page3)))
```

Chapter 4

Storage Principles

The objective of this chapter is two-fold: firstly, to introduce some of the important principles behind the storage mechanism of LISP, and secondly, to illustrate how a knowledge of these principles can provide a better understanding of the way some of the LISP functions work. We will describe the storage mechanism from a conceptual point of view without getting involved in the fine details of LISP implementations. A model for the internal representation of atoms and lists will be described. This model will then be used to explain exactly how list manipulation functions work. We will also introduce a number of destructive list manipulation primitives, which surgically alter list structures.

Other topics included in this chapter are: storage allocation and deallocation, and dotted pairs – a data structure which has been intentionally avoided thus far in this book.

4.1 Representation of s-expressions

LISP maintains a symbol table for keeping track of symbolic atoms. Each entry in the table is usually a structure of four components, as shown below.

symbol name	value binding	function binding	property list

The first component stores the so called print name of a symbol. Other components are pointers, depicting the value binding, the function binding, and the property list of the symbol. (Property lists will be discussed in Chapter 8.) All or some of the latter three entries may be unused at any point in time, in which case they point to some special locations in the store. Using this convention, LISP knows whether any of these is being used. For example, an atom x which has a value binding of 10, but no function binding or property list is represented as:

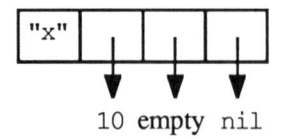

10 empty nil

where *empty* denotes a special location in the stores to which the second and the third component may point (to indicate that they are not used).

Lists are represented differently; each list consists of a collection of dynamic memory units, called *cons-cells*. A cons-cell is a small structure of two components, both of which are pointers:

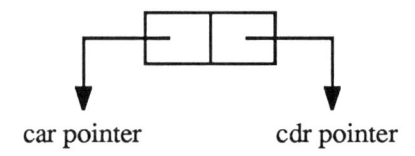

car pointer   cdr pointer

One of the pointers is called the *car pointer* (the pointer on the left above), the other the *cdr pointer*. A list structure is composed by having cons-cells pointing to one another, in a way which resembles a binary tree. For example, the list (x y z) is represented as:

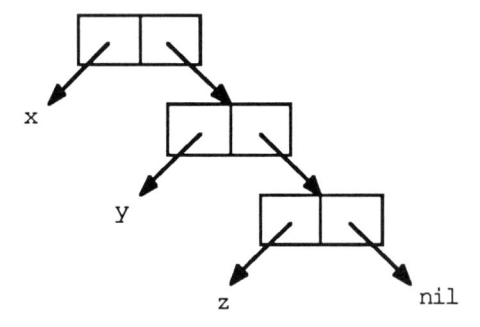

Here, the car of the first cons-cell points to the first atom in the list. Its cdr points to the next cons-cell. Similarly, the car of the second cons-cell points the second atom in the list, with its cdr pointing to the next cons-cell. The last element of the list is represented by a cons-cell whose cdr points to `nil`.

List manipulation functions follow the pointers in this tree structure to do their job. The functions `car` and `cdr`, for example, simply return the car and cdr pointer of the first cons-cell. The following diagram illustrates the effect of various applications of these functions.

4.1 Representation of s-expressions

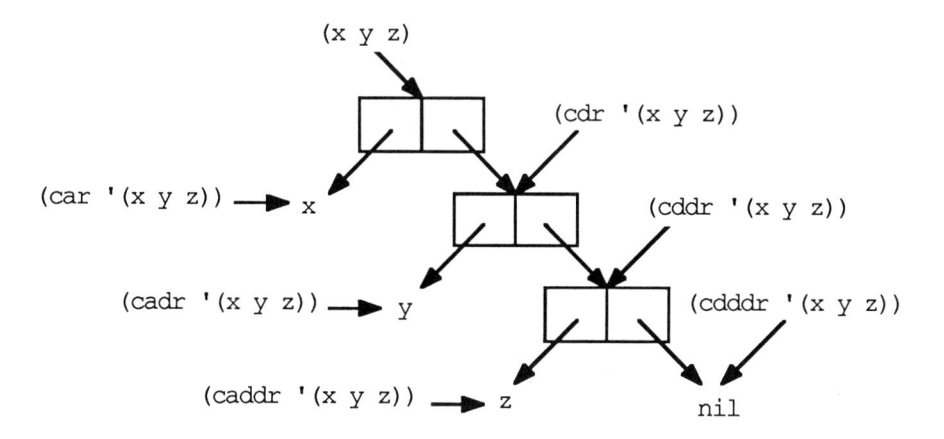

It is easy to show that every list structure has an equivalent binary tree representation. The next example shows the tree representation of a slightly more complicated list.

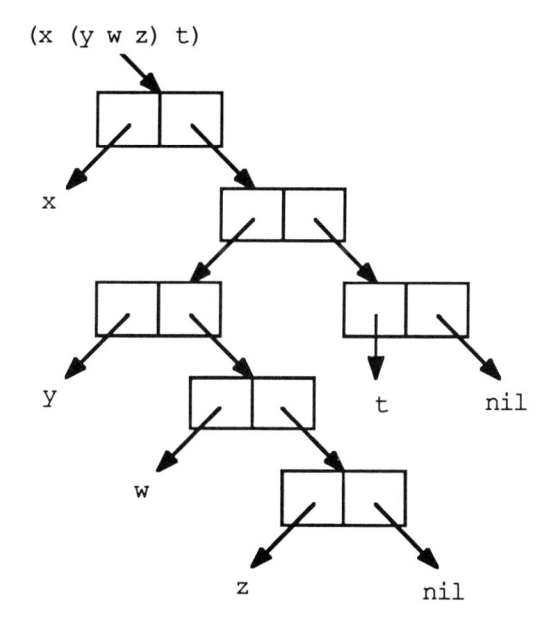

Cons-cell allocation

Many of the list manipulation functions consume new cons-cells each time they are called. Each application of `cons`, for example, requires a new cons-cell to insert an element in front of a list:

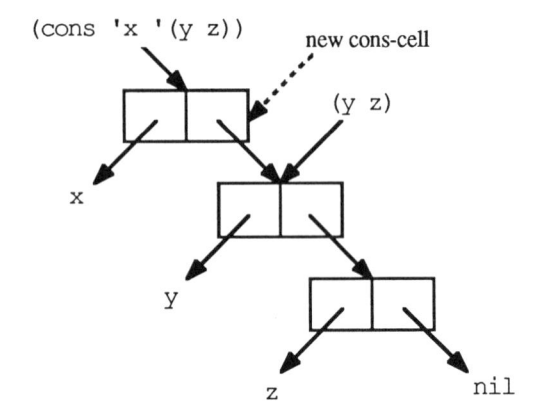

[Figure: (cons 'x '(y z)) showing a new cons-cell pointing to x and to the existing list (y z)]

The function list is even more expensive. It requires as many new cons-cells as there are arguments to list:

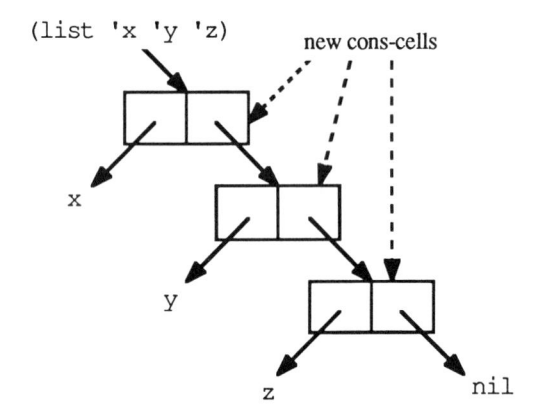

[Figure: (list 'x 'y 'z) showing three new cons-cells forming the list structure with x, y, z, and nil]

Append is slightly more complicated; (append list1 list2 ... listn) requires as many cons-cells as the total number of elements of its first n − 1 arguments. This is because append makes a copy of the top-level structure of the first n − 1 lists. For example, (append '(p q) '(r s)) consumes two new cons-cells for copying the top-level of (p q):

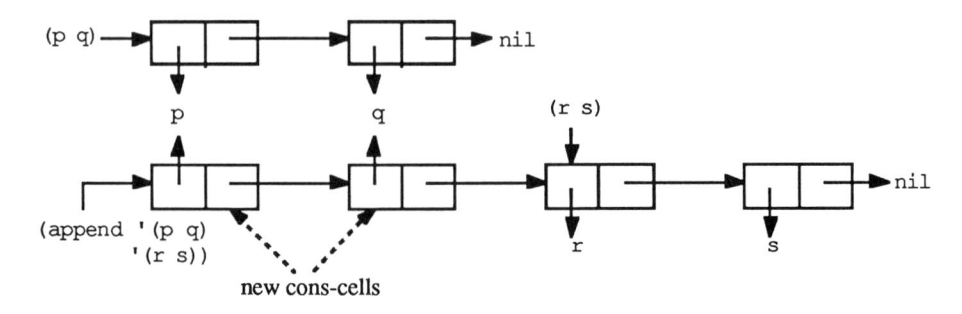

[Figure: diagram showing (p q) and (r s) as separate lists, and (append '(p q) '(r s)) creating two new cons-cells that point to p and q but share the tail (r s)]

4.1 Representation of s-expressions

Eq *revisited*

In Section 2.3 we mentioned that eq is a weaker form of equal, which tests for identity rather than equality. Using representations of list structures the difference can now be made clearer. Consider x, y, and z, three variables which are bound as follows:

```
-> (setq x '(p q r) y x)
(p q r)
-> (setq z '(p q r))
(p q r)
->
```

The variables x and y are identical since they point to the same list structure; x and z are equal since they refer to equivalent lists, but are not identical since these lists are two different copies of the same thing:

```
-> (eq x y)
t
-> (eq x z)
nil
-> (equal x z)
t
->
```

The following diagram illustrates the difference between what x, y, and z refer to:

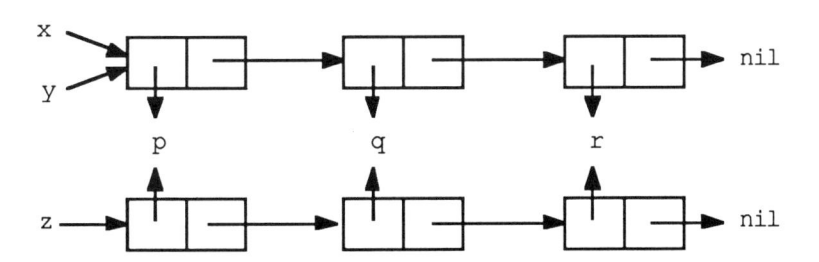

EXERCISE 4.1
Draw a binary tree representation of each of the following lists:

```
(a b c)
(a (b) c)
(a (b (c (d))))
(a (b (c) d) ((e)))
((((nil))))
```

EXERCISE 4.2
> Use binary tree representations to illustrate the effect of evaluating each of the following forms:

```
(cons 'a (cons 'b nil))
(list (list 'a) (list 'b))
(append (list 'a) (list 'b) (list 'c))
```

EXERCISE 4.3
> Write `append-cost`, a function which takes a list of lists and returns the number of new cons-cells required for applying append to that list.

4.2 Destructive primitives

An important property of the list manipulation primitives described thus far in this book is that they make no changes to their arguments. For example, `remove` creates a new list rather than actually removing elements from a list:

```
-> (setq x '(7 9 9 2))
(7 9 9 2)
-> (remove 9 x)
(7 2)
-> x
(7 9 9 2)
->
```

Such functions are called *pure* since they do not cause any side-effects; they use fresh cons-cells if necessary to avoid disturbing list structures. Certain LISP primitives do not share this property; they make implicit changes to their arguments and for that reason are called *impure or destructive*. We have already encountered one such function, `setq`, which was relatively straightforward. The functions that we shall be describing below have more subtle effects: they destructively change list structures.

Destructive composition and transformation

The pure composition function `append` has a destructive counterpart called `nconc`. Like `append`, it sticks two or more lists together. Unlike `append`, it does so by making changes to all its nonempty arguments except the last:

```
-> (setq x '(p q) y '(r s))
(r s)
```

4.2 Destructive primitives

```
-> (nconc x y)
(p q r s)
-> y
(r s)
-> x
(p q r s)
->
```

Nconc, therefore, concatenates lists by altering the cdr pointer of a list so that it will point to the next list:

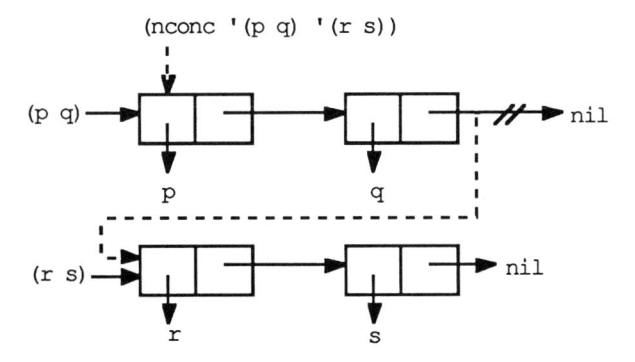

Here, the last cdr pointer in (p q) is altered and forced to point to (r s). The result of this is that we are left with one list: (p q) no longer exists; it is now (p q r s).

Similarly, remove, subst and reverse have destructive equivalents called delete, dsubst and nreverse, respectively:

```
-> (setq x '(a b c d))
(a b c d)
-> (delete 'a x)
(b c d)
-> x
(b c d)
-> (dsubst 'm 'c x)
(a m d)
-> x
(a m d)
-> (nreverse x)
(d m a)
-> x
(a)
->
```

Changing head and tail

The head of a list can be changed destructively by a function called `rplaca` (standing for replace car). Similarly, the tail of a list can be changed by `rplacd` (standing for replace cdr). Here are two simple examples:

```
-> (setq x '(a b c))
(a b c)
-> (rplaca x 'm)
(m b c)
-> x
(m b c)
-> (rplacd x '(n))
(m n)
-> x
(m n)
->
```

Rplaca and rplacd change the head and tail of a list by destructively changing the car and cdr pointers of the first cons-cell in the list:

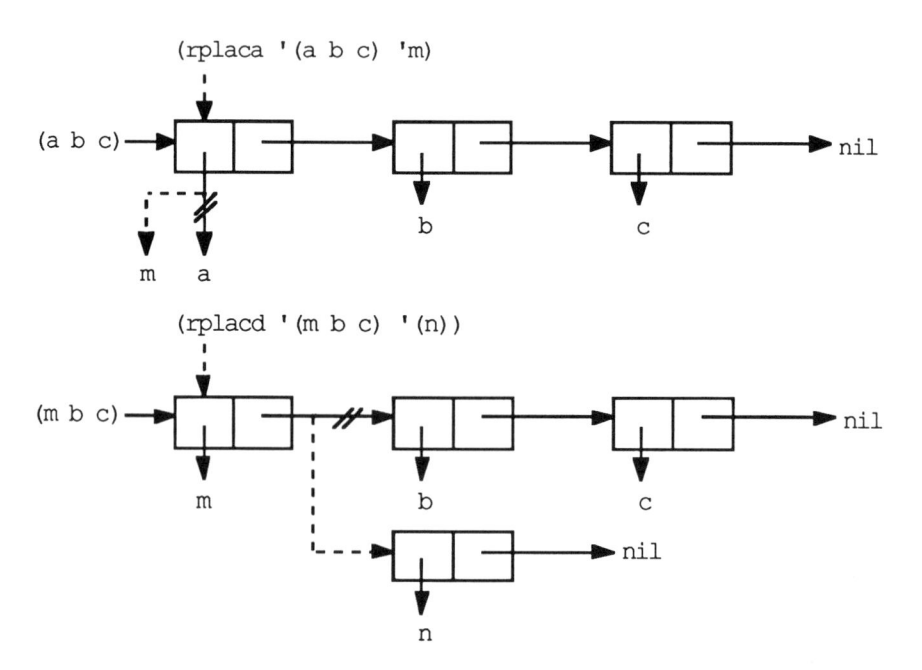

It should be obvious that destructive functions are in general cheaper than the pure ones, for the simple reason that they do not consume any new cons-cells. However, this

4.2 Destructive primitives

advantage is gained at a high price; elegance and clarity are practically lost. The effects created by destructive functions are not always easy to work out and keep track of. Indeed, some of the most subtle and agonizing programming errors are caused by the use of these functions. You are therefore advised to use them only when you are sure what you are doing. If you are not really pressed for efficiency, you might as well ignore these functions altogether.

Having given the warning, it is only fair to say that there are a few situations where the use of destructive functions can be both wise and safe. (See, for example, the use of nconc in Section 5.3.)

Circular lists

One of the worst problems that destructive manipulations of lists can lead to is what is known as a *circular list*. A circular list is a list in which a cons-cell points to an earlier cons-cell. Two examples are shown below.

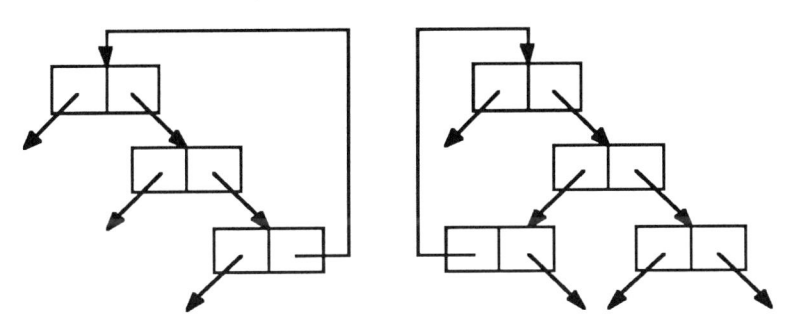

Careless use of destructive functions can easily create circular lists. For example,

```
(rplacd (cddr (setq x '(p q r))) x)
```

will create the following circular list.

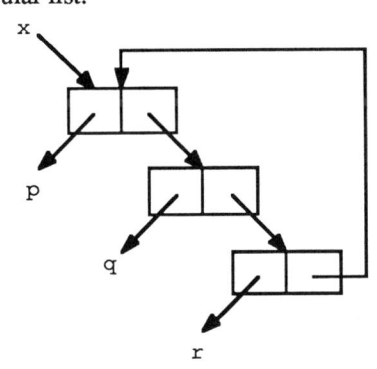

Circular lists are dangerous because one can get caught up in them forever. To convince yourself, just try giving x to LISP for evaluation. You will notice that the LISP system will get into an infinite loop, out of which there is no escape except by brutally interrupting the program.

EXERCISE 4.4

Evaluate the following, in the order given. After each evaluation examine x, y and z, and try to explain their values.

```
(setq x (list 'LISP) y (list 'excites) z (list 'me))
(append x '() y z)
(nconc x y z)
(dsubst 'bores 'excites y)
(nreverse y)
(nreverse x)
(delete 'me z)
```

EXERCISE 4.5

Use append to write copy, a function which takes one list as argument and returns a copy of the top level of the list. Test copy by checking that

```
(nconc (copy '(a b c)) '(d e f))
```

is equivalent to:

```
(append '(a b c) '(d e f))
```

EXERCISE 4.6

Evaluate the following s-expressions, in the order given, and explain the results.

```
(setq x '(a b) y '(c d) z '(e f))
(setq p (append x y z))
(setq q (nconc x y z))
(equal p q)
(eq p q)
(eq p x)
(eq x q)
```

EXERCISE 4.7

Write down expressions, using rplaca, rplacd, car and cdr only, which change the symbols in the following lists, one by one, from lower case to upper case.

```
(birds can fly)
(pigs ((cannot)))
(programs (have (bugs)))
(((computers)) have ((not)))
```

4.3 Storage management

The random access memory of a LISP system is usually divided into a number of partitions, each responsible for storing certain categories of objects. For example, we may have a section for storing lists, another for storing small fixed numbers, and yet another for storing strings, etc. Some LISP systems employ this style of partitioning in order to keep track of the type of objects.

The largest and most important storage area is that of lists. It consists of a block of contiguous memory cells arranged in the following fashion:

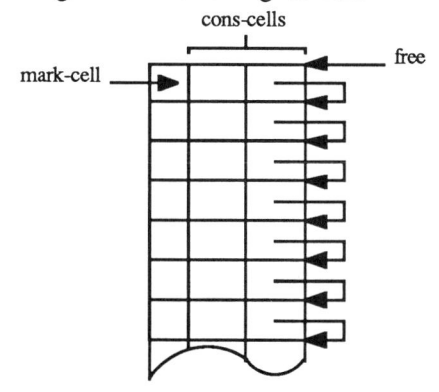

Each structure consists of a cons-cell and a mark-cell. The role of a mark-cell will be explained later. Originally, the entire list storage is arranged as a huge list by having the cdr pointer of each cons-cell pointing to the next cons-cell. Each time a new cons-cell is required, LISP sets the cdr pointer of the current cell (i.e., the cell pointed to by *free*) to nil, returns that cons-cell, and moves the free pointer to the next cell. For example,

```
(setq x (list 'p 'q))
```

will cause the following rearrangement (where the mark-cells have been dropped for clarity):

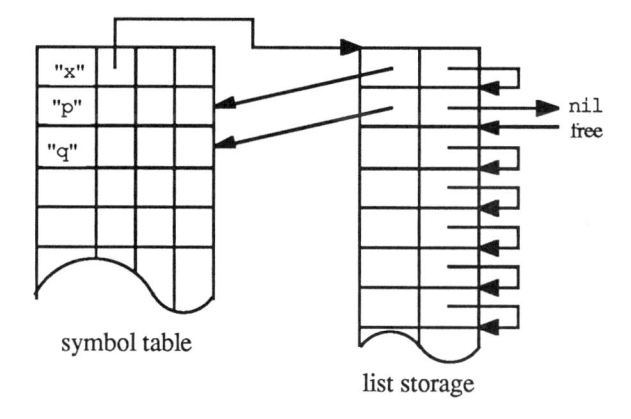

symbol table

list storage

The operation causes the allocation of two cons-cells. The value binding of the symbol x (in the symbol table) is set to the first cell, and the car pointer of the first two cells are set to point to the entries of p and q in the symbol table.

Garbage collection

In the above example, if we change the value of x by setting it to something else

(setq x 'p)

then the pointer to the first cons-cell will be lost:

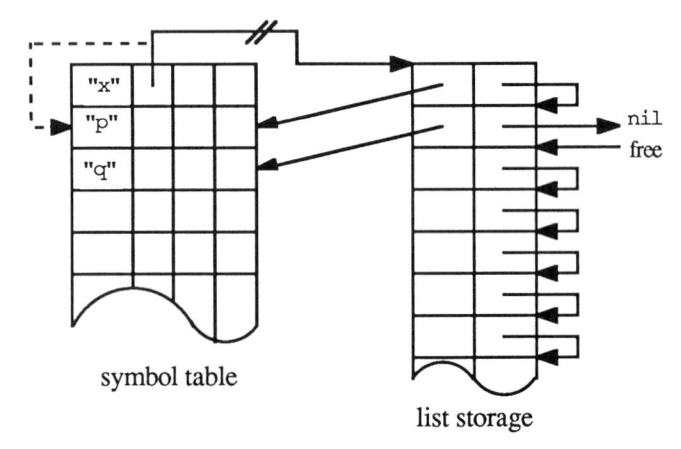

symbol table

list storage

As a result, the first two cons-cells will be inaccessible, and may safely be added back to the free list for reuse. Any previously accessible data which becomes inaccessible is referred to as *garbage*. The process which liberates such garbage is called *garbage collection*.

Garbage collection is typically done in two steps. The first step, called *mark*, goes through the symbol table, and follows the value binding, the function binding, and the property list of every atom, marking every cons-cell it encounters by setting its mark-cell. Since garbage cells cannot be accessed in this way, the process will ensure that all cells but the garbage cells will be marked. The second step of garbage collection, called *sweep*, goes through all the cons-cells and adds the unmarked cells to the free list. It also resets the mark-cells so that the next garbage collection phase may be carried out correctly.

Garbage collection is usually done automatically, without the intervention of the user. The specific strategy used for this varies across different LISP implementations. For example, some LISP systems do a bit of garbage collection after a certain number of cons-cells have been used. Others postpone garbage collection until the free list has been exhausted, and then do one big garbage collection. The advantage of the former approach is that the effect of the process remains almost transparent to the user, and in fact is rarely noticed. The advantage of the latter approach is that it is more efficient, since the overall time

4.4 Dotted pairs

spent on garbage collection is considerably less.

Incidently, the concept of garbage is not limited to cons-cells. Many other data structures, such as strings and arrays, can become garbage, too. The way in which these are garbage collected is very much nonstandard. Some LISP systems, for example, do not garbage collect strings at all; others do so only when the storage is completely exhausted.

4.4 Dotted pairs

It is possible for a cons-cell to have its cdr pointer pointing to an atom rather than another cons-cell or `nil`. The result of this is called a *dotted pair*. The cons-cell

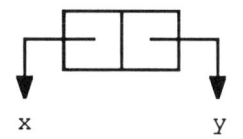

is an example. Dotted pairs are produced when the second argument of `cons` is a nonnil atom. For example, the above dotted pair is produced by:

```
-> (cons 'x 'y)
(x . y)
->
```

A dotted pair is represented by a list of two elements with a dot in the middle.

Early implementations of LISP made extensive use of dotted pairs, mostly for no other reason than saving storage space. Advances in hardware technology and a rapid drop in the cost of memory have made this practice relatively obsolete. Indeed, dotted pairs are best avoided since they can create some very disturbing programming errors.

EXERCISE 4.8

Evaluate the following s-expression and explain the results:

```
(cons 'c (cons 'b (cons 'c 'd)))
(cons (list 'a 'b) 'c)
(list (cons 'a1 'b1) (cons 'a1 'b2) (cons 'a3 'b3))
(cons (cons 'a1 'b1) (cons 'a2 'b2))
```

4.5 Summary

In this chapter we have described the main principles behind the storage mechanisms of LISP. We can summarize them as follows.

- LISP keeps track of symbols using a symbol table, with one entry per symbol.
- List structures are made out of *cons-cells*.
- A cons-cell consists of two components: a *car pointer* and a *cdr pointer*.
- A list is represented as a binary tree of cons-cells.
- Most *pure* list manipulation functions consume cons-cells.
- *Destructive* list manipulation functions economize by destructively changing pointers in list structures.
- Nconc, delete, dsubst and nreverse compose or transform lists destructively.
- Rplaca and rplacd change the head and tail of a list respectively and destructively.
- Destructive manipulation of lists can lead to *circular lists*. This problem must be carefully avoided.
- Con-cells are dynamically allocated.
- LISP automatically *garbage collects* its store.
- A cons-cell whose cdr pointer points to a nonnil atom is called a *dotted pair*.
- Dotted pairs are economic but dangerous.

Project

4.1 Write a simple LISP-like memory manager in Pascal or any other procedural language that you are familiar with. Your program should consist of two major functions: allocate, and collect. Allocate returns a new cons-cell each time it is called, while collect does a complete garbage collection of the store. Design allocate so that it calls collect after every 100 cons-cell allocations. (If you need a more detailed description of garbage collection principles, you may refer to the book by Knuth [1974].)

Chapter 5

Recursion and Iteration

Almost any programming activity requires some notion of repetition, that is, a way of repeating some computation a number of times. There are two fundamental approaches to programming repetition. The first – the older approach – is based on the repeated execution of a sequence of instructions, either for a predetermined number of times, or until some condition is satisfied. This is called *iteration*. The second approach is based on the use of a function by itself. This is called *recursion*, and functions of this nature are called *recursive*. In this chapter we shall introduce recursion followed by a discussion of iteration which also describes the main LISP function provided for this purpose. Finally, we shall examine some useful mapping functions which support an implicit style of iteration.

5.1 Recursion

Recursion is one of the most important and elegant programming techniques ever invented. As mentioned above, it relies on the notion of functions which refer to themselves. To most programmers (who are used to conventional programming languages) recursion is a difficult concept and rather hard to live with. Luckily, recursion is easy in LISP, provided two simple rules are kept in mind. The first rule concerns the use of recursion; it states that recursion is useful only when a problem can be defined in terms of itself. To give an example, consider the problem of calculating the factorial of a positive integer n. This may be formulated as follows

$$0! = 1$$
$$n! = n*(n - 1)!$$

which states that the factorial of 0 is 1, and that the factorial of n is n times the factorial of $n - 1$. The second line clearly shows that factorial is defined in terms of itself. Here is an example of how factorial works:

$$3! = 3*(3-1)! = 3*2!$$
$$= 3*2*(2-1)! = 3*2*1!$$
$$= 3*2*1*0! = 3*2*1*1 = 6$$

We can readily turn the above definition of factorial into a recursive LISP function:

```
(defun factorial (n)
    (cond [(zerop n) 1]                     ;; termination condition.
          [t (times n (factorial (1- n)))])) ;; recursive step.
```

Each time `factorial` is called, n is examined to see if it is zero, in which case 1 will be returned. However, if n is not zero then `factorial` will be called again, with its argument decremented by 1. If we start with a positive n then at some stage n will eventually become zero, at which time the first clause of `cond` will be satisfied and the recursion will unfold. The first clause of `cond` in `factorial` is called the *termination condition* and illustrates the second rule of recursion: every recursive function must have at least one termination condition. The second clause of `cond` is where `factorial` is called by itself. This is called the *recursive step*.

A graphical representation of `factorial` may help you get a better picture of how it works. Figure 5.1 shows the steps involved in computing `(factorial 3)`.

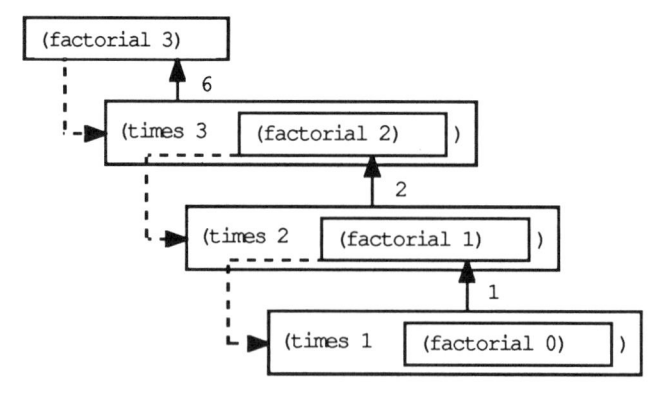

Figure 5.1 The recursive steps in evaluating `(factorial 3)`.

In this figure a dashed line represents a call to `factorial`, and solid line represents the result returned by a `factorial` call when it is completed. The initial call causes three subsequent calls to `factorial`. After each call is completed the result produced by that call is returned to the previous call. Note that the flow of control first works downwards (depicted by dashed lines) and then upwards (depicted by solid lines). The former is called the *folding* process; the latter is called the *unfolding* process.

5.1 Recursion

Many of the list manipulation primitives of LISP can be easily defined as recursive functions. Consider `reverse` for example. The reverse of a list x is `nil` if x is `nil`. Otherwise, it is the same as appending the reverse of the tail of x to a list containing just the head of x:

```
(defun reverse (list)
    (cond [(null list) nil]                 ;; termination condition.
          [t (append (reverse (cdr list))   ;; recursive step.
                     (list (car list)))]))
```

The structure of `reverse` is very similar to that of `factorial`: the first clause of `cond` is the termination condition, and the second clause represents the recursive step. Figure 5.2 shows `reverse` at work when applied to the list (a b c).

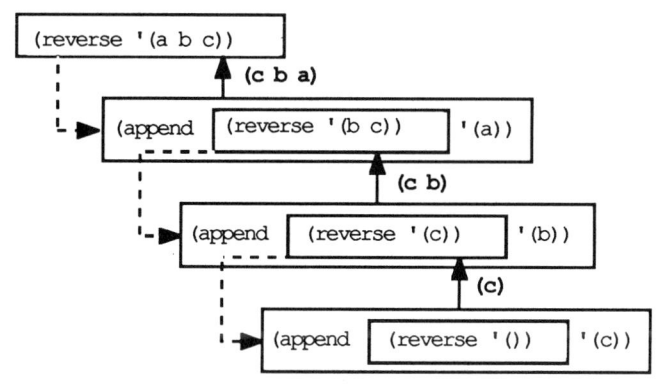

```
(reverse '(a b c))
        ↑ (c b a)
(append (reverse '(b c)) '(a))
                ↑ (c b)
        (append (reverse '(c)) '(b))
                        ↑ (c)
                (append (reverse '()) '(c))
```

Figure 5.2 The recursive steps in evaluating (reverse '(a b c)).

Tail recursion

Consider a function called `nth-element` which when given a list and an integer, depicting the position of an element of the list, returns that element:

```
-> (nth-element 3 '(a b c d))
c
->
```

`Nth-element` may be defined in terms of itself: the nth element of a list x is the head of x if n is one. Otherwise, it is the (n−1)th element of the tail of x:

```
(defun nth-element (n x)
    (cond [(onep n) (car x)]              ;; termination condition.
          [t (nth-element (1- n) (cdr x))])) ;; recursive step.
```

Figure 5.3 shows the steps involved in evaluating (nth-element 3 '(a b c d)).

```
┌─────────────────────────────────────┐
│ (nth-element 3 '(a b c d)       )   │
└─────────────────────────────────────┘
    ╷                   ▲ c
    │    ┌──────────────┴──────────┐
    └──▶ │ (nth-element 2 '(b c d))│
         └─────────────────────────┘
             ╷              ▲ c
             │   ┌──────────┴──────┐
             └──▶│(nth-element 1 '(c d))│
                 └──────────────────┘
```

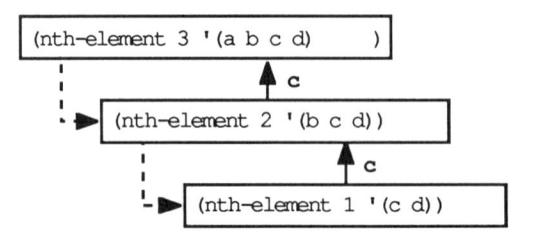

Figure 5.3 The recursive steps in evaluating (nth-element 3 '(a b c d)).

This figure highlights an interesting point about nth-element. Each time recursion is unfolded, the result (i.e., c) is passed to the previous step without alteration. This was not true of the earlier examples. For instance, reverse appended the result to a list and then passed it upwards. This interesting property of nth-element is known as *tail recursion*, and nth-element is itself said to be *tail recursive*.

Until recently, tail recursion was not regarded and handled as a special case; this resulted in inefficient implementations. Modern LISP systems use optimization techniques for the efficient handling of tail recursion.

Multi-arm recursion

Consider a variant of the primitive member which returns t if and only if a given atom is in a list. Let us call this function is-in. Unlike member, we require is-in to search through all the levels of a list if necessary:

```
-> (member 'c '(a (b (c d) e)))
nil
-> (is-in 'c '(a (b (c d) e)))
t
->
```

Is-in may be defined recursively as follows:

```
(defun is-in (atom list)              ;; is atom in list?
  (cond [(null list) nil]              ;; termination condition.
        [(atom (car list))             ;; is head of list a list?
         (or (eq (car list) atom)      ;; atom = head of list?
             (is-in atom (cdr list)))] ;; atom in tail of list?
        [t (or (is-in atom (car list)) ;; atom in head of list?
               (is-in atom (cdr list)))])) ;; atom in tail of list?
```

5.1 Recursion

The first clause of cond checks if list is empty. If so, obviously it cannot contain atom, and nil will be returned. The second clause considers the case when the head of list is an atom. Here t will be returned if atom is the same as the head of list, or if it is in the tail of list. The last clause considers the case when the head of list is a list. This is handled by applying is-in recursively to the head and the tail of list. Figure 5.4 illustrates the steps involved in an application of is-in.

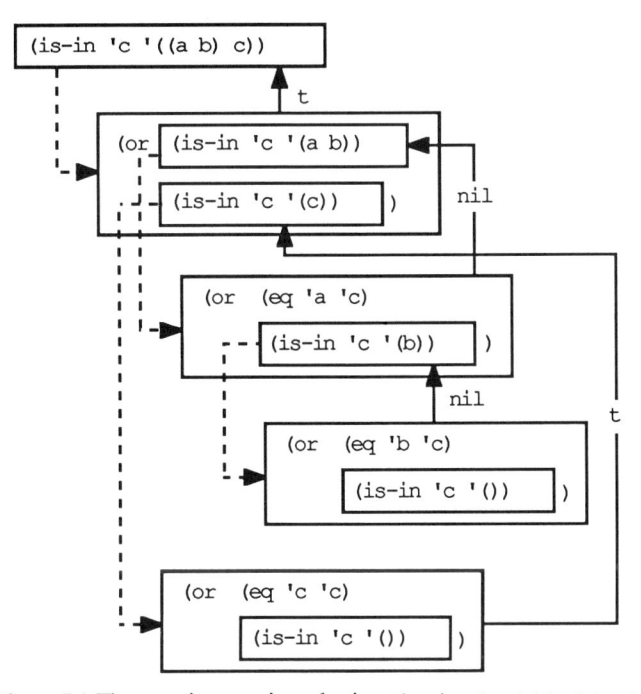

Figure 5.4 The recursive steps in evaluating (is-in 'c '((a b) c)).

Is-in is a *multi-arm* recursive function; all previous examples have dealt with *single-arm* recursion. More precisely, these properties can be defined as follows.

- A function which, when called, calls itself no more than once during that call is single-arm recursive.
- A function which, when called, may call itself more than once during that call is multi-arm recursive.

Note that the body of a function may contain more than one reference to itself and yet the function may be single-arm recursive. This is the case when the conditions triggering the calls are mutually exclusive. Also, note that it is possible for a tail recursive function to be single-arm or multi-arm.

Mutual recursion

A more subtle form of recursion occurs when a function calls itself, not necessarily directly, but via one or more other functions. Such functions are said to be *mutually recursive*. For example, if two functions f1 and f2 call one another (i.e., f1 calls f2, and f2 calls f1) then f1 and f2 are both mutually recursive. Mutual recursion is a viable solution when a problem can be broken down into two or more subproblems, where each subproblem is expressed in terms of the others (and possibly itself).

Let us take a look at a typical problem that can be solved by mutual recursion. Suppose we want to define a function called reduce which when applied to a logical expression (expressed in terms of and and or) reduces it to an equivalent but simpler form. For example, when applied to

```
(and (and a b) (or c (or d e)) f)
```

it should produce:

```
(and a b (or c d e) f)
```

In other words, reduce should get rid of any unnecessary ands and ors in a logical expression. It may be defined as follows:

```
(defun reduce (pred)                                  ;; reduce predicate.
   (cond [(atom pred) pred]                           ;; atomic predicate.
         [(eq (car pred) 'and)                        ;; conjunction.
          (cons 'and (reduce-aux 'and (cdr pred)))]
         [(eq (car pred) 'or)                         ;; disjunction.
          (cons 'or (reduce-aux 'or (cdr pred)))]
         [t pred]))
```

Reduce just reconstructs the predicate pred. If pred is an atom it will return pred itself; if pred is a list whose head is and or or it will reconstruct the list by calling reduce-aux, otherwise, it will return pred. Reduce-aux takes the arguments of an and or or function as a list and reconstructs the argument list by removing the unnecessary ands and ors:

```
(defun reduce-aux (op preds)                          ;; auxiliary.
   (cond [(null preds) nil]                           ;; termination condition.
         [(and (listp (car preds))                    ;; operator in head of preds
               (eq (caar preds) op))                  ;; matches op?
          (append (reduce-aux op (cdar preds))        ;; reduce head.
                  (reduce-aux op (cdr preds)))]       ;; reduce tail.
         [t (cons (reduce (car preds))                ;; reduce head.
                  (reduce-aux op (cdr preds)))]))     ;; reduce tail.
```

5.1 Recursion

`Reduce-aux` takes a logical operator `op` and a list of predicates `preds` which are assumed to be arguments to `op`. If `preds` is an empty list `reduce-aux` will simply return `nil`. If `preds` is nonempty and the first predicate in `preds` is itself a list whose head is the same as `op`, then `preds` will be reduced by applying `reduce-aux` to the arguments in the head of `preds`, and to the tail of `preds`, and the two will then be joined. Otherwise, `preds` is reduced by reducing the first predicate using `reduce` and other predicates using `reduce-aux`:

```
-> (reduce '(or (and (and a b) c) (or d e)))
(or (and a b c) d e)
-> (reduce '(or (or (or a b) c) d (or e f g)))
(or a b c d e f g)
->
```

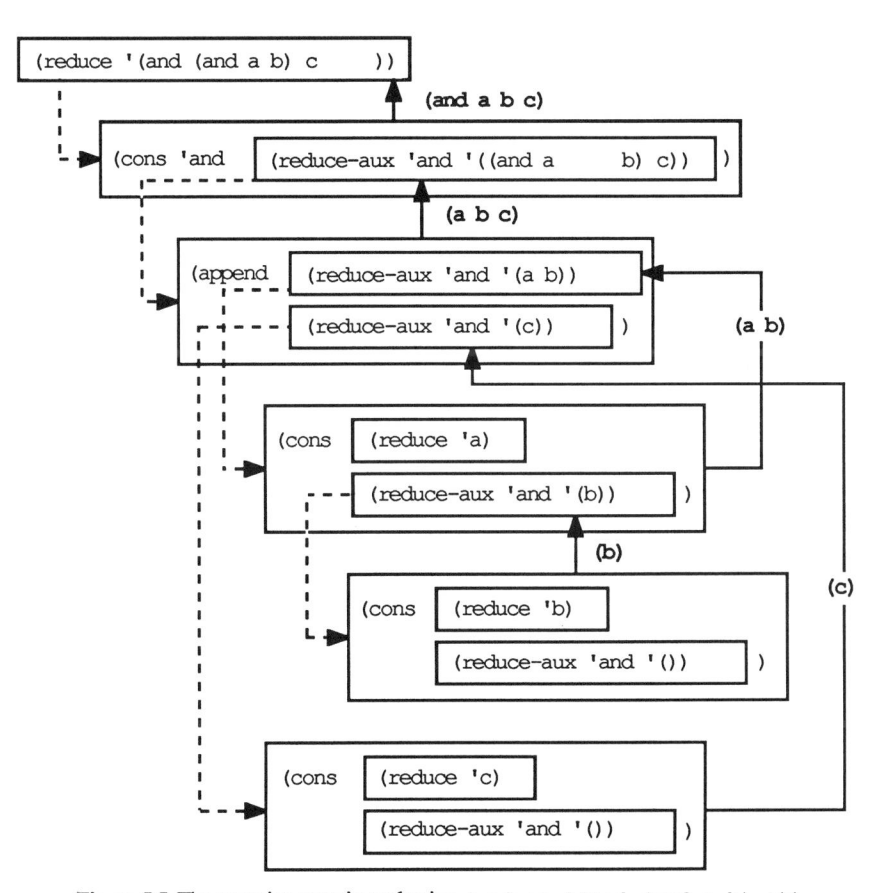

Figure 5.5 The recursive steps in evaluating `(reduce '(and (and a b) c))`.

`Reduce` and `reduce-aux` are mutually recursive since they refer to one another. Figure 5.5 shows the steps involved in reducing a simple logical expression using `reduce`.

It is important to note that mutual recursion can exist between more than two functions as well. Figure 5.6 illustrates two (of the many possible) cases, each involving four mutually recursive functions. Directed lines in this figure depict the calling of one function by another. As a general rule, we can make the following statement.

- Two or more functions are mutually recursive if any of them can be reached from any of the others through a sequence of one or more calls.

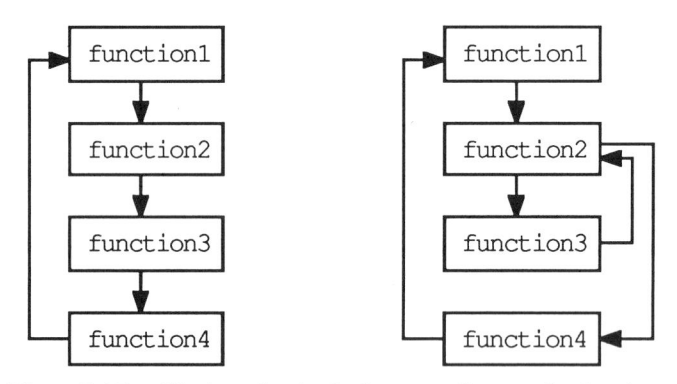

Figure 5.6 Possible dependencies for four mutually recursive functions.

EXERCISE 5.1
Define recursive versions of the LISP primitives: `member`, `length`, and `subst`.

EXERCISE 5.2
Define `nth-tail`, a recursive function which takes an integer n and a list as arguments, and returns the result of cdring n times down the list.

EXERCISE 5.3
Modify the definition of `is-in` above so that both arguments may be lists, and that the function will return the number of occurrences of the first list in all levels of the second list.

5.2 Iteration

As opposed to recursion, which relies on the notion of self-reference, iteration is based on explicit repetition. To iterate is to repeat a computation a number of times. LISP provides two primary functions for iteration. These are described below.

5.2 Iteration

Prog-*based iteration*

Prog is the most elementary iteration function. It supports the following.

- The creation of local variables; in this sense prog is similar to let.
- Elementary loops which are formulated by specifying *labels* (or *tags*) which we may explicitly jump to. A label is simply an atom (i.e., a number or a symbol) in the top level of a prog body.
- The grouping of two or more s-expressions. The body of prog may consist of one or more s-expressions which are evaluated in sequence (rather similar to the body of a function).

A few examples will make these concepts clearer. Suppose we want to write an iterative version of the factorial function using prog. This may be defined as follows:

```
(defun factorial (n)
      (prog (fac)
            (setq fac 1)                    ;; initialize fac.
         loop
            (cond [(zerop n) (return fac)]) ;; term. condition.
            (setq fac (times n fac)         ;; calculate fac.
                  n (1- n))                 ;; decrement n.
            (go loop)))
```

The first argument to prog is always a list of local variables – the list (fac) here. This list may optionally be empty. The body of a prog consists of one or more s-expressions which may be either an atom or a list. The former is assumed to be a label, specifying a position which we may jump to, while the latter is assumed to be a computation. In prog we are usually interested only in the side-effects of such computations. A prog is evaluated by first binding the local variables to nil, and then evaluating each nonatomic s-expression in the body.

Two special function may be used in prog, these being return and go. The former takes an optional argument (which if not present is assumed to be nil) and when evaluated terminates prog and returns the value of its argument. The latter takes one argument which is not evaluated and which must be a label. When evaluated, go transfers control to the point just after the specified label.

In the factorial function, upon evaluation of prog, the local variable fac is bound to nil. The first s-expression in the body is then evaluated which binds fac to 1. The next s-expression is loop which, since an atom, is assumed to be a label and is ignored. The cond expression is then evaluated which checks whether n is zero. If so, the value of fac is returned and the function is terminated. Otherwise, the next s-expression in the body is evaluated which stores the product of n and fac in fac, and decrements n by 1. The last s-expression makes an explicit jump to the loop label. This means that the cond expression will be evaluated again, and so on. The s-expressions between loop and (go loop) are evaluated repeatedly until n becomes zero.

Note that in factorial the only way out of prog is through the return expression. This is because the last s-expression in the prog body is a go expression which causes a jump back to loop. When this is not the case, a prog can also terminate by the flow of control reaching the end of the prog body. In the latter case prog will always return nil:

```
-> (prog (x y)
         (setq x 10)
         (setq y 20))
nil
->
```

Also, note that the choice of a label name is quite arbitrary. For example, in factorial we could have used any other atom instead of loop (e.g., next, label, or even 1) to get exactly the same effect.

The next example defines an iterative version of the reverse primitive. It reverses list by moving down list, one element at a time, and reconstructing list in the reverse order:

```
(defun reverse (list)
   (prog (rev)
      loop
         (and (null list) (return rev))      ;; termination condition.
         (setq rev (cons (car list) rev)     ;; insert next element.
               list (cdr list))              ;; next tail.
         (go loop)))
```

Figure 5.7 shows the general structure of prog.

```
(prog   (var1 ... varn)
        s-expression-1
              :
        s-expression-k )
```

Figure 5.7 The general structure of prog.

Evaluating prog has the following effect.

5.2 Iteration

1. The variables var1 ... varn are all bound to nil.
2. The s-expressions s-expression-1 ... s-expression-k are treated in the following manner.
    2.1 If s-expression-i is an atom it will be assumed to be a label and will be ignored.
    2.2 Otherwise, s-expression-i will be evaluated.
        2.2.1 If this causes the evaluation of a return expression then prog will be terminated and the value of the argument of return will be returned. (If no argument is specified then nil will be returned.)
        2.2.2 If this causes the evaluation of a go expression then control will be transferred to the s-expression just after the label specified by go.
        2.2.3 Otherwise, the value produced as a result of the evaluation of s-expression-i will be thrown away.
3. If flow of control passes the end of prog body then nil will be returned.

Prog has also a number of associated functions which are noniterative. They are useful when we want to group two or more s-expressions into one s-expression, and yet avoid the overhead of using prog. These are prog1, prog2, and progn. Prog1 takes one or more s-expressions, evaluates them in the order they occur, and returns the value of the first s-expression. Prog2 and progn do the same thing but return the value of the second and the last s-expression respectively. Note that, unlike prog, none of these take any local variables or labels. Also, note that return and go are meaningless within the context of these functions.

Do-based iteration

Some programmers believe that prog-based iteration is too crude and can be easily misused. They argue that the use of go can lead to some very complicated flow of control structures which, beside being difficult to understand, are rather error-prone. This problem may be avoided by a disciplined use of prog which enforces a number of good habits such as ensuring that variables are properly initialized, loops are well-structured, labels are proceeded by proper tests for termination of loops, etc. These disciplines may be further enforced by an alternative function called do which is provided by most LISP systems.

Do encourages the programmer to write *structured loops*; these are loops with straightforward control structures. An example will help explaining the use of do. Let us redefine the factorial function, this time using do:

```
(defun factorial (n)
    (do [(fac 1 (times (1+ n) fac))]     ;; initialize and iterate.
        [(zerop n) fac]                   ;; termination condition.
        (setq n (1- n))))                 ;; decrement n.
```

The first argument to do is a list of zero or more local variable specifications. Each variable specification is a list of one to three elements. The head of a list specifies the variable name. The second element in the list specifies an initial value for the variable and the third element in the list specifies a value to which the variable will be bound after each iteration. The second and the third elements are both optional. The second argument to do is a clause – very much like a cond clause. The remaining arguments are s-expressions and act exactly like a prog body.

Do first binds each of its local variables to its initial value (if any). It then evaluates the head of the clause. If this evaluates to nonnil then the remaining s-expressions in the clause will be evaluated and the value of the last s-expression will be returned. Otherwise, do evaluates the s-expressions in the body in the order they occur. Following this, the local variables will be bound to their next value (if any). For example, in factorial, fac will be bound to the value of (times n fac), and the whole process will be repeated.

The general structure of do is shown in Figure 5.8.

```
(do   [(var1 init1 next1) ... (varn initn nextn)]
      [s-expression-c1 ... s-expression-ck]
      s-expression-1
                :
      s-expression-t )
```

Figure 5.8 The general structure of do.

The s-expressions init1 ... initn and next1 ... nextn are optional. The effect of evaluating do is as follows.

1. Var1 ... varn are bound to init1 ... initn in that order and in parallel. When initi is not present it is assumed to be nil.
2. S-expression-c1 is evaluated.
   2.1 If it evaluates to nonnil then s-expression-c2 ... s-expression-ck will be evaluated in that order and the value of s-expression-ck will be returned.
3. S-expression-1 ... s-expression-t are treated as the body of a prog and are evaluated accordingly. Any of s-expression-i may be a label or a list, and may contain explicit gos and returns.
4. Var1 ... varn are bound to the values of next1 ... nextn in that order and in parallel. This step should be ignored if there is no nexti for vari.
5. Go to Step 2.

Since the body of do is exactly like the body of prog, it follows that anything that can be expressed using one, can also be expressed using the other (in possibly a slightly different way). So, although do is more disciplined, it can still be misused just as prog can. Therefore, the question of which one to use is really a matter of taste. The choice should be

5.3 Mapping functions

dictated at best by the problem at hand. Sometimes do matches a problem quite nicely and that is a good enough reason for using it. On other occasions, however, prog provides clearer solutions.

EXERCISE 5.4
> Define iterative versions of the LISP primitives: member, length, and subst.

EXERCISE 5.5
> Define iterative versions of nth-tail (see Exercise 5.2) and nth-element (see Section 5.1). Which version do you consider more reasonable?

EXERCISE 5.6
> Extend the definition of nth-element so that it returns nil when its first argument is less than one. Similarly, extend nth-tail so that it returns nil when its first argument is negative.

EXERCISE 5.7
> Define iterative versions of is-in and reduce (as described in Section 5.1). Which version is more elegant? Which version is more efficient?

5.3 Mapping functions

Certain styles of iteration are directly supported by a number of special functions in LISP, known as the *mapping functions*. These are useful for performing the same computation on all elements of one or more lists. Obviously such iteration can also be accomplished by prog or do. Mapping functions, however, are preferred for this purpose since they offer an *implicit* style of iteration which, beside being efficient, is more elegant and compact.

mapcar

The most commonly used mapping function is mapcar. It takes two or more arguments, the first of which must evaluate to a function. All other arguments should evaluate to lists of equal length. Mapcar applies the function, specified by its first argument, to individual elements of the lists, specified by its subsequent arguments:

```
-> (mapcar 'sqrt '(4 9 16 25))
(2.0 3.0 4.0 5.0)
-> (mapcar 'plus '(1 2 3) '(10 20 30))
(11 22 33)
->
```

Mapcar always returns a list of values, produced as a result of successive applications of the function it maps. Note that the number of lists supplied to mapcar should match the number of arguments required by this function. In the first example above, for instance, only one list is specified since sqrt is a function of one argument. Here sqrt is first applied to 4 to produce 2.0, and then to 9 to produce 3.0, and so on. In the second example, plus is applied to 1 and 10 to produce 11, and then to 2 and 20 to produce 22, and finally to 3 and 30 to produce 33.

Mapcar is often used in conjunction with apply. To give an example, suppose we want to define a function which returns the number of occurrences of one s-expression in the top-level of another. It may be defined easily using apply and mapcar:

```
(defun occurrences (exp1 exp2)
    (length (apply 'nconc
                   (mapcar '(lambda (x)
                              (cond [(equal exp1 x) (list t)]))
                           exp2))))
```

The lambda form defines a function which returns (t) if exp1 and x are equal, and nil otherwise. This function is mapped over exp2. For example, when exp1 is a and exp2 is (a c a d a) it will produce

```
((t) nil (t) nil (t))
```

where the number of ts in this list is equal to the number of elements of exp2 which are equal to exp1. To extract this number, all we have to do is to weed out the nils and then calculate the length of the resulting list. This is done by applying nconc to the list

```
-> (apply 'nconc '((t) nil (t) nil (t)))
(t t t)
->
```

and then getting the length of the resulting list:

```
-> (length '(t t t))
3
->
```

Alternatively, occurrences may be defined as follows

```
(defun occurrences (exp1 exp2)
    (apply 'plus (mapcar '(lambda (x) (cond [(equal exp1 x) 1]
                                            [t 0]))
                         exp2)))
```

5.3 Mapping functions

which composes a list of zeros and ones, depending on whether an element of `exp2` is `equal` to `exp1`, and then sums up the list by applying `plus` to it.

mapc

Consider a user-defined variant of the primitive `max`, which takes a list of numbers and stores the largest number in the list, in a free variable:

```
(defun max1 (list)
    (setq max (car list))
    (mapcar '(lambda (x) (and (greaterp x max)
                              (setq max x)))
            (cdr list)))
```

Here the free variable `max` is first set to the first element of `list`. A `lambda` form is then mapped over the rest of `list`, which updates `max` whenever it finds an element of `list` to be greater than `max`. We note that in this function the list returned by `mapcar` is ignored, since we are only interested in the side-effect that the `lambda` form causes. When used in this way, `mapcar` is rather wasteful as it constructs a new list every time it is called. `Mapc` provides a suitable alternative:

```
(defun max2 (list)
    (setq max (car list))
    (mapc '(lambda (x) (and (greaterp x max)
                            (setq max x)))
          (cdr list)))
```

Unlike `mapcar`, `mapc` simply returns its second argument as its final result (in some LISP systems it simply returns `nil`):

```
-> (max1 '(2 9 11 0 20 9))
(9 11 nil 20 nil)
-> max
20
-> (max2 '(2 9 11 0 20 9))
(9 11 0 20 9)
-> max
20
->
```

mapcan

Since `mapcar` is used so often in conjunction with `apply` and `nconc`, another mapping function is especially provided to simplify such use. This function is called `mapcan` and is identical to `mapcar` and `mapc` in terms of the arguments it takes. The overall effect of

```
(mapcan fun list1 ... listn)
```

is equivalent to:

```
(apply 'nconc (mapcar fun list1 ... listn))
```

As a result the function `occurrences`, defined above, may be written more compactly as:

```
(defun occurrences (exp1 exp2)
   (length (mapcan '(lambda (x)
                       (cond [(equal exp1 x) (list t)]))
                   exp2)))
```

Note that `mapcan` is a destructive function, while `mapcar` and `mapc` are both pure. This should cause no alarm, however, since the list constructed by `mapcan` in all (but the most unusual) cases is made up of fresh cons-cells (as is the case in the above example). So a destructive change to the top level of this list will not create any surprising effects.

EXERCISE 5.8
 A *set* is an unordered collection of objects with no repetitions. For example, {1,4,2} is a set of three numbers. The *union* of two sets s1 and s2 is the set containing the elements of s1 and s2. For example, the union of {1,4,2} and {3,2} is {1,3,2,4}. Use the mapping functions of LISP to define `union`, a function which returns the union of two sets of atoms. (Hint: use list structures with nonrepeated elements to represent sets.)

EXERCISE 5.9
 Write `intersection`, a function which returns the *intersection* of two sets of atoms. The intersection of two sets s1 and s2 is defined to be the set containing those elements in common between s1 and s2. For example, the intersection of {1,4,2} and {3,2} is {2}.

5.4 Recursion versus iteration

As suggested by the examples in this chapter, most problems can be solved both recursively and iteratively. Inevitably, this raises the question of which is better. This question, however, cannot be properly answered without reference to a problem. For certain problems, recursion is more advisable; for others, iteration is.

Take the factorial problem for example. Here, there is no doubt that the iterative solution is preferable to the recursive solution. This is because in the recursive version there will be n + 1 recursive calls to `factorial` for a number n. Now, each recursive call involves the setting up of yet another environment on the system's stack and is costly. Bearing in mind that the LISP stack has limited space, a large n could easily overflow the stack. The iterative version of stack, although less elegant, is more efficient and less likely to fail.

This, of course, is not necessarily true of other problems. Most problems involving the manipulation of lists, for example, are often better expressed recursively. The recursive functions `is-in` and `reduce` are good examples. Both of these are efficient and much clearer than any alternative iterative solution.

Overall, making a proper judgement about recursion and iteration requires some degree of programming experience. As you experiment more and more with LISP, you will gradually develop an intuition for justifiable use of recursion and iteration. In particular, you will develop an appreciation for the fact that there is usually more than one factor involved, affecting your choice. While elegance and efficiency are two factors that immediately come to mind, others such as compactness, memory requirements, robustness, etc., may also be important.

5.5 Summary

In this chapter we have discussed two important techniques for programming repetition. The main points of the chapter may be summarized as follows.

- *Recursion* is an approach to programming repetition based on the notion of functions which refer to themselves.
- *Iteration* is another approach to programming repetition, whereby a sequence of instructions is executed a number of times.
- A problem can be solved recursively if it can be expressed in terms of itself, or if it can be broken down into a number of subproblems, each of which can be expressed in terms of the others (and possibly itself).
- A recursive function must have at least one *termination condition*.
- A recursive function which passes the result of a call to a previous call, without alteration, is called *tail recursive*.
- A recursive function which makes at most one call to itself during each call is *single-arm* recursive, otherwise, it is *multi-arm* recursive.
- Two or more functions are *mutually recursive* if any of them can be reached by any of the others through a sequence of one or more calls.
- Explicit iteration is supported by `prog` and `do`.

- Explicit iteration requires some discipline to ensure the proper formulation of loop structures.
- Do-based iteration is more disciplined than prog-based iteration.
- Mapping functions enable *implicit* iteration over list structures.
- Mapcar and mapc are pure while mapcan is destructive, but usually safe.
- Recursion is more elegant than iteration, but often less efficient.
- The choice between recursion and iteration is guided by experience and the use of common sense.

Projects

5.1 Write an extended version of reduce (see Section 5.1) which has the following capabilities.

- It accepts any s-expression as argument, so there may be other functions in the s-expression in addition to and and or.
- It also reduces not forms, by transforming (not (not pred)) to pred.
- It substitutes eq for every occurrence of equal which has two symbols or small fixed numbers as arguments.

5.2 Write transform-to-or, a recursive function which transforms any predicate, expressed in terms of and, or, and not, into a predicate expressed in terms of or and not only. Similarly, write transform-to-and, a recursive function which transforms any predicate to a predicate in terms of and and not only. Use the following transformation rules for these two functions:

```
(and p1 p2)    transforms to    (not (or (not p1) (not p2)))
(or  p1 p2)    transforms to    (not (and (not p1) (not p2)))
```

Now, redefine transform-to-or and transform-to-and as two iterative functions, and comment on aspects such as elegance, clarity, and efficiency of the two versions.

5.3 Write do-to-prog, a function which takes a do form as argument and returns an equivalent prog form.

5.4 Write check-prog, a function which takes a prog form as argument and checks that its loops are structured. A structured loop here is defined to be of the general form:

```
label1
   ...
   ... loop body ...
   ...
label2
```

where label2 is optional, and the loop body should start with a proper termination condition. The loop body may contain gos to label1 and label2, but not any other label. It may also contain any number of returns. Check-prog should return t when the loops in a prog are structured, and nil otherwise.

Chapter 6

Input and Output

Most computer programs need to communicate with users in order to be useful at all. So far our means of communication with LISP programs have been very crude: input was provided as arguments to functions, and output was merely the result returned by a function. This implicit style of I/O is probably adequate for experimentation and learning, but totally insufficient for writing realistic programs. In this chapter we describe the facilities of LISP for performing explicit I/O. These will include functions for printing data to the VDU screen, reading data from the keyboard, and doing I/O with external devices. We shall also briefly look at some of the facilities of LISP for 'pretty printing'. Finally, we shall describe how the LISP top level may be redefined according to our taste using some simple I/O functions.

6.1 Ordinary I/O

Input and output performed between LISP, the VDU terminal and the keyboard is referred to as ordinary I/O or default I/O. The primary LISP functions provided for this purpose are print and read.

Print takes one argument which must evaluate to an s-expression. It prints the value of this s-expression to the VDU screen:

```
-> (print 100)
100nil
-> (print 'hello)
hellonil
-> (print '(this is a list))
(this is a list)nil
->
```

Print always returns nil (this appears just after the output).

Read requires no arguments. When called, it waits for the user to type in an s-expression; it then simply returns the s-expression without evaluating it:

```
-> (read)
hello
hello
-> (read)
(nothing is evaluated)
(nothing is evaluated)
->
```

Here, we first typed hello, and read simply returned hello. We then typed a list, which was again returned without evaluation by read.

Note that read does not produce any prompt for input. A suggestive prompt may be easily provided using print. The following function repeatedly prompts the user for an expression and prints the expression after evaluation:

```
(defun test ()
   (prog (exp)
      loop
         (print 'expression>)                    ;; prompt.
         (and (eq (setq exp (read)) 'stop) (return))   ;; stop?
         (print (eval exp))                      ;; evaluate & print exprn.
         (terpri)                                ;; new line.
         (go loop)))
```

The function terpri starts output on the next line (it always returns nil). test stops when the user inputs the atom stop:

```
-> (test)
expression>'hello
hello
expression>(add 10 20)
30
expression>stop
->
```

Strange atoms and strings

Certain characters are regarded as special in LISP and cannot be used in atom names.

6.1 Ordinary I/O

Spaces, tabs, and brackets are examples. A simple convention, however, allows us to get round this problem: when an atom contains some special characters, the significance of these characters can be taken away by enclosing the atom in two vertical bars:

```
-> '|strange atom|
|strange atom|
-> '|another(strange atom|
|another(strange atom|
->
```

The function `test`, described above, may be slightly improved by adding a space to the end of the `expression>` prompt, to properly separate the prompt from user input. Vertical bars enable us to do this. If we substitute `|expression> |` for `expression>` in `test`, we will get the following effect:

```
-> (test)
|expression> | 'hello
hello
|expression> |
```

Ideally, we would like to get rid of the vertical bars in the output. This may be done by using `princ` or `patom` (these two being identical) instead of `print`. If we substitute `(patom '|expression> |)` for `(print 'expression>)` in the definition of `test`, we will get what we were after:

```
-> (test)
expression> 'hello
hello
expression>
```

An even easier way of getting round the problem of special characters is to use *strings*. A string is any sequence of characters enclosed in two double quotes. Strings will be described in detail in Chapter 8. For the moment, all we need to know is that, like numbers, strings evaluate to themselves:

```
-> "hello"
"hello"
-> "a lot of special characters: ( . [ #"
"a lot of special characters: ( . [ #"
->
```

As with vertical bars, the function `print` prints a string together with its double quotes, while `princ` and `patom` drop the double quotes:

```
-> (setq x "just another string")
"just another string"
-> (print x)
"just another string"nil
-> (patom x)
just another string"just another string"
->
```

Note that, unlike `print`, `patom` returns the value of its argument as its result.

EXERCISE 6.1

Write down the output you expect to get from each of the following s-expressions. Check your answers with LISP.

```
(print (list 'a 'b))
(patom (list 'a 'b))
(print '|strange . atom|)
(patom '|strange . atom|)
(print (list '|strange . atom|))
(patom (list '|strange . atom|))
(print "a string")
(patom "a string")
(print (list "a string"))
(patom (list "a string"))
```

EXERCISE 6.2

Use `read` and `print` to write a calculator which does simple arithmetic according to the syntax suggested by the following examples:

```
calc> 10 + 20
30
calc> 25 * 2
50
calc> 59.9 - 11
48.9
calc> 12 / 4
3
calc>
```

The calculator should stop when given the symbol `stop`.

6.2 External I/O

I/O may also be performed with respect to a data structure known as a *file*. A file is simply an area of external store (usually magnetic disk) which may be used for storing, and subsequently retrieving information. The mnemonics for external I/O functions vary greatly from one LISP system to another. The ones which we shall be using below are peculiar to Franz and are used here just to illustrate the concepts. The correct names of these functions should be given in the user manual of your LISP system.

Two primary functions `infile` and `outfile` enable the opening of files for input and output, respectively. Both take one argument only which must evaluate to a symbol, representing a file name, and return a *port* for subsequent use. A port is an internal name for an opened file which must be used instead of the file name in all subsequent I/O. For example,

```
-> (setq port1 (outfile 'data))
%data
->
```

which opens a file called `data` for output, and stores the port name (i.e., `%data`) in the free variable `port1`.

All I/O functions described in the previous section can take an additional optional argument which must evaluate to a port. This enables their use for reading from and writing to files. For example, to write the string `"this is a simple string"` to `port1`, we may type:

```
-> (print "this is a simple string" port1)
nil
->
```

Once all I/O from/to a file is completed, the file must be closed using `close`. Close takes one argument, which must evaluate to a port name, and closes the file corresponding to that port:

```
-> (close port1)
t
->
```

If `close` manages to close a file properly it will return `t` (as above). Otherwise, it will return `nil`. Similarly, `infile` and `outfile` return `nil` when they fail to open a file.

Now that we have closed the file `data`, we may open it again, this time for reading, to check its contents:

```
-> (setq port1 (infile 'data))
%data
-> (read port1)
"this is a simple string"
-> (read port1)
nil
-> (close port1)
t
->
```

As this example shows, `read` returns `nil` when it reaches the end of a file.

6.3 Pretty printing

Most LISP systems come with one or more 'pretty printing' functions. For example, in Franz the function `pp` pretty prints a function to the VDU screen, nicely formatting the s-expressions in the function:

```
-> (pp test)
(def test
     (lambda nil
         (prog (exp)
            loop
              (print "expression> ")
              (and (eq (setq exp (read)) 'stop) (return))
              (print (eval exp))
              (terpri))))
t
->
```

The output produced by `pp` may seem rather strange, in that it is not exactly how we defined `test`. This is actually the way LISP stores `test` internally and is equivalent to our definition of `test`. The reasons for this will be described in Chapter 7.

There is also a variant of `pp`, called `pp-form`, which pretty prints any s-expression. However, unlike `pp`, `pp-form` evaluates its argument:

```
-> (pp-form '(append (list (subst 'list 'append '(append
(list 'x 'y) (append (list (list 'x)) (list (list 'y)))
(list nil))))))
```

6.3 Pretty printing

```
         (append (list (subst 'list
                              'append
                              '(append (list 'x 'y)
                                       (append (list (list 'x))
                                               (list (list 'y)))
                                       (list nil))))))nil
->
```

Note that `pp` returns `t`, while `pp-form` returns `nil`. Both these functions may also take an optional second argument for sending their output to a file.

Saving and loading LISP programs

Using `pp` we can store our LISP programs in a file. For example, to store the function `test` in a file called `lisp1`, we may type:

```
-> (pp (F lisp11) test)        ;; pretty print test to file lisp1.
t
->
```

An optional argument, `(F file)`, instructs `pp` to send its output to `file`.

Once a program is stored in a file, it can be reloaded into the LISP environment by the `load` function. Load takes one argument which must evaluate to a file name. It opens that file and reads the s-expressions in the file, evaluating each:

```
-> (load 'lisp1)
t
->
```

When writing large LISP programs, `load` can be most helpful. A LISP program can be created using an interactive editor, or any other means available, and then loaded into LISP whenever it is needed. In this way, one can save a lot of retyping effort.

EXERCISE 6.3
Define `verbose-load`, a variant of the `load` function which acts like `load`, but also prints the name of each function in a file. For example, if a file called `program1` contains the definition of two functions `fun1` and `fun2`, `verbose-load` should read and evaluate these functions, and produce the following output:

```
-> (verbose-load 'program1)
fun1
fun2
nil
```

EXERCISE 6.4

Use `pp-form` to define `pp-file`, a function which reads the functions in a file and pretty prints them to another file. For example,

```
(pp-file 'program1 'program2)
```

should read the functions in `program1` and pretty print them to `program2`. Extend `pp-file` so that it sends its output to the VDU screen when its second argument is VDU.

6.4 The LISP top level

The LISP top level was mentioned in Chapter 1. This is a part of the LISP interpreter responsible for interacting with the user. Top level is in fact nothing but a simple function which repeatedly reads, evaluates and prints s-expressions:

```
(defun top-level ()
   (prog ()
      loop
         (patom "-> ")              ;; prompt.
         (print (eval (read)))      ;; read-eval-print.
         (terpri)                   ;; new line.
         (go loop)))
```

Every time round the loop, `top-level` prints the prompt `->` and then reads an s-expression which is printed after evaluation. This loop is commonly referred to as the *read-eval-print* loop.

LISP has no objection to the user defining the `top-level` function. This enables us to reconfigure the read-eval-print loop according to our taste and requirements. For example, we may redefine `top-level` so that it will not print the result of evaluation when it is `nil`:

```
(defun top-level ()
   (prog (x)
      loop
         (patom "=> ")                      ;; prompt.
         (cond [(setq x (eval (read)))      ;; read-eval.
                (print x) (terpri)])        ;; print & new line.
         (go loop)))
```

The new `top-level` is brought into operation by typing `(reset)`:

```
-> (reset)
[Return to top level]
=> (eq 'a 'a)
t
=> (eq 'a 'b)
=>
```

EXERCISE 6.5
Redefine the LISP top level so that it maintains a copy of all your activities in a log file. It would be a good idea also to define two supplementary functions which start and stop the logging process:

```
-> (start-log 'log)      ;; start recording in file log.
...
-> (stop-log)            ;; stop recording.
```

6.5 Summary

A number of LISP facilities for input and output were described in this chapter. The main points of the chapter may be summarized as follows.

- Print prints an s-expression after evaluation.
- Read reads and returns an s-expression without evaluation.
- Terpri starts output on the next line.
- Strange atom names, containing special characters, may be composed using vertical bars.
- Print prints a strange atom together with its vertical bars while princ and patom hide the vertical bars.
- A *string* is any sequence of characters enclosed in two double quotes.
- Strings evaluate to themselves and are useful for displaying prompts and messages.
- Print prints a string together with its double quotes while princ and patom hide the double quotes.
- A *file* is an area of external store used for storing and retrieving information.
- I/O may also be performed with respect to files.
- Pretty printing functions enable neat presentation of functions and s-expressions.
- Load allows the loading of previously-written LISP programs.
- The LISP top level is merely a *read-eval-print* loop and can be redefined according to the user's taste.

Projects

6.1 Use reduce (see Project 5.1) to write reduce-program, a function which simplifies all predicates in a program. Reduce-program should take two arguments

   (**reduce-program** input-file output-file)

where input-file is a LISP program file to be simplified, and output-file is the result of simplification.

6.2 Extend check-prog (see Project 5.4) so that it produces meaningful messages, indicating any unstructured aspects of a prog.

6.3 Use the I/O functions of LISP to write a simple editor for editing LISP programs. The editor should work as follows. The command

   (**edit** input-file output-file commands)

should edit input-file, using the commands in commands, to produce output-file. Commands is a list of commands, where each command may be one of the following.

   (**del** s-expr1 n)
      Deletes the first n occurrences of s-expr1 in the file.

   (**ins** s-expr1 s-expr2 n)
      Inserts s-expr2 before the first n occurrences of s-expr1.

   (**app** s-expr1 s-expr2 n)
      Inserts s-expr2 after the first n occurrences of s-expr1.

   (**subs** s-expr1 s-expr2 s-expr3 n)
      Substitutes s-expr2 for the first n occurrences of s-expr3 in all occurrences of s-expr1. When s-expr1 is *, it will denote any s-expression.

A value of 0 for n in any of the commands will denote all occurrences. For simplicity, you may ignore comments in your input files.

6.4 Use the I/O functions of LISP (except pp and pp-form) to write pretty-print, a function similar to pp-form, which pretty prints list structures. Pretty-print should take three arguments: a list, a left margin, and a right margin. It should pretty print the list within these margins. There are two LISP primitives, flatc and nwritn, which you might find useful. The former returns the number of characters required for printing an s-expression using patom while the latter returns the number of pending characters in a port.
     When you have completed pretty-print, use getd to extend it so that it also pretty prints functions. (See Appendix 1 for a description of flatc, nwritn, and getd.)

Chapter 7

Macros and Other Functions

The user-defined functions described so far, have been subject to two important restrictions. Firstly, they all take a fixed number of arguments, that is, the number of arguments to a function must be determined at the time of definition and observed throughout its subsequent use. Secondly, such functions always evaluate their arguments at the time of call. This feature is not always desirable, and occasionally the opposite is required. This chapter will expand our choice of function definition styles by introducing three new function definition facilities which overcome these restrictions. These are fexprs, macros, and lexprs. (These categories and their basic structures may be slightly different in other LISP dialects. Those described here are based on Franz LISP.)

7.1 Defining fexprs

All the functions we have defined so far are said to be *exprs*. Exprs represent the most common form of functions: they take a fixed number of arguments, each of which is evaluated. In this section we describe *fexprs* – functions which take a variable number of arguments, none of which is evaluated. Let us begin with an example which illustrates some of the differences.

Suppose that the much needed function `setq` is not provided by LISP, and that we want to define `assign`, a simplified version of `setq` which takes just two arguments. Fexprs allow us to do this easily:

```
(defun assign fexpr (args)
       (set (car args) (eval (cadr args))))
```

The keyword `fexpr`, appearing just after the function name, instructs `defun` that `assign` should be defined as a fexpr. Fexprs always take exactly one parameter (`args` here) which is bound to the list of arguments to the function when it is called. So, for example, given the call

```
(assign x (+ 5 10))
```

then args will be bound to:

```
(x (+ 5 10))
```

Individual arguments may then be extracted from this list using the list extraction functions.

Assign works as follows. The first argument is extracted by (car args) which produces x. The second argument is similarly extracted by (cadr args) which produces (+ 5 10). The latter expression is then evaluated using eval to produce 15. Finally set is used to store 15 in x. The following examples illustrate the equivalence of assign and setq:

```
-> (assign x (+ 10 20))
30
-> x
30
-> (assign y (list 10 (list 20)))
(10 (20))
-> y
(10 (20))
->
```

It should be obvious that assign cannot be defined as an expr since its first argument must not be evaluated. It should also be obvious that assign can take any number of arguments, regardless of the fact that here we made use of the first two arguments only.

Given the last observation, we can write a more general version of assign which, just like setq, takes any number of arguments and stores the values of the even-positioned arguments in the odd-positioned variables:

```
(defun multi-assign fexpr (args)
       (cond [(cddr args)                        ;; more than 2 args?
              (set (car args) (eval (cadr args)))
              (apply 'multi-assign (cddr args))]
             [t                                  ;; at most 2 args.
              (set (car args) (eval (cadr args)))]))
```

When given only two arguments, multi-assign acts exactly as assign. Additional arguments will cause multi-assign to call itself recursively for the remaining arguments:

```
-> (multi-assign x (+ 5 6) y (list 10))
(10)
-> x
11
-> y
(10)
->
```

EXERCISE 7.1
    Define if, a fexpr which takes three or five arguments as illustrated by the following examples:

        (**if** (> x 0) **then** (setq x (1- x)))
        (**if** (> x 0) **then** x **else** (abs x))

    If should return the value of its third argument if the predicate depicted by its first argument evaluates to nonnil. If the predicate evaluates to nil, if should return the value of its fifth argument, if any, and nil otherwise.

7.2 Defining macros

A *macro* is identical to a fexpr in all respects but two. Firstly, when called, a macro's single parameter is bound to the entire list representing the call, rather than just the list of arguments. Secondly, whatever is returned by a macro receives an extra evaluation. Because of this latter property, a macro always returns an s-expression which is a recipe for what the macro is supposed to do, rather than doing the computation and then returning the final result.

    To better illustrate the differences, let us redefine assign, this time as a macro:

```
(defun assign macro (args)
        (list 'set (kwote (cadr args)) (caddr args)))
```

The keyword macro instructs defun that assign should be defined as a macro. As before, there is only one parameter, namely args. Unlike before, however, this parameter is bound to an entire call list. For example, given the call

```
(assign x (+ 10 20))
```

then args will be bound to

```
(assign x (+ 10 20))
```

The function `kwote` is similar to `quote` but first evaluates its argument and then quotes it. In other words, `(kwote x)` is equivalent to `(list (quote quote) x)`. Given the above call, `assign` will return the list:

```
(set 'x (+ 10 20))
```

This list is then evaluated to produce 30.

We observe that `assign` (and in fact any other macro) takes a piece of code, transforms it into a new piece of code, and then evaluates that code to achieve its ends. This process of transformation, from the initial code to the final code, is called *macro expansion*.

But why should we want to do things in such a convoluted way? Why not just use fexprs? There are at least two good reasons. Firstly, macros provide an efficient way of extending LISP by defining new facilities. This is because, for each macro call, LISP does the full expansion only once during the first evaluation of that call so as a result, any subsequent call will be very efficient. This is especially true of compiled LISP code. When a LISP program is compiled, all macro calls are replaced by their appropriate expansions. This means that the overhead of an additional function call for each reference to a macro will disappear altogether.

Secondly, macros are superior to fexprs in that they can avoid name clashes. This issue will be discussed in detail in Section 7.3.

Data manipulation

Suppose that a personnel program uses a list structure to represent each employee:

```
(setq employee '(name id-code address salary ...))
```

Each element of the list may be extracted by appropriate combinations of `cars` and `cdrs`:

```
(car employee)          ;; employee's name
(cadr employee)         ;; employee's id-code
(caddr employee)        ;; employee's address
...                     ;; ...
```

Such style of referencing is not advisable since, beside being cryptic, it leads to programs which are hard to maintain. For example, if an additional component, `age` say, is inserted in the list between the first and the second element, it will require all references to the second through to the last element of the list to be updated. This may involve a lot of work and is potentially error-prone. One way to get round this problem is to define each reference as a function with a mnemonic name, for example:

```
(defun employee-address (employee)
      (caddr employee))
```

Use of (employee-address employee) instead of (caddr employee) will ensure that any changes to the position of address in the list will be confined to the definition of employee-address.

Unfortunately, neither of the two approaches is entirely satisfactory. The former is evidently cryptic and error-prone while the latter is potentially inefficient: every reference to the list carries the overhead of an additional function call. Luckily, macros offer the best of both worlds. For example, given the macro definition:

```
(defun employee-address macro (employee)
      (list 'caddr (cadr employee)))
```

every reference of the form

```
(employee-address employee)
```

will be automatically replaced by the equivalent form:

```
(caddr employee)
```

This not only leads to a good level of readability, but also ensures optimal efficiency. It is therefore advisable that data manipulations, especially those appearing a number of times in a program, should be abstracted and defined as macros.

Use of defmacro

The convention for extracting individual arguments of a macro is arguably cryptic and rather tedious. Most LISP systems provide an alternative way of defining macros, which is more in line with the way exprs are defined. The facility is provided by a function called defmacro. Using defmacro, we can define assign in a considerably more readable way:

```
(defmacro assign (var value)
      (list 'set (kwote var) value))
```

The parameter mechanism of defmacro is very much like that of exprs with the exception that none of the arguments are evaluated. It therefore follows that defmacro is only suitable for defining macros which take a fixed number of arguments.

Incidently defmacro is itself a predefined macro. If your LISP system does not provide it, you may wish to define it yourself.

Use of backquote

Macro definitions are further simplified by a facility called the *backquote* macro. Backquote is a character macro[1] and is supported by a number of LISP systems. It is represented by the backquote character ` and may be used to enforce selective evaluation of a list's components. When used on its own, its effect is similar to that of the quote character:

```
-> `(x y z)
(x y z)
->
```

Putting a comma character (,) before any component of a backquoted list will enforce the evaluation of that component. Furthermore, a comma followed by the @ character will evaluate and splice the component that proceeds it:

```
-> (setq z '(p q))
(p q)
-> `(x y ,z)                      ;; evaluate z.
(x y (p q))
-> `(x y ,@z)                     ;; evaluate and splice z.
(x y p q)
->
```

It is easy to see that the backquote macro provides a convenient way of defining macros:

```
(defmacro assign (var value)
         `(set ,(kwote var) ,value))
```

The backquote macro liberates one from the burden of constructing a macro's result piece by piece: a macro's body is written as if it were an expr. The entire body is then backquoted and each occurrence of a parameter is preceded by a comma.

The let *and* do *macros*

The let and do functions were described earlier in this book. Both these are in fact predefined macros in most LISP systems. As a nontrivial example, we will give a macro definition of let below. The definition of do is rather similar and is deferred as an exercise.

We recall that a let expression can be equivalently defined as a lambda form. For

---

[1] A character macro is a macro associated with a character, and is invoked as soon as the LISP reader detects that character.

7.2 Defining macros

example,

```
(let [(x 10) (y 20) z]
     s-expression-1
     ...
     s-expression-n)
```

is equivalent to

```
((lambda (x y z)
     s-expression-1
     ...
     s-expression-n) 10 20 nil)
```

Our task therefore is to produce a macro definition which transforms the former to the latter. The following macro will do the job:

```
(defun let macro (list)
   (prog (head vars inits)
         (setq head (cadr list))            ;; variables in a let.
    loop
         (cond [(null head)                 ;; no more variables?
                (return (cons (cons 'lambda ;; equivalent lambda form.
                                    (cons (nreverse vars)
                                          (cddr list)))
                              (nreverse inits)))]
               [(atom (car head))           ;; var with no initial value?
                (setq vars (cons (car head) vars)    ;; variables.
                      inits (cons nil inits))]       ;; initial value = nil.
               [t (setq vars (cons (caar head) vars) ;; variable.
                        inits (cons (cadar head) inits))])
         (setq head (cdr head))             ;; next variable.
         (go loop)))
```

The prog in the body of let defines three local variables while head is used for storing the first argument to let, i.e., the list of local variables and their initial values. A loop then goes through this list and separates the variables from their initial values. The former are stored in the variable vars. The latter are stored in inits. The loop also checks whether a variable definition is just an atom, in which case it assumes the initial value for that variable to be nil. Once all variables in head are processed, a lambda form is built and returned as the final result. Prior to this, vars and inits are reversed to keep the order of their elements compatible with those in a let call. This is, of course, not essential and can be omitted.

EXERCISE 7.2

Define `head` and `tail`, macro versions of `car` and `cdr` respectively. Similarly, define `change-head` and `change-tail`, macro versions of `rplaca` and `rplacd`.

EXERCISE 7.3

Define `if` (see Exercise 7.1) as a macro.

EXERCISE 7.4

Extend the `if` macro so that it can incorporate `elseif` parts, as suggested by the following example:

```
(if (> x 0) then (setq x (1- x))
    elseif (= x 0) then x
    else (setq x (1+ x)))
```

Your definition should allow any number of `elseif` parts.

EXERCISE 7.5

Define `case`, a macro which has the following general call form

```
(case s of
    [s-expr-1-1 ... s-expr-1-k]
    ...
    [s-expr-n-1 ... s-expr-n-m])
```

and is equivalent to

```
(cond [(equal s s-expr-1-1) ... s-expr-1-k]
      ...
      [(equal s s-expr-n-1) ... s-expr-n-m])
```

7.3 Name clashes

Consider `do-times`, a function which takes two or more arguments, where the first argument specifies the number of times subsequent arguments should be evaluated. For example,

```
(do-times 3 (setq x (1+ x)))
```

will evaluate `(setq x (1+ x))` three times. We can define `do-times` as a fexpr:

```
(defun do-times fexpr (args)
    (prog (n body)
        (setq n (eval (car args))              ;; no. of evaluations.
              body (cons 'progl (cdr args)))   ;; body of do-times.
```

7.3 Name clashes

```
   loop
    (cond [(plusp n)                    ;; more evaluations?
           (eval body)                  ;; evaluate body.
           (setq n (1- n))              ;; decrement n.
           (go loop)])))
```

The definition may appear flawless, and indeed many examples will work as expected:

```
-> (setq x 10 y 20)
20
-> (do-times 10 (setq x (1+ x)) (setq y (1- y)))
nil
-> x
20
-> y
10
->
```

There is, however, a serious flaw in the definition of do-times which can easily be overlooked. The following example highlights the flaw:

```
-> (setq n 4 sum 0)
0
-> (do-times 2 (setq n (1- n)) (setq sum (+ sum n)))
nil
-> sum
1
->
```

Although we expected the final value of sum to be 3 + 2, it turned out to be 1. The reason for this is that the variable n appears in both the arguments to do-times and in the definition of do-times. This leads to a *name clash*. As a result, the initial value of n will be 2, not 4. Furthermore, the loop will be executed only once since n will be decremented twice, leaving the value 1 in sum.

The definition of do-times contains three variables (i.e., args, n and body) and any of these could clash with variables in arguments to the function. Any name clash involving args may be avoided by defining do-times as a macro. This is because the macro will construct a list in which args will not take part, but rather its components will. Name clashes involving n and body are avoided using a different technique.

The function gensym is a LISP primitive which returns a unique symbol each time it is called:

```
-> (gensym)
g00001
-> (gensym)
g00002
->
```

Provided we are not tasteless enough to use variable names such as g00001, g00002, etc. in our programs, use of gensym in a macro can ensure that no name clash will occur:

```
(defun do-times macro (list)
    (let [(n (gensym))]
       `(prog (,n)
              (setq ,n ,(cadr list))          ;; no. of evaluations.
          loop
              (cond [(plusp ,n)               ;; more evaluations?
                     (eval ,(cons 'prog1 (cddr list)))
                     (setq ,n (1- ,n))        ;; decrement n.
                     (go loop)]))))
```

The definition uses two variables: n and list. N is substituted for by a unique symbol using gensym and the backquote macro; on the other hand, list disappears altogether in a macro expansion. As a result, any chance of a name clash will be as remote as possible:

```
-> (setq n 4 sum 0)
0
-> (do-times 2 (setq n (1- n)) (setq sum (+ sum n)))
nil
-> sum
5
->
```

The name clash problem is the best reason why fexprs should be used very cautiously. Fexprs are in fact rarely used by LISP programmers; the reason for having them is that certain LISP primitives (e.g., cond and prog) are internally defined as fexprs.

EXERCISE 7.6

Most programmers are used to structured loops such as while, repeat and for, as provided by structured programming languages such as Pascal. Define macro versions of these in LISP according to the following specifications:

(while pred **do** s-expr-1 ... s-expr-n)
(repeat s-expr-1 ... s-expr-n **until** pred)
(for var **in** list **do** s-expr-1 ... s-expr-n)

7.4 Defining lexprs

While evaluates pred first and if this evaluates to nonnil it will evaluate s-expr-1 ... s-expr-n. While will repeat this process until pred evaluates to nil. Repeat evaluates s-expr-1 ... s-expr-n first and then evaluates pred. It repeats this process until pred evaluates to nil. For repeatedly binds var to the next element of list and evaluates s-expr-1 ... s-expr-n until list is exhausted.

EXERCISE 7.7
Define do-1, a simplified version of the do macro which has the following general call form:

```
(do-1 (var init next)
      [s-expr-c1 ... s-expr-cn]
      s-expr-1
      ...
      s-expr-k)
```

Do-1 is similar to do except that it takes only one variable. Also, define do-n, an extended version of do-1 which behaves exactly like do.

7.4 Defining lexprs

There is yet another function type, known as a *lexpr*, which supports a style which is halfway between exprs, on the one hand, and fexprs and macros on the other. Lexprs are similar to exprs in that they always evaluate their arguments. They are similar to fexprs and macros in that they take any number of arguments.

To give an example, consider printf, a function which prints an s-expression, starting on a print column specified by an optional argument:

```
(defun printf num
       (and (> num 1)            ;; more than one arg?
            (tab (arg 2)))       ;; use the 2nd arg as tab position.
       (print (arg 1)))          ;; print the first arg.
```

LISP knows that printf is a lexpr because instead of a parameter list it is given just a symbol (i.e., num). When printf is called, num is bound to the number of arguments to the function. Individual arguments are accessed using the function arg. For example, (arg 1) returns the first argument to printf which first checks whether there is more than one argument. If so, it uses the second argument as a tab position. (The function tab simply moves the print column to the position specified by its argument.) Printf then prints the s-expression given by its first argument.

Since the arguments to a lexpr have to be accessed by using arg, such functions are arguably cryptic. Most LISP systems allow lexprs to be defined in a more readable, expr-like style, as suggested by the following redefinition of printf:

```
(defun printf (arg &optional (pos nil))
       (and pos (tab pos))
       (print arg))
```

Here, the keyword `&optional` indicates that `pos` is optional, and will be bound to a corresponding argument if supplied; otherwise, it will be bound to the specified default value (i.e., `nil`). Another keyword, `&rest`, may be used to specify that a parameter should be bound to the list of all remaining arguments. The appearance of `&optional` or `&rest` in the parameter list of a function instructs `defun` to define the function as a lexpr. The conventions for the use of these two keywords are as follows.

`&optional x`	parameter x is optional
`&optional (x init)`	parameter x is optional, with default value `init`
`&rest x`	bind x to the list of remaining arguments

There is also a third keyword, `&aux`, which allows the definition of local variables. As before, `&aux` appears in the parameter list of a function, but does not necessarily cause the function to become a lexpr:

`&aux`	x is local with default value `nil`
`&aux (x init)`	x is local with default value `init`

EXERCISE 7.8
   Extend the definition of `printf`, as defined in Section 7.4, so that it can print any number of formatted s-expressions.

7.5 General structure of definitions

We are now in a position to outline the general structure of function definitions using `defun`. This is shown in Figure 7.1.

```
(defun  fun-name  type  (par1 ... parn)
        s-expression-1
        :
        s-expression-k )
```

Figure 7.1 The general structure of `defun`.

`Type` is optional and if not present, `fun-name` is assumed to be an expr. Also, in the absence of `type`, if we have a single symbol in the place of `(par1 ... parn)` then `fun-name` will be assumed to be a lexpr. Otherwise, `type` should be one of `expr`, `fexpr`, `macro` or args (for lexprs).

Incidently, defun is itself a macro which expands to a def form. Def is the actual function used by LISP for all function definitions. The general structure of def is shown in Figure 7.2.

```
(def  fun-name (type (par1 ... parn)
                s-expression-1
                :
                s-expression-k ))
```

Figure 7.2 The general structure of def.

Here, type must be one of lambda (for exprs), nlambda (for fexprs), macro, or lexpr. One may use def directly for defining functions. Most LISP programmers, however, tend to use defun since it has a slightly more readable syntax.

7.6 Summary

In this chapter we have described three additional function types. The main points of the chapter may be summarized as follows.

- *Fexprs* take a variable number of arguments, none of which is evaluated.
- Fexprs should be used cautiously as they can lead to *name clashes*.
- *Macros* transform a piece of code from one form to another and then evaluate the result.
- Macros are useful for extending LISP and improving program readability.
- Defmacro and the *backquote* macro simplify macro definitions.
- Let, do, defun, and defmacro are all predefined macros.
- *Lexprs* take a variable number of arguments, all of which are evaluated.
- Def is the most basic function of LISP for defining functions.

Project

7.1 Use macros to design a package that will make your LISP dialect resemble another dialect. For example, if you are using Franz LISP, you could define the primitives of Common LISP, Scheme, or any other dialect as macros. For those primitives which are identical in structure but have different mnemonics in different dialects, you might find `make-equivalent` useful. This is a Franz primitive that defines synonyms for symbols. For example,

```
(make-equivalent symbol1 symbol2)
```

makes `symbol1` a synonym of `symbol2`. Put your macro definitions in a file, so that they can be loaded easily when required.

Chapter 8

Further Topics

There are a number of other data structures which are not used as often as the ones described in the earlier chapters of this book. These include property lists, association lists, and array structures. This chapter describes each in some detail, together with the basic functions provided for creating and manipulating such structures. Other material included in this chapter deals with issues concerning the use of strings and symbols; and the ways in which errors can be detected, reported and subsequently handled. The underlying mechanism of error handling is also described as a way of implementing unconventional styles of flow of control. (As with the previous chapter, the notation described in this chapter is based on Franz LISP and may be slightly different in other LISP dialects.)

8.1 Property lists

In Chapter 1 we observed that symbols can play the dual role of variables and function names. Symbols can hold yet extra information, known as *properties*. Loosely speaking, a property is a reference name under which we may store a value in a symbol and subsequently retrieve or alter it. LISP maintains, for each symbol, a *property list* which consists of property names and property values. Initially, the list is empty, but as properties are added to a symbol, the list expands.

To add a property to a symbol, we use the `putprop` function. For example,

```
-> (putprop 'tv 'Sony 'make)
Sony
->
```

adds the property value `Sony` to `tv` under the property name `make`. `Putprop` always returns its second argument, i.e., the property value. A symbol can take as many properties as one wishes. Also, a property value can be any valid s-expression. Here are a few more examples, describing other properties of tv:

```
-> (putprop 'tv '26in 'size)
|26in|
-> (putprop 'tv 'colour 'type)
colour
-> (putprop 'tv '(1987 in Japan) 'manufactured)
(1987 in Japan)
->
```

Property lists can be regarded as a convenient way of describing the properties of an object. Of course, having given some properties to an object, we expect to be able to retrieve them. The function get allows us to do just that:

```
-> (get 'tv 'size)
|26in|
-> (get 'tv 'manufactured)
(1987 in Japan)
-> (get 'tv 'voltage)
nil
->
```

As the last example illustrates, get returns nil when it is asked about a property which is not yet defined.

Putprop can also change the value of a previously defined property. When putprop is used to define an already defined property, the new property value will replace the old one:

```
-> (putprop 'tv '24in 'size)
|24in|
-> (get 'tv 'size)
|24in|
->
```

The entire property list of a symbol is obtained by the plist function. It takes one argument which must evaluate to a symbol and returns the property list of that symbol:

```
-> (plist 'tv)
(manufactured (1987 in Japan)) type colour size |24in| make Sony)
-> (plist 'radio)
nil
->
```

8.1 Property lists

`Remprop` removes a property from a symbol. It does so by removing both the given property name and its property value, provided of course they are already there. If successful `remprop` will return that portion of the property list which starts with the specified property (rather like `member`); otherwise, it will return `nil`:

```
-> (remprop 'tv 'voltage)
nil
-> (remprop 'tv 'type)
(colour size |24i| make Sony)
-> (plist 'tv)
(manufactured (1987 in Japan)) size |24in| make Sony)
->
```

Finally, the entire property list of a symbol may be changed by `setplist`:

```
-> (setplist 'radio '(make JVC type mono weight 525g))
(make JVC type mono weight |525g|)
-> (setplist 'my-radio (plist 'radio))
(make JVC type mono weight |525g|)
->
```

`Setplist` is useful when we want to introduce many properties at once, or when we want to copy all properties of one symbol to another.

EXERCISE 8.1

Use property lists to build a small database of facts about the countries of the world. The following examples illustrate the kind of information one may be interested in:

```
(putprop 'Europe '(England France Germany ...) 'contains)
(putprop 'England 'Europe 'in)
(putprop 'England 'country 'is)
(putprop 'England '(about 60 million) 'population)
(putprop 'England 'London 'capital)
(putprop 'London 'city 'is)
(putprop 'London 'England 'in)
...
```

EXERCISE 8.2

A software system usually consists of a number of subsystems, where each subsystem consists of a number of programs, and each program consists of a number of modules. A module may contain other modules, which may in turn consist of other modules, and so on. This hierarchical organization may be represented by property lists. For example,

```
(putprop 'system '(subsystem1 subsystem2) 'uses)
(putprop 'subsystem1 '(program1 program2) 'uses)
(putprop 'program1 '(module1 module2 module3) 'uses)
(putprop 'module1 ...)
...
```

represents a possible system. Write `uses`, a function which takes a component (i.e., system, subsystem, program or module) and returns all other components that the given component uses down to the lowest module level.

8.2 Association lists

An *association list* is simply a list of lists, and is usually used as an alternative to property lists. Like property lists, as association list is normally used for storing some properties or facts about an object. Unlike property lists, an association list is not attached to a symbol, and may appear anywhere, even as the value binding of a symbol.

For example, the object `tv` (as defined in the previous section) may be represented by the following association list:

```
-> (setq tv '((make Sony) (size 24in) (type colour)
              (manufactured 1987 in Japan)))
((make Sony) (size |24in|) (type colour) (manufactured 1987
in Japan))
->
```

The head of a sublist of an association list is called a *key*. For example in `tv`, `make`, `size`, `type` and `manufactured` are all keys. Individual sublists are extracted using the `assoc` function. It takes two arguments, a key and an association list, and returns an element of the list whose head is `equal` to the key:

```
-> (assoc 'size tv)
(size |24in|)
-> (assoc 'manufactured tv)
(manufactured 1987 in Japan)
->
```

Since `assoc` is only interested in the head of each element of an association list, it follows that the elements can be lists of arbitrary length and structure. Dotted pairs are occasionally used for the sake of efficiency.

Incidently, `assoc` has a special form called `assq` which searches for a key using `eq` rather than `equal`. Obviously, it is more efficient but it will not necessarily work for nonatomic keys.

EXERCISE 8.3
> Use association lists to represent information about books, as illustrated by the following example:
>
> ((**author** Jones) (**title** Software Development) (**year** 1980)
> (**publisher** Prentice Hall))
>
> Use the free variable books to hold a list of such association lists. Now write new-book, a function which adds a book to books if it is not already there, and list-all, a function which lists a given attribute of all books. For example, (list-all 'author) should produce a list of all authors.

8.3 Array structures

An *array* structure is a contiguous block of storage. Like lists, arrays consist of elements. Unlike lists, an array is of a fixed, predetermined size which cannot be changed.

Arrays are useful for representing data which is to be accessed randomly. For example, consider a table which records the monthly rainfall in ten regions of a country over a period of one year:

Region	Jan	Feb	Mar	. . . .	Dec
1	2.1	2.2	2.6		1.9
2	1.5	2.1	1.6		2.2
3	1.8	1.5	1.7		1.6
.					
.					
10	2.2	1.8	1.9		1.5

This table is conveniently represented by a two-dimensional array of size 10 rows by 12 columns. The function array creates arrays in LISP:

```
-> (array table t 10 12)
array[120]
->
```

The first argument to array is an array name. The second argument specifies the type of the array's elements, which when t, allows the elements to be arbitrary s-expressions. The remaining arguments specify the dimensions of the array. Theoretically, there is no bound on the number and size of dimensions. Note that array does not evaluate any of its arguments.

A newly created array is initially empty; that is, it contains empty slots. Each slot (or element) may be referenced by specifying its position. For example,

    (table 1 2)

refers to the third column in the second row of table (i.e., rainfall in region 2 during March). The numbers 1 and 2 are called *indices*. Note that an array's indices start at 0, not 1. For example, the indices of table run from 0 to 9, and 0 to 11.

An array's slot is filled by the function store. This is a function of two arguments, where the first argument specifies a slot to be filled, and the second argument specifies the value to be stored in that slot. For example,

    -> (store (table 1 2) 2.5)
    2.5
    -> (store (table 1 3) 2.6)
    2.6
    -> (table 1 2)
    2.5
    ->

stores the values 2.5 and 2.6 as the rainfall for the months of March and April in region 2.

There are also a number of other array-oriented functions, most of which are used for interrogating various attributes of an array. Arraydims, for example, returns a list of the type and the dimensions of an array:

    -> (arraydims (getd 'table))
    (t 10 12)
    ->

Getd is a LISP primitive which returns the function binding of a symbol. (In Franz, array structures are internally stored as functions.)

Getlength returns the length of an array, which is defined to be the product of the dimensions of that array (i.e., the total number of slots in the array):

    -> (getlength (getd 'table))
    120
    ->

Arrayp returns t if and only if its argument evaluates to an array structure:

    -> (arrayp (getd 'table))
    t
    ->

8.3 Array structures

The use of arrays in LISP is not as common as in most other programming languages. One reason for this is that symbol manipulation applications requiring such data structures rarely arise. Another reason is that the role of arrays is in most cases adequately fulfilled by lists.

Hunk structures

In addition to arrays, Franz LISP provides an array-like data structure of contiguous memory cells called *hunk*. Hunks are limited in two respects: they may only be one-dimensional, and their size should be from 1 - 128 elements. Being structurally simple and limited in size, hunks are extremely efficient.

There are two primary functions for creating hunks. Hunk creates a hunk whose elements are the arguments to hunk. For example,

```
-> (hunk 'a 'b 'c 'd)
{a b c d}
->
```

creates a hunk of four elements. Note that the way a hunk is represented is similar to a list, except that curly brackets are used instead of round brackets.

Alternatively, a hunk may be created using makhunk. This function takes one argument only which must evaluate to either a list or a fixed number. In the former case, it creates a hunk whose elements are the same as the elements of the list, in the same order. In the latter case, it creates a hunk of the specified size, whose elements are all initialized to nil:

```
-> (makhunk '(a b c d))
{a b c d}
-> (makhunk 4)
{nil nil nil nil}
->
```

Individual elements of a hunk are accessed by cxr. This is a function of two arguments, the second of which must evaluate to a hunk, and the first of which must evaluate to an index (a fixed number) to that hunk:

```
-> (setq x (hunk 'a '(b c) 'd))
{a (b c) d}
-> (cxr 2 x)
d
->
```

Note that like arrays, the index of a hunk starts at 0.

Rplacx changes an element of a hunk. The first two arguments to rplacx are like those of cxr and specify an element; the third argument specifies a new value for that element:

```
-> (rplacx 2 x 'n)
{a (b c) n}
-> (cxr 2 x)
n
->
```

There are two predicates associated with hunks; hunkp returns t if and only if its argument evaluates to a hunk, and hunksize returns the size (i.e., the number of elements) of a hunk.

EXERCISE 8.4
  Write maximum, a function which searches through an array of numbers and returns the largest number in the array. Maximum should take one argument only – the array to be searched.

EXERCISE 8.5
  Let h be a hunk whose elements are arbitrary lists. Write sort, a function which sorts the elements of h in ascending order of their lengths. For example, when h is

    {(a b c) (d) (e f)}

  Sort should rearrange h to

    {(d) (e f) (a b c)}

  As before, your function should take one argument only – the hunk to be sorted.

8.4 String and symbol manipulation

As mentioned earlier, a string is an arbitrary sequence of characters enclosed in double quotes. There is some degree of similarity between strings and symbols. The primary reason for this is that symbols are internally stored as strings in the LISP symbol table. The string representation of a symbol is called its *print name* and is extracted by the get_pname function:

```
-> (get_pname 'symbol)
"symbol"
->
```

8.4 String and symbol manipulation

Note, however, that the similarity between strings and symbols is limited to their representation and does not extend to their actual properties. For example, a string cannot have a value or a function binding, whereas a symbol can. In Chapter 5 we saw that strings and symbols may both be used for printing messages:

```
-> (patom '|Good morning|)
Good morning|Good morning|
-> (patom "Good morning")
Good morning"Good morning"
->
```

Strings are always preferred for this purpose. The reason for this is that LISP has to maintain an entry for each symbol in the symbol table. This is rather wasteful since each symbol will be allocated space for its value binding, function binding, and property list. Most probably these will never be used.

Two predicates are provided for identifying strings and symbols; stringp returns t if and only if its argument evaluates to a string, and symbolp returns t if and only if its argument evaluates to a symbol:

```
-> (stringp "hello")
t
-> (stringp 'hello)
nil
-> (symbolp 'hello)
t
-> (symbolp "hello")
nil
->
```

Most string manipulation functions also work on symbols, in which case they assume the print name of a symbol, rather than its value binding. For example, alphalessp takes two arguments (each of which must be a string or a symbol) and returns t if and only if the former alphabetically precedes the latter:

```
-> (alphalessp "goodbye" "hello")
t
-> (alphalessp "goodbye" 'hello)
t
->
```

The function concat concatenates zero or more symbols, strings, or numbers to produce a symbol whose print name is the same as the result of concatenation:

```
-> (concat "my" 'x)
myx
-> (concat "s-" 'expression- 1)
 -expression-1
->
```

Explode breaks an s-expression down into a list of its constituent characters while implode does the opposite by putting the characters back together to produce a symbol:

```
-> (explode 'man)
(m a n)
-> (explode "man")
(|"| m a n |"|)
-> (implode (explode 'man))
man
-> (implode (explode "man"))
|"man"|
-> (explode 123)
(|1| |2| |3|)
-> (explode '(sad man))
(|(| s a d | | m a n |)|)
->
```

The last function to be described here is boundp. This takes one argument which must evaluate to a symbol and returns nonnil if and only if its argument is bound to some value:

```
-> (boundp 'x)
nil
-> (setq x 10)
10
-> (boundp 'x)
(nil . 10)
->
```

EXERCISE 8.6
   Use alphalessp to write sort-names, a function which sorts a hunk of strings in alphabetical order.

EXERCISE 8.7
   Use explode to write subpattern, a function which returns t if and only if the characters in a symbol's name appear in another symbol's name. The following examples illustrate:
      (subpattern 'man 'human)   ;; returns t.
      (subpattern 'man 'median)   ;; returns t.
      (subpattern 'man 'made)   ;; returns nil.

8.5 Error handling

A function can only produce meaningful results for certain classes of input values, commonly referred to as *valid data*. Any invalid data could lead to erroneous results or even total chaos. For clarity, issues concerning invalid data have been intentionally ignored thus far in this book. We now discuss this matter in some detail.

When writing programs, ideally we would like to detect any invalid data and report it as error to the user. One possible approach is to test for invalid data within each function and report it as error using the normal printing functions of LISP. For example, consider an iterative version of the function `nth-element` (as defined in Chapter 5):

```
(defun nth-element (n list)
    (cond [(not (fixp n))                          ;; n is not a fixed number?
           (patom "nth-element: arg 1 must be a fixnum")
           (terpri)]
          [(not (listp list))                      ;; list is not a list?
           (patom "nth-element: arg 2 must be a list")
           (terpri)]
          [t (prog ()                              ;; actual nth-element.
                loop
                   (cond [(> n 1)
                          (setq list (cdr list) n (1- n))
                          (go loop)])
                   (return (car list)))]))
```

The first two clauses of `cond` test that the first argument is a fixed number, and that the second argument is a list. If not, `nth-element` will simply display an appropriate error message and return `nil`:

```
-> (nth-element 2 '(a b c))
b
-> (nth-element 'second '(a b c))
nth-element: arg 1 must be a fixnum
nil
-> (nth-element 2 'list)
nth-element: arg 2 must be a list
nil
->
```

A better approach is to use `error`, a built-in function that LISP primitives use for reporting errors. This has the advantage that an error will be immediately followed by a debug loop, allowing the user to detect exactly what has gone wrong. Furthermore, use of `error` will ensure some degree of uniformity and coherence amongst functions. Rewriting `nth-element` using `error`, we arrive at the following definition:

```
(defun nth-element (n list)
    (cond [(not (fixp n))                        ;; n is not a fixed number?
           (error "nth-element: arg 1 must be a fixnum")]
          [(not (listp list))                    ;; list is not a list?
           (error "nth-element: arg 2 must be a list")]
          [t (prog ()                            ;; actual nth-element.
              loop
                 (cond [(> n 1)
                        (setq list (cdr list) n (1- n))
                        (go loop)])
                 (return (car list)))]))
```

Now, `nth-element` is indistinguishable from LISP primitives in its handling of errors:

```
-> (nth-element 'second '(a b c))
Error: nth-element: arg 1 must be a fixnum
<1>:
```

It should be obvious that `nth-element` could still produce an error message, even if we did not test for the validity of its arguments. However, such error messages would be rather obscure and difficult to trace back to their actual sources. For example, if we removed the first `cond` in the definition of `nth-element`, the following would happen

```
-> (nth-element 'second '(a b c))
Error: Non-number to minus second
<1>:
```

which is not very informative, since relating this back to the fact that `second` is not a fixed number will require a close look at the definition of `nth-element` and is not immediately obvious.

The error mechanism described so far is appropriate only as far as a programmer is concerned. Finished LISP programs which are to be used by other people (most possibly nonprogrammers) are required to behave rather differently: they should report errors, but should not suspend execution by entering a debug loop. Ideally, they should handle an error in such a way that allows the user to continue without disruption. Such behavior is implemented using `errset`.

`Errset` is a function of one or two arguments. It evaluates its first argument, and if no errors occur during the evaluation, it will return a list of one element which is the result of evaluation. Otherwise, `errset` will return `nil`. The second argument is a flag which indicates whether an error message should be displayed or not. If this argument is not present or if it evaluates to a nonnil object, `errset` will display error messages. Otherwise, it will ignore them:

```
-> (errset (nth-element 2 '(a b c)))
(b)
-> (errset (nth-element 'second '(a b c)))
nth-element: arg 1 must be a fixnum
nil
-> (errset (nth-element 'second '(a b c)) nil)
nil
->
```

EXERCISE 8.8
Use `error` to report potential errors in `sort-names` and `subpattern` (see Exercises 8.6 and 8.7).

EXERCISE 8.9
Use `errset` to redefine the LISP top level so that errors will be reported, but will not cause the system to enter a debug loop.

8.6 *Catch* and *throw*

Consider a sequence of functions `f1, f2, ..., fn` where `f1` calls `f2`, `f2` calls `f3`, etc. Sometimes it is useful to find a shortcut which takes us from `fn` back to `f1`, without waiting for the intermediate functions to complete their jobs. A typical example is when `f1, ..., fn` are functions which search a hierarchical data structure, where each function is responsible for searching one level of hierarchy within the structure. Obviously, as soon as the required item is found, the search need no longer continue and it is convenient to return directly to `f1`. This is illustrated by Figure 8.1.

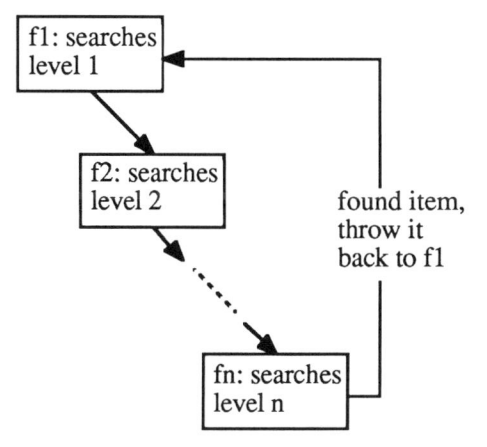

Figure 8.1 Short cut from `fn` to `f1`.

This unusual style of flow of control is supported by catch and throw; throw evaluates an s-expression and throws its value upwards while catch evaluates an s-expression and catches a value which has been thrown during the evaluation of that s-expression, and returns that value as its result. For example, the above situation may be formulated as:

```
(defun f1 (...)
       ...
       (setq item (catch (f2 ...)))
       ...)
(defun f2 (...)
       ...
       (f3 ...)
       ...)
...
(defun fn (...)
       ...
       (cond [(found-item) (throw item)])
       ...)
```

Here, fn finds the required item and throws it. This item is caught by the first catch in the sequence of nested calls, i.e., by the catch in f1. As a result, all the intervening calls are ignored. The transfer of control from fn to f1 is direct and immediate.

Catch and throw can take an additional argument, called a *tag*, to enable more selective catching of values. Tags are useful when more than one value is thrown in an s-expression. For example, in

```
(catch (... (throw value1 tag1)
            (throw value2 tag2)) 'tag1)
```

catch will only catch value1. However, in

```
(catch (... (throw value1 tag1)
            (throw value2 tag2)) '(tag1 tag2))
```

it will catch both value1 and value2. The latter case may also be written as

```
(catch (... (throw value1 tag1)
            (throw value2 tag2)))
```

since a tagless catch will catch anything.

Careful readers have probably noticed some similarity between `catch` and `throw`, on the one hand, and `error` and `errset` on the other. This is not a coincidence; `error` and `errset` are in fact implemented using `throw` and `catch`.

8.7 Summary

In this chapter we have looked at a number of other data structures in LISP and have briefly discussed error handling. We may summarize the main points of the chapter as follows.

- Symbols may have *properties*. These are stored in a symbol's *property list*.
- `Putprop` and `remprop` change and remove the properties of a symbol, respectively.
- `Get` retrieves a property value while `plist` retrieves the entire property list of a symbol.
- `Setplist` defines a new property list for a symbol.
- An *association list* is a list of lists, recording properties or facts about an object.
- `Assoc` retrieves information from an association list.
- An *array* is a contiguous block of storage.
- Arrays are defined using the `array` function.
- Array references are like function calls.
- `Store` stores a value in an array's slot.
- *Hunks* are one-dimensional arrays of limited size (1 - 128 elements.)
- `Hunk` and `makhunk` create hunks.
- `Cxr` and `rplacx` access and change an element of a hunk, respectively.
- Strings are more efficient than symbols for representing messages.
- Most string manipulation functions also work for symbols.
- `Error` and `errset` facilitate LISP-compatible error handling.
- `Catch` and `throw` facilitate unconventional flow of control.

Project

8.1 Write `match`, a pattern matching function for matching the atoms in an s-expression against a general pattern. The general call

```
(match s-expression pattern)
```

should return a list of atoms in `s-expression` which match `pattern`. `Pattern` should be a string, formulated according to the following conventions:

`-`	will match any single character.
`*`	will match any sequence of zero or more characters.
`+`	will match any sequence of one or more characters.
`/-`	will match the character `-`.
`/*`	will match the character `*`.
`/+`	will match the character `+`.
`//`	will match the character `/`.

any other character will match itself.

The following examples illustrate:

```
(match "an example" "a*e")      ;; match
(match "man" "m-n")             ;; match
(match "caadr" "c+r")           ;; match
(match "function" "fun-")       ;; do not match
```

Extend your program by writing `match-file`, a function which matches the s-expressions in a file against a pattern, and prints the matched atoms in alphabetical order.

Chapter 9

Advanced Topics

This chapter deals with a number of topics which are not essential for writing LISP programs, but will help you to debug your programs more easily, and once completed, make them run faster. The first section is devoted to the debugging and tracing facilities of LISP. It shows how you can examine the behavior of a program during its execution to detect potential errors. The section on compilation will show you how to compile your LISP programs to achieve greater efficiency. Franz LISP allows the use of functions written in other UNIX-based programming languages. This will be illustrated using an example. Finally, we will describe ways of bootstraping your programs so that they will run as stand-alone programs.

The topics covered in this chapter are very dialect dependent. Readers using other LISP dialects should consult the user manual of their system to find the exact commands for the described facilities.

9.1 Debugging and tracing

When a program fails, the next logical step is to go through the program to detect the source of the error and correct it. This practice is called *debugging*. Debugging is a tedious, mentally demanding job. To make life easier, most programming environments provide one or more debugging tools to assist the programmer in this difficult task. LISP is no exception.

Debugging in LISP is somewhat easier than in other programming languages, since the LISP interpreter keeps good track of the source code during interpretation. This information is kept on a stack which grows and shrinks as s-expressions are evaluated. The stack provides a good starting point for investigating what might have gone wrong.

Interrogating the stack

LISP sets up a *stack frame* for each s-expression being evaluated. For example when evaluating

```
(list (cons 'a '(b c)) 'd)
```

a stack frame is first set up for evaluating (list ...). The evaluation of this expression requires the evaluation of (cons ...) for which another stack frame is set up. Once the latter expression is evaluated, its stack frame is disposed of and the result (a b c) is passed to the previous stack frame, which is in turn completed and disposed of, returning the result ((a b c) d). What happens on the stack, therefore, directly conforms to the way the program is executed. This implies that the information held on the stack can be very valuable in detecting the source of errors.

The function showstack allows the user to get a listing of what is stored on the stack at any point in time. To illustrate its use, consider the following faulty LISP function:

```
(defun atoms (list)
   (prog (count)
     loop
        (cond [(null list) (return count)]
              [(atom (car list)) (setq count (1+ count))]
              [t (setq count (+ count (atoms (car list))))])
        (setq list (cdr list))
        (go loop)))
```

Atoms is supposed to return the number of atoms in a list, but fails in the midst of execution:

```
-> (atoms '(a b))
Error: 1+: non fixnum argument   nil
<1>:
```

In this case the error message is clear and shows what has gone wrong. This is not always the case. For example, in a large program where 1+ has been used in many places, it is not immediately obvious which of these the error message could be referring to. Showstack allows the pinpointing of the actual position where the failure has occurred:

```
<1>: (showstack)
(showstack)
break-err-handler
(|1+| count)
(setq count <**>)
```

9.1 Debugging and tracing

```
(cond ((null list) (return count))
      ((atom &) <**>) (t (setq count &)))
(prog (count) loop <**> ...)
(atoms '(a b))
nil
<1>:
```

`Showstack` shows the contents of the stack from top to bottom; so, more recent stack frames are displayed first. The top two stack frames correspond to `showstack` itself and the error handling mechanism of LISP. The third stack frame is where the error has actually occurred. Note the two conventions used for displaying the stack: the symbol <**> is used as an abbreviation for the next stack frame, and ellipses are used to abbreviate long s-expressions.

Using a debugger

Although `showstack` is adequate for most purposes, it is not as flexible as one might wish. For example, it does not allow one to go back to the context of an expression in the middle of the stack and evaluate a variable in that context. Such additional flexibility is provided by an interactive debugger, which allows the programmer to move up and down the stack easily to investigate what might be wrong.

The standard Franz LISP debugger is called *fixit* and is invoked by typing (debug):

```
<1>: (debug)
[fasl /usr/lib/LISP/fix.o]
<------debug------>
:
```

The debugger is not always resident in LISP and is brought in when required. When invoked, it comes up with a colon prompt indicating that it is ready for your requests. The debugger has its own set of commands. The command `where`, for example, displays your current position in the stack:

```
: where
<------debug------>
you are at top of stack.
there are 0 debug's below.
:
```

The commands u and dn move one frame up or down the stack:

```
:dn
(eval (debug))
:dn
(break-err-handler (ER%misc 0 nil |1+: non fixnum argument |    nil))
:dn
(|1+| count)
:u
(break-err-handler (ER%misc 0 nil |1+: non fixnum argument |    nil))
:dn
(|1+| count)
:where
(|1+| count)
you are 3 frames from the top.
:
```

Bk prints a back-trace of the stack, showing the exact position we are at:

```
:bk
<------debug------>
(eval (debug))
(break-err-handler (ER%misc 0 nil |1+: non fixnum argument |    nil))
(|1+| count)      <--- you are here
(setq count (|1+| count))
(cond (& &) (& &) (t &))
(prog (count) loop (cond & & &) (setq list &) ...)
(atoms '&)
(eval (atoms &))
<bottom of stack>
:
```

Most of the debugger commands also accept additional arguments and/or suffixes. For example, u and dn may be given an integer argument, indicating the number of stack frames we wish to move up or down. Moreover, bk accepts a variety of suffixes which may be mixed: f shows only function names, v shows variable bindings, etc.:

```
:bkf
<------debug------>
eval
break-err-handler
|1+|    <--- you are here
setq
cond
```

9.1 Debugging and tracing

```
prog
atoms
eval
<bottom of stack>

:bkfv
<------debug------>
eval
break-err-handler
|1+|    <--- you are here
setq
cond
    count = nil
prog
    list = (a b)
atoms
eval
<bottom of stack>
:
```

A useful feature of the debugger is that one can move to any stack frame and evaluate or change the binding of variables in the context of that frame. In this way, one can temporarily fix an error and try out its effect:

```
:count
      count = nil
:(setq count 0)
0
:redo
2
->
```

Here, we first examined the value of count, which turned out to be nil. The right value for count at this point is obviously 0; so, we then set count to 0. Finally, we used redo to resume evaluation from the point we were in the stack. As we expected, this worked and atoms returned 2. Note that by completing the evaluation of atoms, we automatically got out of the debugger. Another command for getting out of the debugger is ok. It simply resumes processing from the top of the stack:

```
:ok
t
<1>:
```

There is not enough room here for describing all the features of the debugger. The reader is therefore referred to the Franz LISP manual for more information. Here is a brief summary of the commands understood by the debugger, which you may yourself obtain by typing help:

:help	
u / u n / u f / u n f	go up, i.e., more recent (n frames of function f)
up / up n	go up to next (nth) nonsystem function
d / dn	go down, i.e., less recent (opposite of u and up)
ok / go	continue after an error or debug loop
redo / redo f	resume computation from current frame (or at fn f)
step	restart in single-step mode
return e	return from call with value of e (default is nil)
edit	edit the current stack frame
editf / editf f	edit nearest fn on stack (or edit fn f)
top / bot	go to top (bottom) of stack
p / pp	show current stack frame (pretty print)
where	give current stack position
help / h / ?	print this table -- /usr/LISP/doc/fixit.ref
help ...	get the help for ...
pop / ^d	exit one level of debug (reset)
bk / bk n / bk f / bk n f /	backtrace (to nth frame of fn f)
..f function names only	..a include system functions
..v show variable bindings	..e show expressions in full
..c go no deeper than here	*** combinations are allowed ***

Using a tracer

A useful debugging technique is to follow the sequence of function calls in a program, listing out what each function is given as arguments, and what it returns as result. This is called *tracing*. Franz LISP offers a trace package which does the job for us. To trace a program, we should first inform the tracer which functions we want to be traced. For example, consider the following corrected version of atoms:

```
(defun atoms (list)
   (prog (count)
        (setq count 0)
      loop
        (cond [(null list) (return count)]
              [(atom (car list)) (setq count (1+ count))]
              [t (setq count (+ count (atoms (car list))))])
        (setq list (cdr list))
        (go loop)))
```

9.1 Debugging and tracing

To trace all calls to this function, we do the following:

```
-> (trace atoms)                          ;; mark atoms for tracing.
[autoload /usr/lib/LISP/trace]
[fasl /usr/lib/LISP/trace.o]
(atoms)
-> (atoms '((a (b c)) (d e)))             ;; test atoms.
1 <Enter> atoms (((a (b c)) (d e)))
|2 <Enter> atoms ((a (b c)))
| 3 <Enter> atoms ((b c))
| 3 <EXIT>  atoms  2
|2 <EXIT>  atoms  3
|2 <Enter> atoms ((d e))
|2 <EXIT>  atoms  2
1 <EXIT>  atoms  5
5
->
```

The call to trace informs the tracer that calls to atoms should be traced. Like the debugger, the trace package is not normally resident in LISP and is demand-loaded. The above call to atoms shows the way atoms is traced. The lines containing <Enter> correspond to calls to atoms. The lines containing <EXIT> correspond to returns from atoms. These lines also contain the arguments passed to the function and the results returned from it. Furthermore, each line is labelled with the depth of the call, and properly indented to show the way calls fold and unfold.

The trace package allows the tracing of any number of functions. Functions which are no longer needed to be traced, should be untraced using untrace:

```
-> (untrace atoms)
(atoms)
->
```

Both trace and untrace may take any number of function names as arguments.

Beside debugging, a trace package is also useful for studying the behavior of a program, for example, to find out how it works.

Code instrumentation

Code instrumentation is one of the most effective techniques for debugging programs. Here, those parts of a program that are suspected to be misbehaving are first located. One or more variables which are likely to manifest the source of the misbehavior are then chosen and instrumented so that their values will be displayed during execution. This is usually done using a simple output function such as the one shown below:

```
(defun SHOW (pos item)
   (patom "** ") (patom pos) (patom " **   ")
   (patom item) (patom " = ") (patom (eval item)) (terpri))
```

To illustrate the code instrumentation technique, suppose we have decided to instrument atoms so that intermediate values of list will be displayed. Here is how it may be done:

```
(defun atoms (list)
   (prog (count)
         (setq count 0)
      loop
(SHOW 1 'list)
         (cond [(null list) (return count)]
               [(atom (car list)) (setq count (1+ count))]
               [t (setq count (+ count (atoms (car list))))])
         (setq list (cdr list))
         (go loop)))
```

Calling atoms now produces detailed information about list each time round the loop:

```
-> (atoms '((a b) (c)))
** 1 **    list = ((a b) (c))
** 1 **    list = (a b)
** 1 **    list = (b)
** 1 **    list = nil
** 1 **    list = ((c))
** 1 **    list = (c)
** 1 **    list = nil
** 1 **    list = nil
3
->
```

The reason for having the first argument to SHOW is that a program may be instrumented at more than one point. This parameter allows us to find out to which call to SHOW the output corresponds.

Incidently, note that we did not indent the call to SHOW like the rest of the program. This enables such calls to be easily located and removed once the program is fully debugged. Alternatively, calls to SHOW may be commented out, in case they might be needed in the future. To avoid confusion, however, all such comments should be clearly labelled to correspond to code instrumentation.

9.2 Compilation

So far our use of LISP has been confined to the LISP interpreter. The interpreter, as we saw, keeps track of many things. For example, it maintains detailed information about each s-expression being evaluated on the stack. The behavior of the interpreter has an advantage from a programming and debugging point of view: it allows us to examine the state of affairs during execution and especially when things go wrong. However, as far as completed and fully debugged programs are concerned, the interpreter does a lot of unnecessary work which only slows programs down.

Compilation of LISP programs is a way of getting round the overhead of the interpreter. A LISP compiler is like any other high-level programming language compiler; it is a program which translates LISP source code to its equivalent machine code representation. The fundamental difference between an interpreter and a compiler is that the former works directly on the source code, by accessing and then evaluating individual s-expressions, while the latter first produces a machine code representation of the source code – usually called the *object code* – and then executes the object code directly. This is illustrated in Figure 9.1.

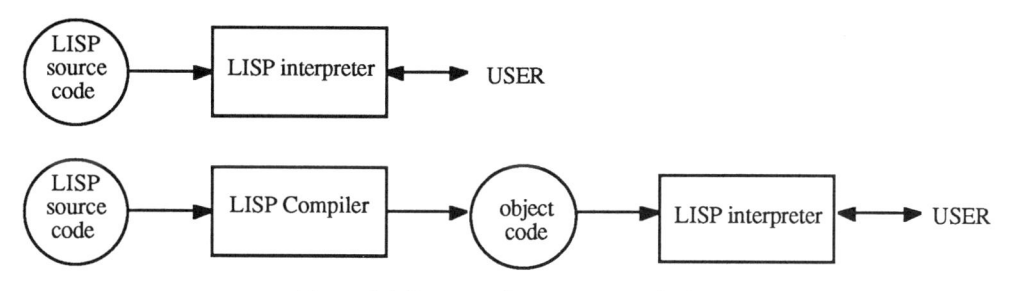

Figure 9.1 Interpretation versus compilation.

The standard Franz LISP compiler under UNIX is called *liszt*. To illustrate its use, consider the following function and suppose that its definition is stored in a UNIX file called rev.l:

```
(defun rev-list (list)                          ;; reverse a list.
        (prog (res)
           loop
              (cond [(null list) (return res)])
              (setq res (cons (car list) res)
                    list (cdr list))
              (go loop)))
```

To compile this program we feed rev.l through the compiler by typing:

```
$ liszt rev.l
Compilation begins with Liszt vax version 8.36
source: rev.l, result: rev.o
rev-list
%Note: rev.l: Compilation complete
%Note: rev.l:   Time: Real: 0:4, CPU: 0:0.47, GC: 0:0.00 for 0      gcs
%Note: rev.l: Assembly begins
%Note: rev.l: Assembly completed successfully
$
```

The compiler produces some output regarding what it is doing. Note the naming conventions for the files: a Franz LISP source file always ends in .l, and an object file always ends in .o. Once the compiler has completed its job, the system comes up with the UNIX $ prompt.

Now that we have successfully compiled the program, we are ready to load it into LISP and run it:

```
@ lisp
Franz Lisp, Opus 38.79
-> (load 'rev)
[fasl rev.o]
t
-> (rev-list '(a b c d))
(d c b a)
->
```

Note that load, when asked to load rev, automatically assumed the object file and loaded rev.o. The general rule is that, when given an abbreviated file name (i.e., without its ending), load always looks for an object file with that name. If it finds it, it will load it; otherwise, it will look for a source file and load that. This convention may be overridden by specifying the full name of a file. Also note that load uses fasl for loading object files. Alternatively, fasl may be used directly.

Compiler options

If you find the excessive output produced by the compiler disturbing, you can suppress much of it by specifying an option which will run the compiler in 'quiet' mode:

```
$ liszt -q rev
$
```

9.2 Compilation

This option will not suppress warning and error messages, so its use is safe. There are also other compiler options which allow you to alter various attributes of the compiler. Each option is specified (as above) by a minus symbol, followed by a letter. More than one option may appear after a minus symbol. The most commonly used options are as follows.

- m Compile the file in MacLISP mode.
- o Specifies a different object file name, for example, `liszt rev -o r.o` produces the object file in `r.o` instead of `rev.o`.
- q Run in quiet mode; compiler notes and function names will be suppressed.
- r Include bootstraping code in the object code (see Section 9.4 below).
- u Compile the file in UCI-LISP mode.
- w Suppress warning messages.
- x Produce a cross-reference file; this will be stored in a `.x` file. For example, `liszt -x rev` will produce the cross-reference in `rev.x`.

Compiler declarations

Ideally, one would expect a program that works when interpreted, to also work when compiled. In reality this is rarely the case. Minor difficulties often arise because the compiler needs to know certain additional information about the program. Such information is provided in the form of a compiler declaration in the program's source code. This subsection describes declarations that you need to know in order to ensure that your compiled programs will behave correctly.

A declaration to the compiler should be of the form

```
(declare ...something...)
```

where ...something... is one or more lists of compiler-specific information. All such declarations usually appear at the beginning of a file and are ignored by the interpreter. Each form of declaration is briefly described below.

(declare (special var1 ... varn))
  All free variables must be declared to be special (e.g., var1 ... varn above). If you fail to do so, the compiler will produce a warning message, indicating that such variables are assumed to be special. Do not be misled by this message; your program could still fail. It is best to make all special declarations at the beginning of a file.

(declare (unspecial var1 ... varn))
  This does the reverse of special, and makes variables that were previously declared to be special, unspecial. Obviously, the right place for such a declaration is somewhere in the middle of a file where a variable is no longer needed to be special (e.g., a

variable which was previously free and is now needed to be local).

(declare (specials t))
: Declares all variables to be special. Make sure you really mean this before using this declaration.

(declare (lambda fun1 ... funi))
(declare (lexpr fun1 ... funi))
(declare (nlambda fun1 ... funi))
: Declare functions `fun1 ... funi` to be `lambda`, `lexpr`, or `nlambda`, respectively. The first two declarations are not really necessary and are included for the sake of consistency. The last declaration might be necessary for `nlambda` functions (see below). For compatibility with MacLISP, the keywords `*expr`, `*lexpr`, and `*fexpr` may be used as synonyms instead of `lambda`, `lexpr`, and `nlambda` respectively.

(declare (macros t))
: The LISP compiler performs macro expansion at compile-time, and leaves no trace of macros in the object code. This declaration asks the compiler to include the definition of macros in the object code, so that they can be called from the top level.

(declare (localf fun1 ... funi))
: Asks the compiler to treat functions `fun1 ... funi` as local to the file being compiled. The effect of this is that references to such functions will be properly compiled but no run-time reference will be allowed (as if these functions never existed). The advantages are that the object code will be more efficient, and that the same function names can have different definitions in different files, without any risk of a name clash.

Multiple declarations may be made using one `declare` form. For example,

```
(declare (macros t)
         (special var1 var2)
         (localf fun1))
```

is equivalent to:

```
(declare (macros t))
(declare (special var1 var2))
(declare (localf fun1))
```

It is worth noting that, because the compiler performs macro expansion at compile time, you should ensure that each macro definition appears before it is referred to. Similarly, each nlambda form must be declared or defined before it is referred to.

9.3 Use of foreign functions 139

To sum up, the following three points need to be taken into account when compiling Franz LISP programs.

- If a variable is free with respect to one or more functions, then declare it as special at the beginning of the file.
- If your file contains any macros, then these should appear before they are referred to.
- If your file contains any nlambdas, then these should either be declared or appear before they are referred to.

9.3 Use of foreign functions

When writing real-life LISP programs, occasionally it is necessary to code parts of the program in some other programming language. This is usually justified when one is trying to overcome the following difficulties.

- To provide access to operating system routines, or to programs written by other people in other programming languages.
- To perform tasks which are not possible in LISP, such as very low-level I/O, interrupt handling, etc.
- To remove the bottlenecks of a LISP program. A bottleneck is a small section of a program which exhibits an unproportionate execution time, often because it cannot be expressed efficiently in LISP (e.g., character-oriented file processing).

Fortunately, Franz LISP allows the loading and use of code written in other UNIX-based programming languages. These are collectively called *foreign functions*, and are classified into four categories.

- *Subroutines*. These do not return anything, but LISP always returns `t` for them.
- *Functions*. These must return a valid LISP object.
- *Integer-functions*. These return an integer value which is converted by LISP into a fixed number.
- *Real-functions*. These return a double precision value which is converted by LISP into a float number.

To illustrate the use of foreign functions, we will show below how two C functions may be compiled, loaded into LISP, and subsequently referred to as LISP functions. Here is the definition of the C functions. The first function, `maximum`, returns the largest integer in an array of integers. The second function, `last_elem`, returns the last element of a list:

```
#define nil 0
typedef struct cell {
          struct cell *cdr, *car;
} *cons_cell;                                    /* cons-cell type */

int maximum (nums, n)                            /* find the largest integer in nums */
int nums[], *n;
{
   int i, max = nums[0];

        for (i=1; i < *n; ++i)
            if (nums[i] > max)
                max = nums[i];
        return (max);
}

cons_cell last_elem (list)                       /* return the last element of list */
cons_cell list;
{
        if (list == nil)
            return (nil);
        while (list->cdr != nil)
            list = list->cdr;
        return (list->car);
}
```

Next, we compile the C functions. Assuming that they are stored in a file called `for.c`, we do the following:

```
$ cc -c for.c
```

The C compiler stores the resulting object code in `for.o`. We can now use `cfasl` to load `for.o`, and at the same time set up the definition of `maximum`:

```
@ lisp
Franz Lisp, Opus 38.79
-> (cfasl 'for.o '_maximum 'maximum "integer-function")
/usr/lib/LISP/nld -N -x -A /usr/ucb/bin/LISP -T 95800 for.o
-e _maximum -o /tmpc
#95800-"integer-function"
->
```

`Cfasl` is called only once for each object file; subsequent functions are then loaded using `getaddress`. When setting up a foreign function, we may give it a new name; `last_elem`, for example, is renamed as `last-elem`:

```
-> (getaddress '_last_elem 'last-elem "function")
£9583e-"function"
->
```

Having set up the functions, we can now try them out:

```
-> (setq x (array nil fixnum-block 3))
array[3]
-> (store (funcall x 0) 5)
5
-> (store (funcall x 1) 15)
15
-> (store (funcall x 2) 10)
10
-> (maximum x 3)
15
-> (last-elem '(a b c d))
d
->
```

The steps taken above are typical of the process, and are similarly done for code written in other programming languages. Readers interested in more detail about the use of foreign functions should refer to the user manual.

A final word of advice: do not over use foreign functions; leave them for situations where there is no other reasonable alternative. It is generally a good idea to deal with foreign functions only when all other parts of a program are in place. If your use of foreign functions is purely for efficiency reasons, then the right approach is to code everything initially in LISP. Once you have everything working, then gradually replace the bottlenecks by individually-tested foreign functions.

9.4 Autorun and snapshot

When you have completed a serious program in LISP, it is most likely that you will want to use it as a stand-alone program. It is rather inconvenient to go through the process of invoking LISP, loading your program, and then calling the appropriate function, each time you want to use the program. For example, if you have a LISP program called myprog, having a main function called main, you usually have to go through the following steps to get it running:

```
$ lisp
Franz Lisp, Opus 38.79
-> (load 'myprog)
[fasl myprog.o]
-> (main)
...
```

It would be much more convenient if you could just type myprog so that everything would get going immediately. Fortunately, there are two ways of arranging this in Franz LISP.

The first approach uses the r option of the LISP compiler to bootstrap a program. To give an example, consider a simple program which prints a short message and then terminates:

```
(defun test ()
       (patom "This program is autorun.")
       (terpri)
       (exit))
(setq user-top-level 'test)              ;; call test automatically.
```

Assuming that this code is in a file called foo.l, compiling foo using the r option of the compiler will produce the desired effect:

```
$ liszt -qr -o foo foo.l
$ foo
This program is autorun
$
```

When a program is compiled using the r option of liszt, the object code will contain a piece of bootstrapping code which will automatically load the program and then look for the binding of the symbol user-top-level. If this symbol is bound to nonnil, then the function represented by the value of the binding (i.e., test here) will be called. This causes the program to run automatically without going through the usual manual steps.

This approach is reasonable for small programs. With large, frequently-used programs it is more convenient to take a snapshot of the whole LISP environment once the program is loaded. The snapshot may then be used as a stand-alone program, without going through the normal loading procedure. The following piece of code illustrates a way of doing this. Here we have assumed that the user program has a main function called main:

```
(declare (special BOOT))
(setq BOOT t)
```

```
(defun top-level ()
  (cond [BOOT
          (setq BOOT nil)                    ;; make future snapshot impossible.
          (patom "Booting the program.") (terpri)
          (dumpLISP)                         ;; take a snapshot of LISP.
          (exec mv -f savedLISP myprog)      ;; move the snapshot to myprog.
          (exit)])
  (main))                                    ;; run the user program.
```

Let us assume that the above code and the user program are in a file called `myprog.1`. The following steps should be taken:

```
$ liszt -q myprog
$ lisp
Franz Lisp, Opus 38.79
-> (load 'myprog)
[fasl myprog.o]
t
-> (reset)
[Return to top level]
Booting the program.
$
```

The process works as follows. Once the program is compiled and loaded, doing `reset` causes our definition of `top-level` to take over. Since this is the first execution, `BOOT` will be bound to `t`, hence the s-expressions in `cond` will be evaluated, causing a snapshot of LISP to be taken and then moved to `myprog`. In the meantime, the value of `BOOT` is changed to `nil` to ensure that subsequent runs will not go through this process. From now on, each time we type `myprog`, the program will run automatically.

9.5 Summary

In this chapter we have described some of the advanced facilities of LISP, e.g., debugging and compilation. We can summarize them as follows.

- LISP maintains a run-time stack consisting of *stack frames* for evaluating individual s-expressions.
- `Showstack` displays the contents of the run-time stack, from top to bottom.
- LISP programs may be *debugged* using an interactive debugger which allows one to

move up and down the stack, evaluate expressions in different contexts, and change the values of variables.
- A program *trace* is a listing of the program's run-time function calls (including their arguments and results).
- `Trace` marks functions for tracing; `untrace` does the reverse.
- *Code instrumentation* is a technique whereby output commands are inserted at specific points of interest in a program to display the values of variables.
- LISP programs may be compiled just like programs in other programming languages.
- Compilation improves performance but makes debugging more difficult.
- Franz LISP allows the loading and execution of code written in other programming languages – *foreign functions*.
- *Autorun* and *snapshot* are two techniques for transforming LISP programs into stand-alone programs.

Projects

9.1 Write a LISP program which consists of two main functions `instrument` and `uninstrument`. `Uninstrument` takes a LISP file which has been instrumented using `SHOW` and comments out all calls to `SHOW` by placing a semicolon in front of them. `Instrument` does the reverse by getting rid of the semicolons.
Compile your program program once it has been completed, taking into account the points mentioned in Section 9.2. (Note: `uninstrument` is easy; it involves reading each form in a file and searching through it for occurrences of `SHOW`. `Instrument` is slightly more difficult, since comment lines are ignored by `read`. Instead, you should use a lower-level input function such as `readc` – see Appendix 1. You may assume that each call to `SHOW` begins at a new line.)

9.2 Implement `instrument` and `uninstrument` as two Pascal or C functions. After thorough testing, load them into LISP as foreign functions (see Section 9.3).

Chapter 10

Programming Style

Learning to program in a new programming language is one thing; learning how to write good programs is another. This chapter addresses the issue of style: how to write well-designed, clear, and easy-to-understand programs. Many of the stylistic issues are language-independent; they concern the way a program should be designed, refined, and decomposed into units expressible in the target language. These will be tackled in the first section. The second section provides some guidelines on how LISP programs should be documented. The remaining two sections introduce the reader to two popular styles of programming: functional, and object-oriented programming.

This chapter is not essential for readers who are interested in learning LISP only. It does, nevertheless, make a few points – though brief they may be – which you will find very useful when tackling complicated LISP programs.

10.1 Software design

One can classify programs into two main categories: those that are written for experimentation, teaching, and learning (e.g., the programs in this book), and those that are written for real-life use (e.g., commercial programs). It is rather difficult to illustrate the importance of good design using programs in the first category, since these are often too simple to show the subtleties involved, and in most cases too trivial to need detailed explanation. It is only in the latter category that the importance of this issue comes to life.

Unfortunately, no introductory book has enough space to describe a large real-life program, nor can the reader be expected to be patient enough to embark on such a task. The alternative is to sketch only the principles involved, and this is what we shall be doing in this section. For the moment, we shall not give any concrete examples. The use of the methods, however, will be illustrated in subsequent chapters, when we go through specific case studies, and when we feel that a problem is difficult enough to illustrate the power of the design methods involved. When appropriate, we shall also give references to the literature for those who seek more explanations and examples.

The study of the software development process and the constituent steps of software projects is the premise of *software engineering* [Sommerville 1982]. Software design is one of the major topics of software engineering. To put the concept and its role in better perspective, let us begin our discussion by defining a few useful software engineering terms.

- A *requirements specification* is a statement of *what* a program is supposed to do. It must not, in any way, indicate how it should be done.
- *Design* is the act of producing solutions that satisfy the specification. It is an iterative process which progressively produces more detailed descriptions of *how* the problem is to be solved.
- The end product of a design stage is a *design specification*. This is a documentation of the design decisions in a form suitable for initiating the next design stage.
- The final design stage is called *implementation* (or *coding*). This occurs when the design is in a suitably detailed form to be expressed in a programming language.

It should be obvious that any program requires a requirements specification to establish the goals of the program. Requirements can be expressed in various ways. In their simplest form, they are written as English prose (see, for example, the end-of-chapter projects in this book).

Our interest here lies mainly in design, since it is usually the dominant part of program development. A good design will make life easier not only for yourself, but also for those who will be using or maintaining your programs.

Design iteration

To succeed, a design should always start with an abstract view of the problem. This is done by concentrating one's attention on important issues of interest, and ignoring lower-level details which are initially unimportant. Next, follows the design iteration, which attempts to break the problem down into a number of smaller, more manageable subproblems. This process is iteratively applied to subproblems until the final subproblems are sufficiently simple to be expressed in a programming language. This practice is called *top-down* design, and is illustrated in Figure 10.1.

Stepwise refinement [Wirth 1971] is one design method that employs such a strategy. Refinement is a term applied to the process of moving from the abstract to the detailed. Stepwise refinement distinguishes between two forms of refinement: *program specification* refinement, and *data specification* refinement. It argues that the refinement of these two should be carried out gradually and in parallel.

10.1 Software design

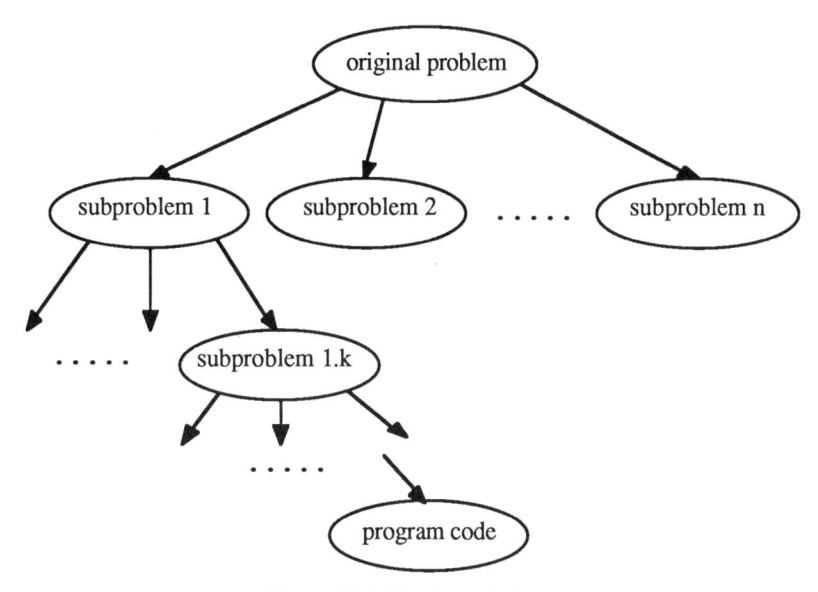

Figure 10.1 Top-down design.

A design process is best seen as a process of decision making, where each decision deals with a choice from a number of alternatives. To make better decisions, the design space should be explored as fully as possible so that the designer is aware of the alternatives available to him. This represents the harder half of design. The easier half is that of making the decisions. Such decisions are usually guided by design guidelines (as well as intuition). The three major guidelines of stepwise refinement [Wirth 1971] are as follows:

- 'Decompose decisions as much as possible.'
- 'Untangle aspects which are only seemingly independent.'
- 'Defer those decisions which concern details of representation as long as possible.'

In stepwise refinement an algorithmic style of English prose is used to describe the refinements. In Section 12.4 we shall see examples of the use of the method, where two complicated programs for graph searching are developed.

Kernighan and Plauger [1981] provide further insight into designing clear, easy-to-understand, and flexible programs. They propose a programming style which is based on the notion of a *tool*. A tool is a computer program which solves a general, rather than a special problem. The intention of the tool approach is to make programming easier and more productive: because of being general, a tool is likely to serve future, as well as present requirements. This means that programs will not be written, used, and then simply forgotten. They will also come in handy when a similar need arises in the future.

Tools should be constructed so that they can be used and combined easily. Two properties contribute towards this.

- *Simplicity*. A tool should have a simple, well-defined function.
- *Clean interface*. The interface of a tool to the outside environment should be simple and clean.

Tools which exhibit these properties can be easily combined to construct more complicated tools. This reflects another design strategy which is commonly called *bottom-up* design. Despite their appearance, top-down and bottom-up design are not contradictory, but rather complementary: individual tools may be designed in a top-down manner, and then combined in a bottom-up manner.

The simplest, most useful, and flexible tools are those that receive only one input, perform a simple, well-defined transformation on the input, and produce a single output. Such tools are called *filters*. Filters are combined easily by placing them sequentially, one after the other. Each tool processes the data handed over to it, and passes it to the next tool, as shown in Figure 10.2. Chapter 13 will describe a symbolic differentiation program which is constructed in this manner, using four simple filters.

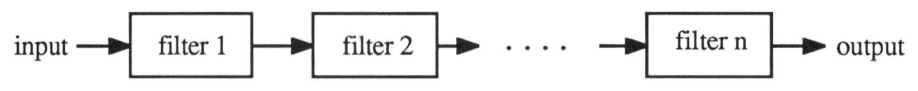

input → [filter 1] → [filter 2] → . . . . → [filter n] → output

Figure 10.2 Program design using filter tools.

On decomposition

The way a program is decomposed and refined determines its final structure. Based on the decomposition, a program is organized as a collection of functions which communicate by calling each other and by passing arguments. There are always numerous ways in which a program can be decomposed, few of which represent clear designs. To ensure a clear design, one should follow strategies which improve desirable qualities such as simplicity, structure, and ease-of-change.

If we use a small box to represent a function, and use arrows to represent what functions a function may call, then we arrive at a graphical representation of the structure of a program. Two examples of such diagrams are shown in Figure 10.3. In the first diagram, for example, function A may call functions B, C, and D. Such diagrams are usually called *structure diagrams* or *reference diagrams*.

Most design disciplines favor simple structure diagrams. *Structured design* [Basili and Baker 1981], for instance, favors diagram 1 (which has a tree structure) to diagram 2 (which has a graph structure). The argument is that the less dependent a function is on other functions, the easier it is to work on that function in isolation to other functions. This is a valid argument, but is sometimes pushed to the extreme, in which case, it will have adverse effects. For example, certain programming languages (e.g., FORTRAN) do not even allow diagram 2.

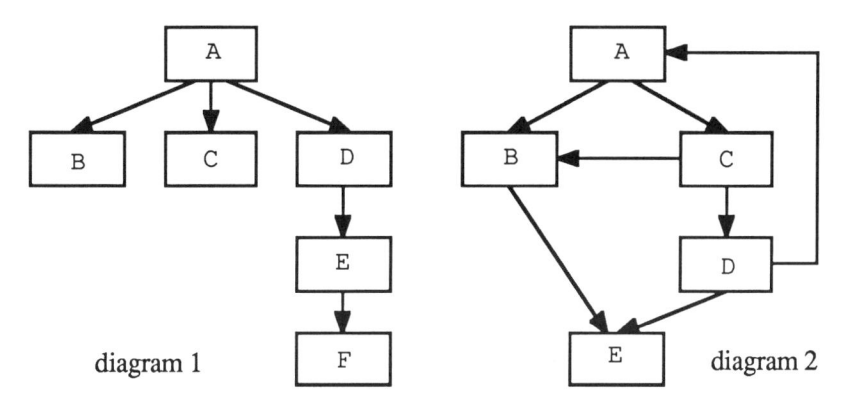

Figure 10.3 Two sample structure diagrams.

It is unfortunate that newcomers to software design are often taught two dogmatic design criteria that are not only unreasonable, but also often counter-productive. The first criterion is that a software design should resemble a tree structure. This is unreasonable since for many design problems a tree structure acts as a superficial framework, hiding other structures which may reflect the essence of the program more naturally. The correct criterion is to choose a structure which fits the problem more naturally than others. If this happens to be tree-like, so much the better; if not, one has to admit that the problem is a complex one that requires a complex solution.

The second criterion – and this is even more absurd – is to impose a size limit on each function. One often comes across statements such as that no function should be more than eight lines long. One objection to this criterion is that it is ambiguous: one can type the same function in two or ten lines say, using different indentation and spacing. Another objection is that it totally ignores what goes into a function. Making functions smaller does not necessarily make them easier to write or understand, but it certainly increases their number. The source of this criterion is a number of empirical studies which have suggested a correlation between clearer designs and small module size. The evidence against this criterion is a good number of well-designed, existing software products in which many modules are even pages long.

Design criteria

Currently, the most respected criteria for software design and decomposition are those suggested by Parnas [1972, 1979]. Parnas has argued that a design should start with a list of difficult design decisions. Modularization should then be carried out in such a way that each module hides a major design decision from others. Furthermore, each module should do one and only one thing, which in turn must be well-defined. Two advantages are gained from the use of these criteria. Firstly, such modularization increases the independence of modules, so one can work on them in isolation and secondly, it does not impose any arbitrary infrastructure on the design. For example, it does not limit a module's size or require the design to be necessarily tree-like.

Software design is currently an active and large research area. Consequently, it is not possible to include all on-going ideas in an introductory book of this nature. Readers interested to know more about this topic are referred to any standard book on software engineering [e.g., Shooman 1982, Sommerville 1982] and other publications on software design [Meyer 1982, Booch 1986, Yau 1986]. Below, we list a number of guidelines which you are advised to follow when designing your LISP programs. The intention is not to apply them dogmatically; much better results are obtained by also using common sense. The guidelines are as follows.

- Always write down a clear statement of the problem, i.e., what is required. During design refer back to the requirements to ensure that the objectives are met.
- Identify the main difficulties and, based on this, follow a top-down design strategy, by working from the abstract to the detailed.
- Do not jump from requirements to code. Refine and decompose gradually, and revise your decisions.
- Hide each major design decision by a function. Do not include more than one decision in a function [Parnas 1972].
- Design each function in such a way so that its use will not require a knowledge of how it works, but only what it does.
- Identify the domain of each function, i.e., the range of acceptable values for its parameters. If required, ensure that the function can deal with values outside its domain adequately by reporting errors.
- For each function, identify the side-effects that it assumes and produces. Also, clearly identify what a function returns.
- Test each function thoroughly in isolation (if possible), and then in association with related functions. A big-bang strategy where everything is written and then tested at once rarely works – see Meyer [1978] for more details.
- Avoid the use of global and free variables when possible. Leave the use of such variables to situations when you think too many parameters are being passed without alteration through a sequence of nested calls. Always initialize all global variables at the beginning of the program.
- Use meaningful and mnemonic symbols that reflect their intentions.
- When designing, always attempt to define the problem in terms of itself, to see if it has a recursive solution. If so, and if the recursive solution is reasonable and satisfies your constraints, then adopt it. Otherwise, stick to an iterative solution.
- Avoid the use of unstructured loops. A loop should have a simple, clear flow of control. Make sure that all loops terminate.

- Make sure that all recursive functions have a satisfiable termination condition.
- If you make compromises for efficiency and/or space, clearly state your reasons.
- Present your functions in a logical manner. Start with higher-level functions and end with lower-level ones.
- Document your code by meaningful comments (see the next section).
- For large programs use a number of files, each containing a set of related functions.
- Finally, be consistent in whatever style you use. A changing style is no style.

10.2 Documentation

The purpose of documentation is to make a program more understandable to those who will have to study and possibly change it. Almost every aspect of a program is subject to documentation: its requirements, its design, its code, its testing, etc. In this section we concentrate on code documentation; other related aspects are extensively dealt with in the literature [Aron 1983].

Like other programming languages, LISP programs are documented by inserting meaningful comments in the program text. Such comments serve four purposes.

- To describe information specific to a program, e.g., its author, version, target machine, copyrights, etc.
- To describe changes to a program, i.e., what has changed, who has changed it, and when it was changed.
- To describe the purpose of individual functions, e.g., what they do, what they assume, and how they may be used.
- To explain things that are not obvious from the program text.

It is best to use a consistent style for documentation. One might, for example, document individual functions using the following template:

```
; (function-name ...arguments...) -------------- [function type] ---
; WHERE:          describes each argument's role and structure.
; ASSUMES:        describes the conditions assumed by the function.
; RETURNS:        describes what is returned by the function.
; SIDE-EFFECTS:   describes the function's side-effects.
; ERROR:          describes the function's error conditions.
; GLOBALS:        describes any global variable referred to in the function.
; USES:           lists the functions called by this function.
; USED BY:        lists the functions that call this function.
; NOTE:           emphasizes any unusual aspects of the function.
```

The template starts by outlining a general call to the function. The type of individual arguments in this call may be indicated using a simple prefix convention. For example, one may use a prefix of l, x, or f to show that an argument must be a list, a fixed number, or a float number respectively. Function type (appearing on the top right hand side of the template) indicates whether the function is a lambda, macro, etc. Each field that follows, describes one aspect of the function. Obviously, not all fields are always required. The following example serves as an illustration.

```
; (extract-id-list 'l_user-recs) -------------------- [lambda] --
; WHERE:      l_user-recs is a list of user records.
; RETURNS:    a list of all user id's in l_user-recs, in that order.
; USES:       extract-id.
; USED BY:    process-users, sort-users.

(defun extract-id-list (user-recs)
    (prog (id-list)
       loop
          (cond [(null user-recs)
                    ;; id-list was constructed in reverse order
                    ;; using cons, so it must be reversed now:
                    (return (nreverse id-list))])
          (setq id-list (cons (extract-id (car user-recs))
                              id-list))
          (setq user-recs (cdr user-recs))    ;; next user record.
          (go loop)))
```

This example also illustrates another type of comment as classified above: the use of nreverse is justified by stating that id-list was constructed in the reverse order.

We conclude our discussion on documentation by drawing your attention to three points which, although seemingly trivial, are often overlooked.

- The use of comments for documentation is secondary to software design. A well-designed program is readable on its own, and needs few comments. A badly designed program, on the other hand, is always unreadable, no matter how many comments are inserted in it.
- Good indentation often reduces the need for detailed comments.
- There is nothing worse than a misleading, loose comment. Comments should be designed as carefully as programs themselves.

10.3 Functional programming

Most of us are familiar with traditional programming languages such as FORTRAN and Pascal which are based on *procedures* – recipes for computation. In these languages the procedure is the basic building block for creating programs. A procedure carries out its duty by relying on side-effects, that is, by overwriting the contents of variables by newly computed values so that computation may progress. For example, consider the following simple Pascal procedure:

```
procedure factorial (n: integer; var fac: integer);
begin
     fac := 1;
     while (n > 0) do begin
          fac := fac * n;
          n := n - 1
     end
end;
```

This procedure computes the factorial of n by progressively changing the contents of n and `fac`. It is now widely acknowledged that programs written using this style of computation are generally inelegant, often subtle and difficult to follow, and more or less intractable as far as their correctness is concerned.

Functional programming[Henderson 1980] which represents a different style of programming, does not suffer from these disadvantages. Here, *functions*, as opposed to procedures, are the basic building block for creating programs.

LISP is usually referred to as a functional programming language. This is not strictly true, since, although based on functions, it also allows the use of side-effects. LISP therefore supports a mixed style which offers both procedural and functional programming. This implies that LISP does have a purely functional subset. In fact, if we remove all impure functions of LISP (e.g., `set`, `setq`, `nconc`, etc.) what we will be left with will be a purely functional language.

The factorial program, for example, may be expressed elegantly as a purely functional program in this subset:

```
(defun factorial (n)
     (cond [(plusp n) (* n (factorial (1- n)))]
           [t 1])))
```

Functional programming is important because of the simplicity that it offers: functional programs are generally easier to write, understand, and modify. In addition, since functional programming rests on a sound mathematical foundation (called *lambda calculus*), a functional program can be proved correct with little difficulty. Currently, there are theorem proving tools which can automatically verify the correctness of a large class of functional program.

Although better known than most others, LISP is not the only functional programming language around. Numerous such languages have been developed in recent years: HOPE [Burstall *et al.* 1980], KRC [Turner 1982], ML [Harper 1986], and Miranda [Turner 1986] are examples. As opposed to LISP, which has an explicit style, these languages offer an implicit, *declarative* style for defining functions. Programs written in these languages typically consist of a set of assertions from which deductions may be made.

To illustrate the declarative style, consider the following Miranda program which implements the quick sort algorithm [Turner 1986]:

```
qsort[] = []
qsort(a:b) = qsort[x←b|x ≤ a] ++ [a] ++ qsort[x←b|x > a]
```

It consists of two assertions. The first assertion states that sorting an empty list is the same as an empty list. The second assertion states that sorting a list whose head is a and whose tail is b, is the same as sorting the list of those elements of b that are less than a, appended by the list containing a, appended by the result of sorting the list containing those elements of b that are greater than a. The careful reader will appreciate the expressive power of the declarative style, and the conciseness that it leads to.

Incidently, there is also a third approach to programming, called *logic programming* [Kowalski 1979, Genesereth and Ginsberg 1985], which also offers a declarative style. The main difference between functional programming and logic programming is that, in contrast to the former which relies on functions, the latter rests on *relations*. The most well-known programming language in this category is PROLOG, which uses resolution as its basic mechanism for execution. Figure 10.4 summarizes our categorization of programming styles.

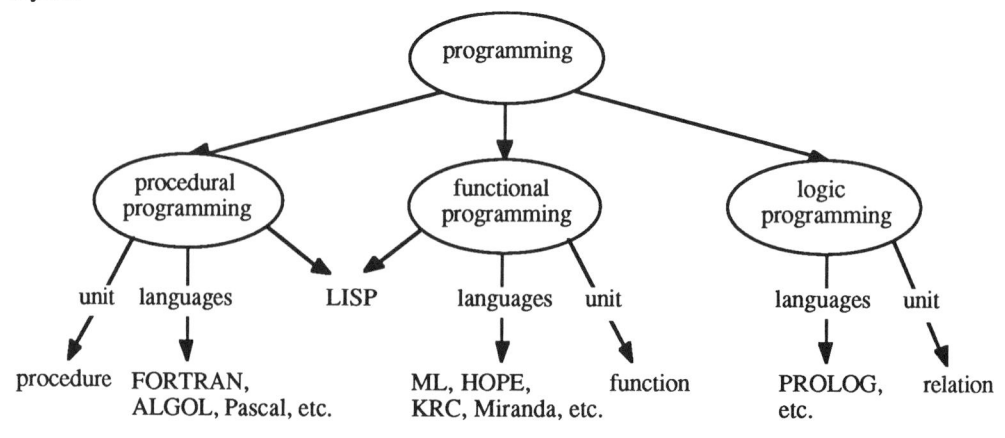

Figure 10.4 Styles of programming.

In Chapter 14 we will describe a number of purely functional extensions to LISP. These, together with the basic functional subset of LISP, provide a powerful functional notation in which programs may be formulated very concisely.

10.4 Object-oriented programming

One style of programming which is becoming increasingly more popular is *object-oriented programming* (OOP for short) [Xerox 1981, Cox 1986, ACM 1986]. This approach was not included in the previous section as a fourth style, since it is not independent of the three approaches described there, but rather complementary to them: procedural, functional, and logic programming can all support object-oriented programming.

Much has been written about OOP and there are numerous definitions of the term in the literature, few of which are correct. Genuine object-oriented programming rests on two concepts: *abstract data types* and *inheritance*. Abstract data types allow the creation of new data types, i.e., ones which are not directly provided by a programming language. These elaborate on the concrete, elementary types of the language by creating data types which match the problem at hand more naturally.

Take sets for instance. In a conventional programming language, one would represent a set using a concrete type such as array, and then implement each set operator as a procedure. In an object-oriented language, one can define a set as an abstract data type. This new type automatically becomes an extension of the language and may be used just like the elementary types (e.g., integers). Members of this new data type are commonly called objects – hence the term 'object-oriented'. The advantages of the latter approach are that objects of the new data type may be manipulated through their private operators only, and that implementation details of these objects are completely hidden from their users. None of these is true in the former case. The significance of abstract data types is that they avoid many common, accidental design errors.

Inheritance, the second cornerstone of OOP, allows the creation of new data types from those already defined, by defining the ways in which these new types differ from the old ones. The obvious advantage of inheritance is that it avoids unnecessary duplication of code.

Unlike traditional design techniques, which have the objective of breaking a system into modules, object-oriented design decomposes a system into a collection of objects that communicate with each other by passing messages [Booch 1986]. The object-oriented approach is evidently closer to the real world, since real world objects can be directly modelled by software objects.

Because of LISP's weak typing, object-oriented programming in LISP is conceived rather differently. Furthermore, most LISP systems do not support OOP directly, but are easily extended to do so – see, for example, [Winston and Horn 1984] and [Hurley 1985] for ways of doing this in Common LISP and Franz LISP, respectively.

10.5 Summary

In this chapter we have briefly discussed some of the important issues concerning the way programs should be developed. Here is a summary of the main points.

- A *requirements specification* specifies what a program should do.
- A *design specification* articulates how a program should do it.
- *Implementation* is the final stage of design where the design is expressed in a programming language.
- A program should be designed *top-down*, by moving from the abstract to the detailed.
- *Stepwise refinement* is a top-down design method which encourages gradual and in-parallel refinement of program specification and data specification.
- A *software tool* is a program that does a general, as opposed to special task.
- Tool-oriented development combines top-down and bottom-up design.
- Tree-like structure diagrams and small module sizes are inadequate, and often misleading design criteria.
- *Information hiding* is the right design criterion.
- A good designer always considers alternative designs before committing himself to a design.
- Comments improve the readability of well-designed programs. They do very little for badly designed programs.
- Program comments should be designed as carefully as programs themselves.
- *Procedural programming* is based on procedures – recipes for computation which cause side-effects.
- *Functional programming* is based on functions – side-effect free computations.
- LISP offers a mixed style of procedural and functional programming.
- *Declarative programming* is an implicit programming style based on assertions.
- *Object-oriented programming* is based on abstract data types and inheritance.
- *Abstract data types* allow the definition of new data types.
- *Inheritance* allows the derivation of new data types from old ones.

Project

10.1 In their excellent book, Kernighan and Plauger [1978] describe an extensive number of guidelines for writing clear and elegant programs. They use FORTRAN programs to illustrate their arguments. Make a list of the described guidelines and relate them to LISP programs.

Chapter 11

Pattern Matching

This chapter describes pattern matching – a process which involves the comparison of similar s-expressions. We begin our discussion by looking at natural language processing as a potential application area for pattern matching. We then describe the concepts of pattern symbols and pattern variables, and their use in formulating patterns. A simple pattern matcher will be developed which incorporates these ideas and which is of immediate utility in many pattern matching problems.

11.1 Introduction

Suppose we have built a database of facts about the countries of the world as suggested in Exercise 8.1. We now wish to build a flexible user interface to this database, which allows us to ask questions about the given facts in plain English, to which the system should respond appropriately. The following examples serve as an illustration.

```
-> (where is England)
(England is in Eurpoe)
-> (what other countries are in Europe)
(France Germany Italy Spain Holland ...)
-> (what is the capital of England)
(London)
-> (what is London)
(London is a city)
-> (is France a city)
(no France is a country)
-> (how many people do live in France)
(about 65 million people)
```

```
-> (what is the population of Mars)
(I don't know)
```

How would one write such an interface? One possible approach is to look at each question, atom by atom, and try to work out what the question is about. A more promising (and general) approach is to use what is known as *pattern matching*.

Pattern matching is a technical term applied to the process of comparing similar s-expressions. It is an important technique and has extensive uses in many areas of computing such as natural language processing, programming language translation, and theorem proving. The notion of a pattern is central to the process and denotes a generalized expression.

To describe the concept in more simple terms, take the first question in the above dialog:

```
(where is England)
```

If we substitute the name of any country or city for England in this question the result will be still a valid question. This suggests a pattern which depicts a whole class of similar questions:

```
(where is France)
(where is Italy)
(where is Amsterdam)
   ...
```

This may be represented more compactly as

```
(where is -)
```

where the symbol - stands for the name of any country or city. This generalized form is called a *pattern*. The symbol - is called a *pattern symbol*. Pattern matching involves the comparison of patterns, as such, to other s-expressions to see whether they are similar. A program which allows us to do this is called a *pattern matcher*. For example, when given

```
(match '(where is -)
       '(where is England))
```

the pattern matcher will produce t, indicating that the given expressions match.

The use of a pattern matcher allows us to classify questions into a number of categories. This makes subsequent answering relatively straightforward.

11.2 Pattern symbols

We saw an example of a pattern symbol in the previous section (i.e., -). This symbol matches exactly one s-expression. In order to be flexible, pattern matchers also use of a number of additional pattern symbols, which have rather different meanings. Consider the following s-expressions:

(**how many** countries are there **in** the world)
(**how many** English speaking countries are there **in** the world)
(**how many** people do live **in** France)

These suggest a common pattern as depicted by the words appearing in bold. To formulate this pattern we need to say that before and after **in** there may be one or more words. The pattern symbol + specifies this:

(how many + in +)

This pattern will match any of the above three s-expressions. For example, in the first expression, the first + will match countries are there, and the second + will match the world.

Two other pattern symbols are ~ and *. The former will match zero or one s-expression. The latter will match zero or more s-expressions. For example, the following patterns all match

(match '(a ~ c)
       '(a b c))

(match '(a ~ c)
       '(a c))

(match '(a * e)
       '(a b c d e))

(match '(a * e)
       '(a e))

whereas the patterns

(match '(a ~ d)
       '(a b c d))

(match '(a * d)
       '(a g k))

do not match.

All examples we have given so far involve lists of atoms. Patterns can, in general, be much more complicated: pattern symbols may appear at any level of a list and still play the same role. The following examples illustrate this (all the given patterns match):

```
(match '(a (b - c))
        '(a (b k c)))

(match '(a ( b - c))
        '(a (b (m n) c)))

(match '(a (b (c *) d +))
        '(a (b (c e f) d k)))

(match '(a (b (c *) d +))
        '(a (b (c) d (e f (g)))))

(match '(a (b c (~ e) (*)))
        '(a (b c (e))))

(match '(a (b c (~ e) (*)))
        '(a (b c (e) (f (k m) a))))

(match '(a (b c (~ e) (+)))
        '(a (b c (e) (f (k m) a))))
```

Figure 11.1 summarizes the meaning of our pattern symbols. You should note that what is significant about these symbols is their meaning and not their 'names'. Any other set of unique symbols would have also done the job.

PATTERN SYMBOL	MEANING
–	matches exactly one s-expression
~	matches zero or one s-expression
+	matches one or more s-expressions
*	matches zero or more s-expressions

Figure 11.1 Summary of pattern symbols.

Having described the notation, we now write the first version of our pattern matcher. This is shown below.

11.2 Pattern symbols

```
(defun match (pat expr)  ;; --------------------------- match pattern.
  (cond [(null pat) (null expr)]                    ;; empty pattern?
        [(null expr) (and (null (cdr pat))          ;; empty expr?
                         (memq (car pat) '(~ *)))]
        [(equal (car pat) (car expr))               ;; matching heads?
         (match (cdr pat) (cdr expr))]              ;; match the tails.
        [(listp (car pat))                          ;; head of pat a list?
         (and (listp (car expr))                    ;; so must be expr.
              (match (car pat) (car expr))          ;; heads and
              (match (cdr pat) (cdr expr)))]        ;; tails must match.
        [(eq (car pat) '-)                          ;; head is - pattern?
         (match (cdr pat) (cdr expr))]              ;; tails must match.
        [(eq (car pat) '~)                          ;; head is ~ pattern?
         (or (match (cdr pat) expr)                 ;; ~ matches zero.
             (match (cdr pat) (cdr expr)))]         ;; ~ matches one.
        [(eq (car pat) '*)                          ;; head is * pattern?
         (or (match (cdr pat) expr)                 ;; * matches zero.
             (match pat (cdr expr)))]               ;; * matches 1 or more.
        [(eq (car pat) '+)                          ;; head is + pattern?
         (or (match (cdr pat) (cdr expr))           ;; + matches one.
             ;; after the first match, + is like *:
             (match (cons '* (cdr pat)) (cdr expr)))]))
```

Match matches the pattern pat against the expression expr. This is achieved by comparing pat and expr element by element using recursion, and treating each pattern symbol separately according to its specified meaning.

EXERCISE 11.1

A further useful pattern symbol is ^ which introduces a list of alternative patterns. For example, the pattern (^ p1 p2 p3) will match any expression which matches p1, p2, or p3. Note that p1, p2, and p3 may themselves be arbitrary patterns. The following examples illustrate the point.

```
-> (match '(a (^ b c d) e)
          '(a c e))
t
-> (match '(a (^ (b ~ c) (e *)))
          '(a (b c)))
t
-> (match '(a (^ (b ~ c) (e *)))
          '(a (e f)))
t
->
```

Extend the match function to incorporate ^.

11.3 Pattern variables

Using `match`, it is now easy to classify queries to our database. For example, questions of the type `'where is'` are detected by:

```
(cond [(match '(where is -) question) ...]
      ...
```

However, in order to answer such questions, we need to know what a pattern symbol matches against. This is facilitated by *pattern variables*. A pattern variable is a free variable associated with a pattern symbol. When a match between a pattern symbol and an expression is successful, the pattern variable is bound to that expression.

The fact that a pattern symbol may or may not have a pattern variable may lead to confusion. To avoid this, we choose slightly different names for pattern symbols which have pattern variables. For example,

```
(where is -)
```

will be written as

```
(where is -- place)
```

when we require a pattern variable for -. Here, `place` is a pattern variable (since it appears immediately after `--`). This extension will require our pattern matcher to produce `t` when given

```
(match '(where is -- place)
       '(where is England))
```

and at the same time bind `place` to `England`.

Other pattern symbols are extended similarly to support pattern variables. The overall notation of pattern variables is summarized in Figure 11.2.

PATTERN VARIABLE	MEANING
-- var	matches exactly one s-expression
~~ var	matches zero or one s-expression
++ var	matches one or more s-expressions
** var	matches zero or more s-expressions
(where the result of a match is stored in var .)	

Figure 11.2 Summary of pattern variables.

11.3 Pattern variables

Pattern variables associated with -- and ~~ are bound to a single s-expression (if the match is successful). Pattern variables for ** and ++, on the other hand, are bound to a list of matching s-expressions. The following examples serve as an illustration.

```
-> (match '(a -- x b)
          '(a v b))
t
-> x
v
-> (match '(a ** x f)
          '(a b c d e f))
t
-> x
(b c d e)
-> (match '(a ~~ x f)
          '(a f))
t
-> x
nil
->
```

Extending our pattern matcher with facilities to handle pattern variables, in addition to the previously coded pattern symbols, leads to the following definition of match:

```
(defun match (pat expr) ;; ------------------------- match pattern.
   (cond [(null pat) (null expr)]
         [(null expr)
          (cond [(null (cdr pat))                     ;; one pattern?
                 (memq (car pat) '(~ *))]             ;; matches ~ or *.
                [(cddr pat) nil]                      ;; 1<patterns: no match.
                [(memq (car pat) '(~~ **))            ;; ~~ or ** pattern?
                 (set (cadr pat) nil) t])]            ;; bind its var to nil.
         [(equal (car pat) (car expr))
          (match (cdr pat) (cdr expr))]
         [(listp (car pat))
          (and (listp (car expr))
               (match (car pat) (car expr))
               (match (cdr pat) (cdr expr)))]
         [(eq (car pat) '-)
          (match (cdr pat) (cdr expr))]
         [(eq (car pat) '--)                          ;; head is -- pattern?
          (set (cadr pat) (car expr))                 ;; bind its variable.
```

```
              (match (cddr pat) (cdr expr))]         ;; rest must match.
      [(eq (car pat) '~)
       (or (match (cdr pat) expr)
           (match (cdr pat) (cdr expr)))]
      [(eq (car pat) '~~)                            ;; head is ~~ pattern?
       (cond [(match (cddr pat) expr)                ;; matches zero?
              (set (cadr pat) nil) t]                ;; bind its var to nil.
             [(match (cddr pat) (cdr expr))          ;; matches one?
              (set (cadr pat) (car expr)) t])]       ;; bind its var.
      [(eq (car pat) '*)
       (or (match (cdr pat) expr)
           (match pat (cdr expr)))]
      [(eq (car pat) '**)                            ;; head is **?
       (cond [(match (cddr pat) expr)                ;; matches zero?
              (set (cadr pat) nil) t]                ;; set its var to nil.
             [(match pat (cdr expr))                 ;; matches 1 or more?
              (set (cadr pat)                        ;; bind its variable.
                   (cons (car expr) (eval (cadr pat)))) t])]
      [(eq (car pat) '+)
       (or (match (cdr pat) (cdr expr))
           (match (cons '* (cdr pat)) (cdr expr)))]
      [(eq (car pat) '++)                            ;; head is ++ pattern?
       (cond [(match (cddr pat) (cdr expr))          ;; matches one?
              (set (cadr pat) (list (car expr))) t]  ;; bind var.
             [(match pat (cdr expr))                 ;; matches more than 1?
              (set (cadr pat)                        ;; bind its variable.
                   (cons (car expr) (eval (cadr pat)))) t])]))
```

This final version of `match` provides us with enough flexibility to tackle the interface problem described at the beginning of this chapter. For example, the `'where is'` question can now be both detected and properly answered:

```
(cond [(match '(where is -- x) question)
       (cond [(setq y (get x 'in))                   ;; get 'in' property.
              (print `(,x is in ,y))]                ;; print answer.
             [t (print '(I don't know))])]
      ...
```

The reader should note that, for reasons of simplicity, `match` will assign the most recent value to a repeated variable, and will not check for consistency. For example,

```
(match '(-- x likes -- x) '(Pat likes sweets))
```

will succeed, and x will have the value sweets.

Certain uses of pattern matching (for example, for executing programs written in a declarative style) require match to accept pattern symbols and pattern variables in both its arguments. This requires a more complicated matching strategy, and is left for the reader to explore (see Project 11.2). Other applications of pattern matching are described by Kronfeld [1979], and Winston [1979].

DESIGN NOTE
> Both versions of match were simple enough to unwarrant any need for detailed design or description. This is fortunate, but not always the case. In the next chapter we will come across programs which, though not longer, are complicated enough to require careful and detailed design.
>
> Given the unusual length of the second version of match, some programmers might be tempted to break it down by introducing a few auxiliary functions. This is not advisable. Considering the fact that match does not break any of the design criteria outlined in Section 10.1, there is no excuse for using such auxiliary functions. Despite the large cond in its body, the function, as it stands, is straightforward. The introduction of auxiliary functions will only confuse the overall structure. Such functions should be used when they are really needed, and when they can improve the overall structure. (See, for example, reduce in Section 5.1, or optimize in Section 12.3.)

EXERCISE 11.2
> Extend the second version of match to allow ^ to take pattern variables. Use the convention
>
> (^^ var p1 ... pn)
>
> where var is the pattern variable and p1 ... pn are arbitrary patterns.

11.4 Summary

In this chapter we have described pattern matching as a case study. The main points of the chapter may be summarized as follows.

- *Pattern matching* involves comparing similar s-expression to see if they are similar.
- *Patterns* are built using pattern symbols.
- A *pattern symbol* depicts a whole class of expressions.
- The power of a pattern matcher is significantly increased by the use of *pattern variables*.
- A pattern variable is a free variable associated with a pattern symbol and is bound to the s-expression(s) which match that symbol.
- Pattern matching simplifies the problem of natural language processing.
- Pattern matching also has other applications: theorem proving, execution of declarative languages, etc.

Projects

11.1 Use match to write a simple version of the question answering program suggested in this chapter. Your program should be able to answer questions of the form:

```
(where is ...)
(what is ...)
(what is ... of ...)
(is ... a ...)
(is ... in ...)
```

11.2 Extend match so that it accepts pattern symbols and pattern variables in both its arguments. (Note: the use of the same pattern variable in both arguments could lead to binding problems, and should be taken into account.)

Chapter 12

Data Structures for Searching

Many programming tasks involve the search of a collection of data items for a particular item. To enable systematic searching, such data has to be represented by suitable data structures that simplify the task. This chapter introduces a number of search-oriented structures which are commonly used in programming. Each data structure is complemented by one or more search strategies: these will be described in the form of algorithms together with their implementation in LISP. The data structures and algorithms will be introduced in an increasing order of complexity, and will include trees, tables, and graphs.

12.1 Tree structures

One of the most common forms of data structure for searching is a *tree*. An example is shown in Figure 12.1. A tree consists of *nodes* (represented by circles) and *edges* or *arcs* (represented by directed lines). Arcs depict the direction of travel, for example, in Figure 12.1 when at node a, we can move down to one of the nodes b, c, or d. Nodes b, c, and d are called the *children* of a; a is called the *parent* of b, c, and d.

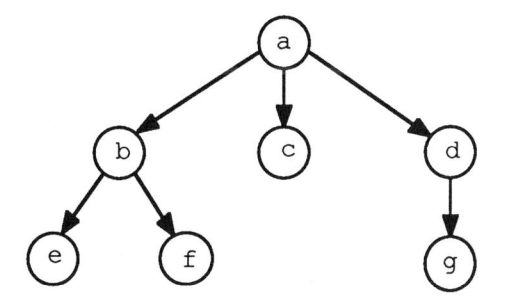

Figure 12.1 Example of a tree structure.

167

The entry point for a tree is denoted by a unique node which has no parent (i.e., node a); this is called the *root* of the tree. All other nodes are required to have exactly one parent. A node may have as many children as desired. Nodes with no children are called the *leaves* of a tree. For example, nodes c, e, f, and g are all leaves.

Trees are easily represented by list structures. The above tree, for example, may be represented by the following list:

```
(a (b (e) (f)) (c) (d (g)))
```

Trees are suitable for representing hierarchical data, for examples: a heredity tree; a tree representing the hierarchy of components in a machine; and a tree representing the structure of a book in terms of chapters, sections, subsections, and paragraphs. Usually, the main objective for creating a tree is to enable one to search for some data item in the data that it represents. For example, one might search a heredity tree to find the immediate relatives of a person.

A tree search always starts at the root node and works its way downwards until the required item is found, or until it is established that no such item exists. Numerous tree search strategies exist. Below we shall describe three of the most common strategies.

Depth-first search

The *depth-first* strategy starts the search at the root node and works its way downwards, following the left nodes until it reaches a leaf. Having searched the subtree below a node, it goes back to the parent of that node and searches the subtree represented by the next child. This procedure is repeated recursively until the required node is found, or until the entire tree is searched. Figure 12.2 illustrates the strategy; dashed lines are used to show the order of traversal of nodes.

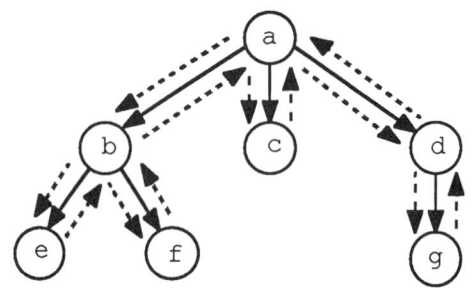

Figure 12.2 The depth-first search strategy.

The implementation of depth-first search is essentially recursive and straightforward, as shown below:

12.1 Tree structures

```
(defun depth (tree item)    ;; ------------------------ depth-first search
   (cond [(atom tree) nil]                              ;; empty tree?
         [(equal (car tree) item) tree]                 ;; item = root node?
         [(depth (car tree) item)]                      ;; search 1st subtree.
         [(depth (cdr tree) item)]))                    ;; search other subtrees.
```

Depth takes, as arguments, a tree and an item to search for. It first compares the item against the root node. If they are not identical, it then takes each child of the node – which itself represents a subtree – and applies the search recursively to that subtree. When successful, depth returns a subtree whose root is the required item; otherwise, it returns nil:

```
-> (setq tree1 '(a (b (e) (f)) (c) (d (g))))
(a (b (e) (f)) (c) (d (g)))
-> (depth tree1 'b)
(b (e) (f))
-> (depth tree1 'g)
(g)
-> (depth tree1 'k)
nil
->
```

Breadth-first search

In contrast to depth-first, a *breadth-first* search works its way in a zig-zag manner from top to bottom, and from left to right. This is illustrated by Figure 12.3. Here node a is visited first, followed by nodes b, c, and d, and finally, nodes e, f, and g. The search therefore progresses level by level, where level *n*+1 is searched only when levels 1 - *n* have already been searched. Unlike the depth-first strategy, the leaves of a tree are always visited last.

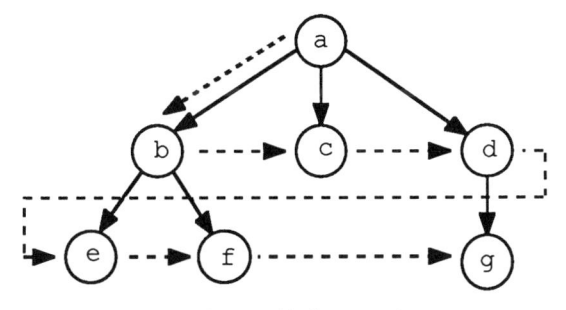

Figure 12.3 The breadth-first search strategy.

The implementation of a breadth-first search is essentially nonrecursive. This is because the strategy cannot be defined in terms of itself:

```
(defun breadth (tree item)    ;; ---------------------- breadth-first search.
   (cond [(eq (car tree) item) tree]         ;; item = root node?
         [t (prog (queue nodes)              ;; root is level 1.
               (setq queue (cdr tree))       ;; queue for level 2.
                     nodes queue)            ;; nodes in level 2.
            loop
               (cond [(null nodes)           ;; nodes exhausted?
                      ;; if last level then item isn't there, return nil:
                      (and (null queue) (return nil))
                      ;; update queue and nodes for the next level:
                      (setq queue (apply 'append
                                         (mapcar 'cdr queue))
                            nodes queue)
                      (go loop)]             ;; try next level.
                     [(eq (caar nodes) item) ;; found item,
                      (return (car nodes))]) ;; return its tree.
               (setq nodes (cdr nodes))      ;; move to next node.
               (go loop))]))
```

Breadth uses a queue to keep track of the nodes visited in a row. For example, having considered node a, it composes a queue containing nodes b, c, and d. After searching this row, it uses this queue to construct a new queue for the next row, which will contain nodes e, f, and g. As before, the search progresses until the required node is found, or until the entire tree is searched. Like depth, breadth returns a subtree whose root is the required item. When unsuccessful, it returns nil:

```
-> (breadth tree1 'b)
(b (e) (f))
-> (breadth tree1 'g)
(g)
-> (breadth tree1 'k)
nil
->
```

Obviously, the nature of different search strategies determines the applications for which they are suitable. A depth-first search, for example, is superior when most of the required items are resident in the leaves, while a breadth-first search is more suitable when most of the required items reside near the root.

Binary trees

A binary tree is a restricted form of tree in which every nonleaf node has exactly two children. An example is shown in Figure 12.4. Binary trees are well-known for their ability to support very efficient search algorithms. This is achieved by keeping the tree sorted, so that for any given nonleaf node *n*, the left child precedes *n* and the right child succeeds *n*. The binary tree of Figure 12.4, for example, is based on this convention and is alphabetically sorted.

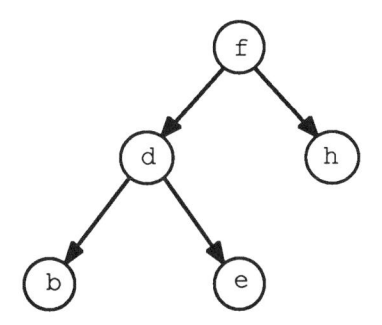

Figure 12.4 A simple binary tree.

Binary trees are easily represented by list structures. The above tree, for instance, is represented by the following list:

```
[(f (d (b nil nil) (e nil nil)) (h nil nil))]
```

In representations, such as the one above, leaves are usually given dummy children (i.e., `nil`). This improves consistency and also simplifies the algorithms that have to deal with binary trees.

A binary tree is constructed by a function which ensures that the tree will remain sorted:

```
(defun insert (tree item)   ;; ---------------------- insert item into tree.
   (cond [(null (car tree))                           ;; tree empty?
          (rplaca tree (list item nil nil))]          ;; make a tree.
         [(eq item (caar tree)) nil]                  ;; item already there?
         [(alphalessp item (caar tree))               ;; item precedes node?
          (insert (cdar tree) item)]                  ;; insert in left subtree.
         [t (insert (cddar tree) item)]))             ;; insert in right subtree
```

Insert inserts `item` into `tree` so that `tree` will remain sorted. It works as follows. When `tree` is empty, it constructs a tree consisting of `item` and two `nil` children. When `item` is identical to the root node, it returns `nil`, indicating that `item` is already there. If `item` precedes the current root node, it recursively applies insert to the left subtree; otherwise, it applies insert to the right subtree. Using insert, we can now construct the binary tree of Figure 12.4:

```
-> (setq tree2 '(nil))
(nil)
-> (insert tree2 'f)
((f nil nil))
-> (insert tree2 'd)
((d nil nil) nil)
-> tree2
((f (d nil nil) nil))
-> (insert tree2 'b)
((b nil nil) nil)
-> (insert tree2 'e)
((e nil nil))
-> (insert tree2 'h)
((h nil nil))
-> tree2
((f (d (b nil nil) (e nil nil)) (h nil nil)))
->
```

The way a binary tree is searched is very similar to the way it is constructed:

```
(defun search (tree item)    ;; ---------------------- search binary tree.
    (cond [(null (car tree)) nil]              ;; tree empty?
          [(eq item (caar tree)) (car tree)]   ;; found item.
          [(alphalessp item (caar tree))       ;; item precedes node?
           (search (cdar tree) item)]          ;; search left subtree.
          [t (search (cddar tree) item)]))     ;; search right subtree.
```

Search returns nil if item does not exist in tree; otherwise, it returns a subtree whose root node is identical to item:

```
-> (search tree2 'b)
(b nil nil)
-> (search tree2 'e)
(e nil nil)
-> (search tree2 'k)
nil
->
```

12.2 Table structures

Figure 12.5 compares the traversals performed by the three search algorithms described above, to find c in the binary tree of Figure 12.4. Binary search is the clear winner. However, one should bear in mind that a binary tree might not always be an adequate representation: occasionally, more general forms of trees (as described earlier) are required.

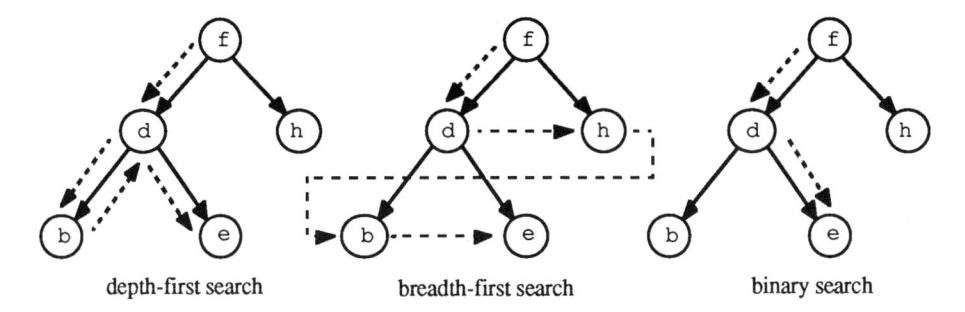

Figure 12.5 A comparison of three search strategies.

EXERCISE 12.1
Use the code instrumentation technique described in Section 9.1 to instrument the above three search functions. Instrument each function so that it prints the visited nodes during a search. Run the instrumented programs to convince yourself that the nodes visited are indeed the ones expected.

EXERCISE 12.2
Define `remove`, a function which removes a node from a binary tree. When successful, `remove` should return a nonnil object; otherwise, it should return `nil`. (Hint: to remove a node, first check its children; if they are both `nil` then simply remove the node; otherwise, first remove the node, and then insert one of the subtrees of the node into the other.)

12.2 Table structures

Unlike trees, table structures are data structures of fixed or semi-fixed nature. Usually, they are based on arrays (especially one dimensional arrays), and data items appear one after the other in a consecutive manner. Like trees, the data items may appear sorted or unsorted. Below we shall concentrate on sorted tables, since they are generally more useful and more interesting.

Binary search

The simplest form of table is one of fixed, predetermined size, where a single data item is stored per slot. Figure 12.6 shows an example of such a table, which contains a list of names.

|Ali|John|Mary|Peter| ⋯ |Roy|Tony|

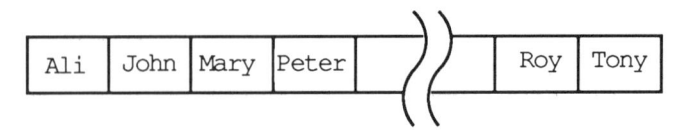

Figure 12.6 A simple fixed table.

By keeping a table sorted one can significantly reduce the search time. The fastest and most well-known algorithm for searching sorted tables is *binary search*.

In binary search, the required item is compared against the mid-item of the table. If they agree then the search stops; otherwise, the algorithm is applied to the lower or the upper half of the table, depending on whether the required item precedes or succeeds the mid-item. This procedure is repeated until the item is found, or until the table shrinks to nothing.

The hunk data structure of Franz LISP is very suitable for implementing the binary search algorithm, since such tables tend to be of small size. Here is an implementation of binary search which uses a hunk structure:

```
(defun search (table size item)  ;; ---------------- search table.
   (prog (low high mid)
         (setq low 0 high (1- size))          ;; initialize.
     loop
         (cond [(> low high) (return nil)]    ;; table exhausted?
               [(equal item                   ;; found it?
                       (cxr (setq mid (/ (+ low high) 2)) table))
                (return mid)]                 ;; return item index.
               [(alphalessp item (cxr mid table)) ;; item precedes mid-item?
                (setq high (1- mid))]         ;; lower half.
               [t (setq low (1+ mid))])       ;; upper half.
         (go loop)))
```

When successful, `search` returns an index which depicts the position of `item` in `table`; otherwise, it returns `nil`:

```
-> (setq table1 (hunk 'a 'c 'g 'k 'x 'z))
{a c g k x z}
-> (search table1 6 'x)
4
-> (search table1 6 'm)
nil
->
```

12.2 Table structures

Beside other applications, binary search is commonly used in compilers for high-level programming languages (e.g., Pascal). The lexical analyzer component of the compiler feeds every identifier in a program through a binary search function which determines whether it is a reserved word or not. Binary search is suitable for this purpose since the reserved words of a language are fixed and known in advance.

Hash-and-link (HAL) structures

Table structures may also be of a semi-fixed nature. In such tables, although the number of slots in the table is fixed and predetermined, the table can hold a variable number of entries. This is achieved by storing, in each slot, a dynamic data structures (e.g., a linked list) which can hold a variable number of entries. An example of such a table is shown in Figure 12.7, and is called a *hash-and-link* structure, or HAL for short.

```
┌──────┐
│      │──▶ (... linked list for slot 0 ...)
├──────┤
│      │──▶ (... linked list for slot 1 ...)
├──────┤
   ~~~
├──────┤
│      │──▶ (... linked list for slot n-1 ...)
├──────┤
│      │──▶ (... linked list for slot n ...)
└──────┘
```

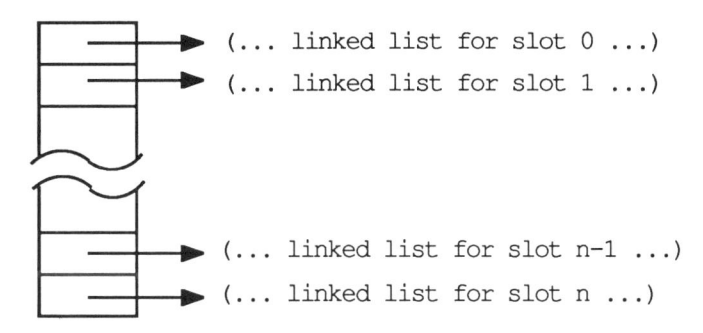

Figure 12.7 A hash-and-link (HAL) structure.

A HAL structure is constructed using a *hash* function – hence the term 'hash-and-link'. The hash function calculates, for any given entry, the slot in which it should be stored. This slot is then accessed and the entry is stored in the linked list depicted by the slot. The hash function is also used by the search algorithm, to find the slot in which an item is stored. Consistency is assured by requiring the hash function to return a unique slot number for an entry. In Figure 12.7, for example, this number will be an integer in the range 0 - n. To achieve better searching efficiency, the insertion algorithm typically ensures that the entries in each linked list are kept sorted at all times.

The number of slots in a HAL structure is often small; the number of entries in the table, however, may be arbitrarily large. As before, hunk structures may be used to implement such tables:

```
(setq table1 (makhunk (setq table-size 64)))
```

A reasonable hash function for this table would be

```
(defun hash (name)
      (remainder (apply '+ (exploden name)) table-size))
```

which ensures that the slot number (also called the *hash address*) is in the range 0 - (table-size - 1).

To construct a HAL table processing program we need to decide on a suitable list structure to represent the linked lists. Let us assume that each entry in the table will be of the form

```
(name ...other information about name...)
```

where name is the atom to which the hash function will be applied (usually called the *key*). As a result, a linked list will look something like this:

```
[nil (name1 ...) (name2 ...) ... (namek ...)]
```

The reason for having a dummy entry (i.e., nil) in front of the list is that it considerably simplifies the insertion algorithm. Below is an insertion function for inserting an entry into a HAL table that uses the above convention:

```
(defun insert (entry)     ;; ------------------------ insert into HAL table.
    (prog (hash-addr entries)
       (setq hash-addr (hash (car entry))       ;; hash address.
             entries (cxr hash-addr table))     ;; entries in slot.
       (and (null entries)                      ;; empty slot?
            (rplacx hash-addr                   ;; make new slot for entry,
                  table (list nil entry))
            (return t))                         ;; and return t.
  loop
       (cond [(null (cdr entries))              ;; end of list?
              (return (rplacd entries           ;; append entry to entries.
                         (list entry)))]
             [(equal (car entry) (caadr entries))  ;; already there?
              (return                           ;; overwrite the old entry.
                 (rplaca (cdr entries) entry))]
             [(alphalessp (car entry) (caadr entries)) ;; precede this?
              (return (rplacd entries           ;; insert it in front.
                         (cons entry (cdr entries))))]
             [t (setq entries (cdr entries))]   ;; next entry.
       (go loop)])))
```

12.2 Table structures

Insert ensures that entry is inserted in table so that the entries in each list are alphabetically sorted. If an entry with the same name already exists in table, the new entry will overwrite the old one. Insert always returns a nonnil object:

```
-> (insert '(John 22))
t
-> (insert '(Tony 25))
t
-> (insert '(Mary 14))
t
-> (insert '(Mary 15))
((Mary 15))
->
```

A HAL table is searched by first finding the linked list for an item, and then searching that list:

```
(defun search (name)     ;; -------------------------- search HAL table.
   (prog (entries)
         (setq entries (cxr (hash name) table))    ;; entries in slot.
      loop
         (cond [(or (null (setq entries (cdr entries)))
                    (alphalessp name (caar entries)))
                (return nil)]                      ;; not in table.
               [(equal name (caar entries))        ;; found it.
                (return (car entries))])
         (go loop)))
```

When successful, search returns an entry whose head is equal to name; otherwise, it returns nil:

```
-> (search 'Mary)
(Mary 15)
-> (search 'Peter)
nil
->
```

HAL structures are typically used in language processors (i.e., assemblers, compilers, and interpreters), where they are commonly referred to as *symbol tables*. When processing a program, the language processor maintains in the symbol table an entry for each identifier (e.g., variable, function name, etc.). Such an entry contains the name of the identifier, and certain additional information about the identifier (e.g., its kind, type, size, scope, etc.).

This allows the language processor to keep track of identifiers and their properties. HAL structures are also used in many other software tools that maintain their own internal, application-dependent databases, for example, cross-reference tools, verifiers, debuggers, and report generators.

EXERCISE 12.3
> Define `slot`, a function for the above HAL structure, which when given a name, returns the contents of the slot in which the entry for that name is stored. Use `slot` to make sure that all slot entries are alphabetically sorted.

EXERCISE 12.4
> Define `remove` and `size` as additions to the HAL structure described above. `Remove` takes the name of an entry and removes that entry from the table. It returns a non`nil` object when successful, and `nil` otherwise; `size` returns the total number of entries in the table.

12.3 Graph structures

As mentioned earlier, tree structures are suitable for representing data which are essentially hierarchical. Not all data satisfy this requirement. For example, consider a representation of the relationships between the various parts and subparts of a machine. It is quite possible for two parts to have a common subpart. This implies that a node (depicted by a subpart) may have more than one parent (depicted by parts). This extra level of complexity produces a data structure which is called a *graph*. A node in a graph may have any number of parents or children, as illustrated by the diagrams in Figure 12.8.

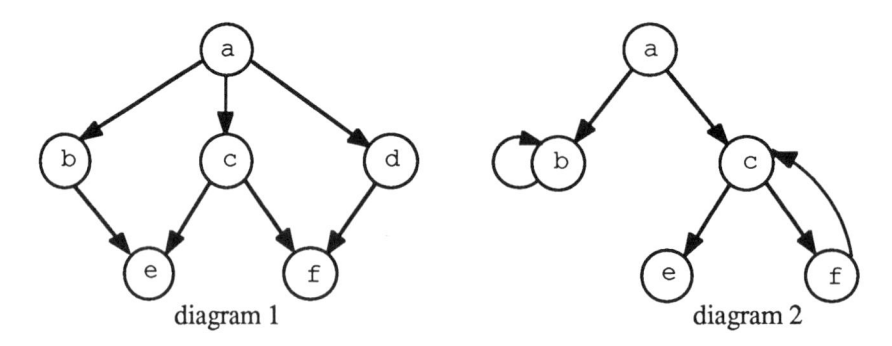

Figure 12.8 Two examples of graphs.

A graph may be even more complicated: a node may have an upper node (e.g., its parent) as its child, or even be its own child. Diagram 2 of Figure 12.8 illustrates this point. It should now be obvious that the structure diagrams described earlier in Chapter 10 are themselves graphs. It should also be obvious that a tree is a restricted, simplified form of

12.3 Graph structures

graph. Note that unlike a tree, a graph does not necessarily have to have a single entry point: generally, more than one entry point (i.e., multiple roots) is allowed.

In LISP there are at least three ways of representing a graph. One way is to expand a graph into a tree by duplicating nodes that have multiple parents. This is obviously wasteful. Another way is to use destructive functions to build a list that mirrors a graph. This has the danger of introducing circular lists. A more reasonable approach is to represent each node by an atom, whose property list or binding is a list of its children. Using this latter approach, the first diagram above is represented by:

```
(setq a '(b c d)
      b '(e)
      c '(e f)
      d '(f)
      e nil
      f nil)
```

Notation

Graphs are the subject of a branch of mathematics called *graph theory* [Even 1979, Temperley 1981]. Various mathematical notations are currently in use for describing and analyzing graphs. It is not the intention of this book to get involved in the complexity of such notations. Below we will outline a very simple notation which will suffice for the purpose of this section.

We define a graph G to be a collection <R,N,E>, where R is the set of root nodes, N is the set of all nodes, and E is the set of edges in G. Each edge is represented by a tuple: for example, (d,f) represents the edge connecting node d to node f.

We will use G(p) to denote a subgraph of G that has p as its root. Similarly, we will use C(p) to denote the children of p. For example, in diagram 1 above, G(c) is the subgraph consisting of nodes c, e, and f; G(a) is the entire graph; and C(c) is the set containing nodes e and f, i.e., {e,f}.

We define a *path* to be an unbroken sequence of nodes and edges in a graph. A path is represented by an ordered list of the nodes it contains. For example, in diagram 2 above, (a,c), (a,c,f), and (c,f,c) are all valid paths. Furthermore, we define a *route* to be a path whose first node is a root node and whose last node is a leaf.

Graph search

Two types of search problems are associated with graphs. The first problem is to search a graph for a particular item. This is a generalization of the tree search problem, and will not be discussed here (see Exercise 12.6). The second problem involves searching a graph for a specific route.

The criterion for selecting a route is dependent on the problem at hand. A typical problem is that of finding the *critical* route in a graph which has a cost associated with each of its arcs. A route is critical (or *optimal*) if it has a minimal cost. An example of such a graph is shown in Figure 12.9, where the critical route is highlighted.

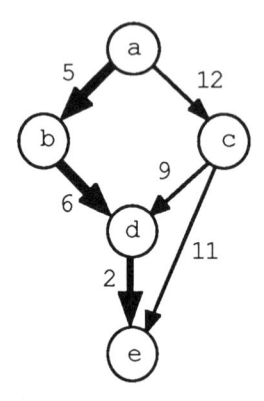

Figure 12.9 A critical route in a graph.

In this section we will concentrate on the problem of finding the critical route in a nonrecursive graph. The next section will generalize the solution by considering recursive graphs and graphs in which various neighboring arcs may be grouped together.

Finding the optimal route in a graph is a rather difficult problem. To be consistent with what we said in Chapter 10, we will follow a top-down design method, and describe the way the program is developed.

Our first task is to find an adequate graph representation that includes the costs associated with edges. By extending the representation convention described above, we arrive at the following representation for Figure 12.9:

```
(setq a '((b 5) (c 12))
      b '((d 6))
      c '((d 9) (e 11))
      d '((e 2))
      e nil)
```

In other words, we include with each child of a node, the cost of reaching that child. Next we define two macro for accessing a node in a list of nodes (e.g., the binding of a above), and the cost of reaching that node:

```
(defmacro node (nodes) `(caar ,nodes))

(defmacro node-cost (nodes) `(cadar ,nodes))
```

12.3 Graph structures

Having disposed of the problem of data representation and access, we now concentrate on the main problem. Obviously, the optimal route can be found by exhaustively searching all routes in a graph, and picking the one that has the lowest cost. This approach, however, is naive and costly, as the number of such routes may be prohibitively large.

We observe that the cost of a valid route provides an upper bound that every other route has to satisfy to have any chance of being optimal. In this way, the searching of routes which break the bound can be avoided. Using this observation, we arrive at our first design, which is described by the following algorithm.

<u>Optimize</u>
    set the bound to a large number
    repeat
        follow a route **until**
            either its cost exceeds the bound
            or a leaf node is reached.
        if the cost is smaller than the bound **then**
            make the route the current optimum, and
            set the bound to its cost
    until there are no more routes to be considered.

To realise this solution, we need a way of systematically trying out routes. The insight for the problem comes from a second observation: we note that if (p1,p2,p3,...,pn) is an optimal route of G(p1), then (p2,p3,...,pn) is an optimal route of G(p2). This is illustrated in Figure 12.10.

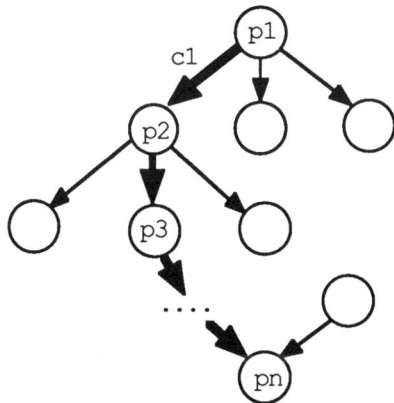

Figure 12.10 The optimal route of a graph decides the optimal route of a subgraph.

The conclusion is that to find the optimal route in the set of routes that share (p1,p2) as their first edge, we should find the optimal route of G(p2), and then insert (p1,p2) in front of it. Note that this implies that the problem has a recursive solution, since the problem of finding the optimal route in a graph reduces to the problem of finding the optimal routes in its subgraphs. The bound mechanism is also easily dealt with: if b is the starting bound for

G(p1) then b - c1 is the starting bound for G(p2). This leads us to a refinement of our original design as follows.

<u>Optimize</u>
   given a bound b and a graph G(p) **do**
      if C(p) is empty **then**
         return p as the optimal route and 0 as the cost.
      while there is another child pi in C(p) **do**
         if c, the cost of edge (p,pi), is below b **then**
            use optimize **to**
               find the optimal route of G(pi) using the bound $b-c$.
         if $c1$, the cost of the optimal route, is below $b-c$ **then**
            set B to $c+c1$.
            set suboptimal route to the optimal route of G(pi).
      if a suboptimal route ($pi, ...,pn$) was found **then**
         return ($p,pi,...,pn$) as the optimal route together with its cost.

Our last design is sufficiently detailed to be directly translated into a recursive LISP function:

```
(defun optimize (node bound)  ;; --------------- find optimal route in a graph.
    (prog (subnodes subbound route op-route cost)
          (and (null (setq subnodes (eval node)))  ;; no children?
               (return (list 0 node)))             ;; return node with cost 0.
    loop
      (cond
        [(null subnodes)                            ;; no more children?
             (return (cond [op-route               ;; had an optimal route?
                            (cons (car op-route)   ;; return it.
                                  (cons node (cdr op-route)))]
                           [t (list bound)]))]     ;; return dummy.
        [(plusp (setq subbound                     ;; edge cost below bound?
                      (- bound (setq cost
                                     (node-cost subnodes)))))
             (setq route                            ;; find optimal subroute.
                   (optimize (node subnodes) subbound))
             (cond [(< (car route) subbound)        ;; cost within bound?
                    ;; update bound and optimal subroute:
                    (setq bound (+ (car route) cost)
                          op-route (cons bound (cdr route)))])])
      (setq subnodes (cdr subnodes))                ;; next child.
      (go loop)))
```

12.3 Graph structures

Given a node *p* in graph G and an upper bound *b*, `optimize` returns the optimal route of G(*p*), provided its cost does not exceed *b*. Note that `optimize` returns a list, whose head is the optimal cost and whose tail is the optimal route.

To try the program out, we set up the graph shown in Figure 12.11, using the conventions described earlier:

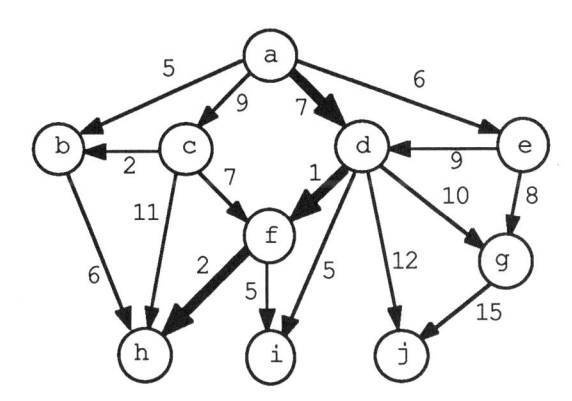

```
-> (setq a '((b 5) (c 9) (d 7) (e 6))
      b '((h 6))
      c '((b 2) (h 11) (f 7))
      d '((f 1) (i 5) (j 12) (g 10))
      e '((d 9) (g 8))
      f '((h 2) (i 5))
      g '((j 15))
      h nil
      i nil
      j nil)
nil
->
```

Figure 12.11 A test case for `optimize`.

We observe that the following routes are all optimal for the given graphs and subgraphs:

```
-> (optimize 'a 100)
(10 a d f h)
-> (optimize 'd 100)
(3 d f h)
-> (optimize 'c 100)
(8 c b h)
->
```

The search strategy described above is in fact a general technique and is called *branch-and-bound* [Sedgewick 1983]. The general idea behind this technique is to limit the scope of a search by progressively producing better bounds which the solution has to satisfy. In this way a large part of the search domain, which cannot possibly contain the optimal solution, is discarded. In contrast to exhaustive search, branch-and-bound search techniques are exceptionally efficient. They are extensively used in operations research and artificial intelligence applications [Winston 1979, Banerji 1980, Sedgewick 1983].

And-or *graphs*

The edges emanating from a node in a graph are considered as alternatives. For example, in Figure 12.11 edges (a,b), (a,c), (a,d), and (a,e) initiate alternative routes. One way of expressing this explicitly is to imagine an *or* operator (here represented by a vertical bar |) inserted between the edges:

(a,b) | (a,c) | (a,d) | (a,e)

If we extend this notion by also allowing the use of the *and* operator (represented by &), we arrive at an extended form of graph which is referred to as an *and-or graph*. Figure 12.12 shows an example of such a graph, which is identical to Figure 12.11, but also contains a few *and* operators. In this figure, a small curve (joining two or more adjacent arcs) is used to represent an *and* operator. For example, edges (d,f), (d,i), and (d,j) are grouped together using an *and* operator.

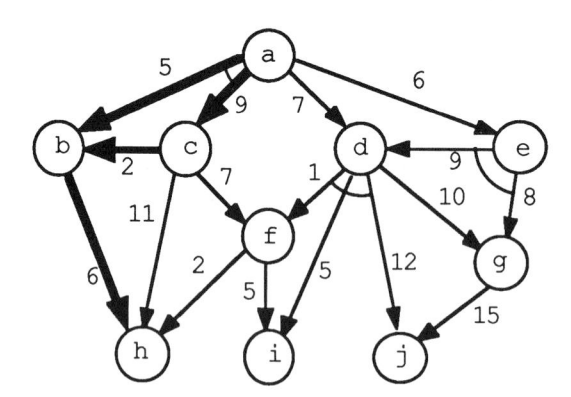

Figure 12.12 An example of an *and-or* graph.

The way an *and* operator is interpreted in straightforward: when at node a, if we choose edge (a,b) then we must also choose edge (a,c). The implication of this is that (a,b,h) is not a valid route, where as (a,b,h) & (a,c,h) is a valid route. The latter may be written as:

12.3 Graph structures

a & ((b,h),(c,h))

And-or graphs are suitable for describing problems in which there is a choice between alternative decisions (as in normal graphs), but where some decisions also force the making of other decisions. Here is an example (represented by Figure 12.13):

> To travel from New York to Amsterdam, one has a choice of three airlines: X, Y, and Z. Airline X offers two flights: one direct (F1), and one via London (F2). The direct flight has a compulsory travel insurance (I), of which there are two types ...

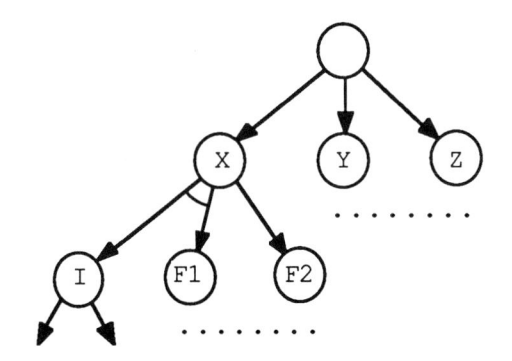

Figure 12.13 Travelling from New York to Amsterdam.

The problem to be tackled here is that of finding the optimal route in an *and-or* graph. As before, we start by formulating an adequate graph representation. By extending the notation used in the previous subsection, we arrive at the following representation for Figure 12.12:

```
(setq a '((& (b 5) (c 9)) (d 7) (e 6))
      b '((h 6))
      c '((b 2) (h 11) (f 7))
      d '((& (f 1) (i 5) (j 12)) (g 10))
      ... )
```

The inclusion of *and* operators requires a new definition for node-cost:

```
(defun node-cost (nodes)
    (cond [(eq (caar nodes) '&)
           (apply '+ (mapcar 'cadr (cdar nodes)))]
          [t (cadar nodes)]))
```

An important point to bear in mind is that a route in an *and-or* graph may involve visiting a node more than once. For example, the optimal route of Figure 12.2 visits node b twice. Care should be taken to ensure that the subgraphs below such a node are only considered once, in other words, the optimal route of the aforementioned graph should be

a & ((b,h),(c,b))

and not

a & ((b,h),(c,b,h))

To make the optimization program aware of this fact, we need to record what nodes have been visited at each stage of the search. Bearing in mind this point and the notion of *and* branches, we are now in a position to outline our design of the optimization program. This is essentially a generalization of the second design which we sketched above for the graph program and is as follows.

Optimize
    given a graph G(p), a bound b, and a set of already visited nodes v **do**
        if C(p) is empty **or** p is in v **then**
            return p as the optimal route with cost 0.
        while there is another child or group of children, pi, in C(p) **do**
            if c, the cost of edge(s) (p,pi), is below b **then**
                use optimize-aux **to**
                      find the optimal route of G(pi) **using**
                          the bound b-c, and a set of visited nodes v and p.
                if $c1$, the cost of the optimal route, is below b-c **then**
                    set b to $c+c1$.
                    set suboptimal route to the optimal route of G(pi).
        if a suboptimal route ($pi,...,pn$) was found **then**
            return ($p,pi,...,pn$) as the optimal route together with its cost.

The refinement refers to an abstraction called optimal-aux; this is refined as follows.

Optimize-aux
    given a graph G with initial edge(s) e,
        a bound b, and a set of already visited nodes v **do**
        if e is a set of *and*-grouped edges **then**
            initialize the set of routes to empty.
            initialize total cost to zero.
            while there is another edge (p,pi) in e **do**
                use optimize **to** find the optimal route starting with (p,pi).
                if $c1$, the cost of the optimal route, is greater than b **then**
                    (this cannot be part of an optimal route, so:)
                    return b as a dummy.
                add the optimal route to the set of routes.
                add the cost of route to the total cost.
            return the set of optimal routes with their total cost.
        else
            use optimize **to** find and return the optimal route starting with e.

12.3 Graph structures

We now code the above refinements as two mutually recursive LISP functions:

```lisp
(defun optimize (node bound visited)   ;; --------- optimize and-or graph.
  (prog (subnodes subbound route op-route cost)
        (and (or (null (setq subnodes (eval node)))   ;; no children?
                 (is-in node visited))                ;; Or node already visited?
             (return (list 0 node)))                  ;; return node with cost 0.
    loop
        (cond
          [(null subnodes)                            ;; no more children?
           (return (cond [op-route                    ;; had optimal route?
                          (cons (car op-route)        ;; return it.
                                (cons node (cdr op-route)))]
                         [t (list bound)]))]          ;; return dummy.
          [(plusp (setq subbound                      ;; edge cost within bound?
                        (- bound (setq cost
                                       (node-cost subnodes)))))
           (setq route                                ;; find optimal subroute.
                 (optimize-aux (car subnodes) subbound
                               (cons node visited)))
           (cond [(< (car route) subbound)            ;; cost within bound.
                  (setq bound (+ (car route) cost)    ;; update.
                        op-route (cons bound (cdr route)))])])
        (setq subnodes (cdr subnodes))                ;; next child.
        (go loop)))
;; -------------------------------------------------------------
(defun optimize-aux (node bound visited)              ;; auxiliary.
  (cond [(eq (car node) '&)                           ;; and branches?
         (prog (nodes route total-cost subbound routes)
               (setq nodes (cdr node)                 ;; the and children.
                     total-cost 0                     ;; initialize cost.
                     subbound bound)                  ;; initialize subbound.
           loop
               (and (null nodes)                      ;; no more children.
                    (return (cons total-cost          ;; return optimal route.
                                  (list (cons '& routes)))))
               (setq route                            ;; optimize subroute.
                     (optimize (node nodes) subbound visited))
               (and (> (car route) subbound)          ;; exceeds bound?
                    (return (list bound)))            ;; return dummy.
               (setq routes (cons (cdr route) routes) ;; update.
                     total-cost (+ total-cost (car route))
                     visited (append (cdr route) visited)
                     nodes (cdr nodes))               ;; next child.
               (go loop))]
        [t (optimize (car node) bound visited)]))    ;; optimize non and.
```

Given a node *p* in an *and-or* graph G, a bound *b*, and a set of already visited nodes *v* (this is initially empty), optimize returns the optimal route of G(*p*), provided its cost is below *b*. As with our previous optimization function, optimize returns a list consisting of the optimal cost and the optimal route. Note that optimize uses is-in – a function which we developed in Section 4.1 – to find out whether a node has already been visited.

We now try the program out by setting up the *and-or* graph of Figure 12.12 and by optimizing the graph and a few of its subgraphs:

```
-> (setq a '((& (b 5) (c 9)) (d 7) (e 6))
         b '((h 6))
         c '((b 2) (h 11) (f 7))
         d '((& (f 1) (i 5) (j 12)) (g 10))
         e '((& (d 9) (g 8)))
         f '((h 2) (i 5))
         g '((j 15))
         h nil
         i nil
         j nil)
nil
-> (optimize 'a 100 nil)
(22 a (& (c b) (b h)))
-> (optimize 'c 100 nil)
(8 c b h)
-> (optimize 'd 100 nil)
(20 d (& (j) (i) (f h)))
->
```

An interesting property of the above optimization program is that, unlike the previous program, it can handle recursive graphs. This is because, by keeping track of nodes visited in each search, we have ensured that no edge will be traversed more than once in a route. As a result, only the cost of one recursive edge to a node will be taken into account and subsequent recursions to that node will be ignored.

EXERCISE 12.5
    Use the examples in Figures 12.11 and 12.12 to go through the above optimization functions, and convince yourself that the implemented strategies have a much better performance than exhaustive search. A typical comparison may list out the paths exercised by either strategy before finding the optimal solution. (Hint: instrument the code of the functions so that they display the visited nodes and the cost of the attempted routes.)

EXERCISE 12.6
    Write search, a function which searches a graph for a given item. Ensure that nodes with multiple parents are searched only once. (Hint: employ the technique used by the *and-or* graph optimization program, by passing an additional argument, visited, which keeps track of the nodes visited in a search.)

12.4 Summary

In this chapter we have introduced a number of useful data structures for formulating search problems and, using these, we have illustrated various search strategies. We have observed the following points.

- A *tree* is a data structure in which there is exactly one root node, each node has exactly one parent (except the root node which has no parent), and each node may have as many children as required.
- *Depth-first* is a recursive search strategy which searches a tree by searching its subtrees from left to right.
- *Breadth-first* is a nonrecursive search strategy which searches a tree level by level from top to bottom and from left to right.
- A *binary tree* is a restricted form of tree in which each node (apart from leaf nodes) has exactly two children.
- A *table* is a fixed or semi-fixed data structure which consists of a number of consecutive slots for storing information.
- A sorted, fixed table may be searched efficiently using *binary search*.
- A *hash-and-link* (HAL) table stores a linked list in each slot, and is searched using a *hash* function which decides in which slot an entry is stored.
- A *graph* is similar to a tree, except that it may have multiple roots, and that a node may have multiple parents. (A tree therefore is a special, restricted form of graph.)
- A *path* is an unbroken sequence of nodes and edges in a graph.
- A *route* is a path that starts at a root node and ends at a leaf node.
- Graphs may be searched for two purposes: to find a particular node, or to find a particular path.
- A *critical* (or *optimal*) route in a graph which has a cost associated with each edge is one which has the lowest cost.
- The critical path of a graph may be found efficiently using a *branch-and-bound* algorithm.
- The branch-and-bound strategy avoids the unnecessary searching of unpromising parts of a graph by using a bound which progressively restricts the search space.
- An *and-or* graph is a generalized form of graph in which neighboring edges may be grouped together using *and* operators.

Projects

12.1 B^+-*tree* is a sophisticated tree structure which supports direct, as well as sequential access to data. You will find a detailed description of this form of tree in work by Wirth [1976] and Comer [1979]. After familiarizing yourself with the concept, write a B^+-tree management program. This will consist of three major functions for inserting an item into the tree, removing an item from the tree, and finding an item in the tree.

12.2 Use the HAL table management program described in Section 12.2 to develop a software tool which automatically inserts USES and USED BY comments into a LISP file (see Section 10.2). Each entry in the table will correspond to one user-defined function f, and will contain the name of f, the list of functions that f calls, and the list of functions that call f:

```
(f  (... functions that f calls ...)      ;; USES list.
    (... functions that call f  ...))     ;; USED BY list.
```

Below is an outline design which does the job in three passes over a file. Your task is to refine this design and implement it in LISP.

Pass1
   given a LISP file F do
      initialize fs, the set of user-defined functions, to empty.
      while there is another function f in F do
         add f to fs.

Pass2
   given a LISP file F, and fs, the list of user-defined functions in F, do
      initialize a HAL table T to empty.
      while there is another function f in F do
         for every function f' in the definition of f do
            update T by adding f' to the *uses* list of f.
            update T by adding f to the *used-by* list of f'.

Pass3
   given a LISP file F, a cross-usage table T, and an output file F' do
      while there is another function f in F do
         find the entry for f in T.
         print to F' the *uses* list of f as a comment.
         print to F' the *used-by* list of f as a comment.
         pretty print f to F'.

12.3 The *and-or* graph is an exceptionally powerful data structure for modelling the design space of a product. In this model, each part of the product is represented by a node, and its alternative subparts are represented by the children of that node. An edge, connecting a part to a subpart, represents the cost of choosing that subpart. This approach is also applicable to software products, where the role of parts and subparts is played by modules and submodules. Take an imaginary software project, explore its design space, and model it as an *and-or* graph. Then use the graph optimization program of Section 12.3 to find the optimal design in this space.

12.4 A *Petri net* is a graph structure for modelling the flow of information in (concurrent) systems [Peterson 1977]. It contains two types of node: *places* (represented by circles) and *transitions* (represented by bars). An example is shown below.

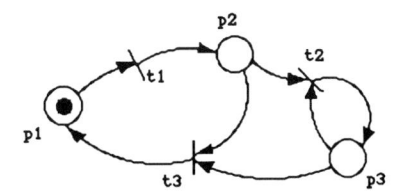

A Petri net may be marked by inserting *bullets* (represented by black dots) in places. This enables the dynamic execution of the net: bullets are *fired* by moving them from one place to another.

Your task is to first familiarize yourself with Petri nets – by reading the first few sections of of the work by Peterson [1977], say – and then develop a LISP program which supports the construction and execution of Petri nets. (Note: there are a number of extended versions of the Petri net notation. You are advised to start with the basic notation and then gradually generalize your solutions to include these extended forms. Once you have covered these, you might like to tackle an even more complicated extension of the notation, such as that described by Varadharajan and Baker [1987].)

Chapter 13

Symbolic Differentiation

The purpose of this chapter is to illustrate how symbol manipulation may be applied to some analytical problems in mathematics. The symbolic differentiation of functions is presented as a case study. We describe a program which can work out the derivative of some nontrivial functions. This program is then supplemented by two additional programs which convert our algebraic notation from a form suitable for human readers to a form suitable for LISP, and viceversa. Finally, we describe ways of simplifying the algebraic results produced by our programs. This leads to a reduction function which is used to formulate an improved version of the differentiation program to produce more meaningful and compact results.

The reader is not required to understand the underlying mathematics in order to follow the discussion in this chapter. All the mathematical formulae are presented as rules which are easily converted into LISP code.

13.1 Introduction

A common problem in calculus is finding the *derivative* (also known as the *differential*) of a function with respect to some variable. Examples are:

$f(x) = x^2+2$ $\Rightarrow$ $df/dx = 2x$
$g(x) = x.\sin x$ $\Rightarrow$ $df/dx = \sin x + x.\cos x$

The notation *df/dx* is read as 'the derivative of *f* with respect to *x*'. The functions *f* and *g* have a single variable (i.e., *x*). For the moment, we restrict our discussion to this type of function.

The differentiation of single-variable functions is governed by a number of simple rules. The first rule states that the derivative of a constant is always zero:

13.2 A differentiation program

$$d/dx[a] = 0$$

The second rule states that the derivative of a function f raised to the power of some constant a is a times the derivative of f, times f to the power of $a - 1$:

$$d/dx[f^a(x)] = a.df/dx.f^{a-1}(x)$$

The third rule concerns the derivative of a composite function:

$$d/dx[f(g(x))] = dg/dx.df/dg$$

The derivatives arising from addition, subtraction, multiplication, and division of functions are governed by the following rules:

$$d/dx[f(x) + g(x)] = df/dx + dg/dx$$
$$d/dx[f(x) - g(x)] = df/dx - dg/dx$$
$$d/dx[f(x) . g(x)] = df/dx.g(x) + f(x).dg/dx$$
$$d/dx[f(x) / g(x)] = [df/dx.g(x) - f(x).dg/dx]/g^2(x)$$

Two rules concern the derivatives of the exponential and the logarithm of functions:

$$d/dx[\exp(f(x))] = df/dx.\exp(f(x))$$
$$d/dx[\log(f(x))] = (df/dx)/f(x)$$

Other rules concern the derivatives of trigonometric and hyperbolic functions:

$$d/dx[\sin(f(x))] = df/dx.\cos(f(x))$$
$$d/dx[\cos(f(x))] = -df/dx.\sin(f(x))$$
$$d/dx[\arcsin(f(x))] = (df/dx)/[1-f^2(x)]$$
$$d/dx[\arccos(f(x))] = - (df/dx)[1-f^2(x)]$$
$$d/dx[\sinh(f(x))] = df/dx.\cosh(f(x))^{1/2}$$
$$d/dx[\cosh(f(x))] = df/dx.\sinh(f(x))^{1/2}$$

Now, given this set of rules, we would like to write a program that takes a function of one variable and produces the derivative of that function with respect to the variable.

13.2 A differentiation program

Our first task is to represent a function in a suitable form for symbol manipulation. The LISP convention for calling functions seems to be adequate. This is exemplified by the following functions:

x^3+2x-1	$\Rightarrow$	`(- (+ (^ x 3) (* 2 x)) 1)`
$\log(x - \sin x)$	$\Rightarrow$	`(log (- x (sin x)))`
$\sin(\cos x) / (\exp x^2)$	$\Rightarrow$	`(/ (sin (cos x)) (exp (^ x 2)))`

This form of representation is called a *prefix* notation, where one writes an expression by first writing an operator (or a function name) and then writing the operands (or the arguments).

Let us now write `der`, a function which takes a function `f`, represented in prefix form, and returns its derivative, again in prefix form. Der is easily written as a recursive function, consisting of a large `cond` where each clause of the `cond` will deal with one rule. For example, the rule

$$d/dx[f(x) + g(x)] = df/dx + dg/dx$$

may be coded as:

```
(cond [...]
      [(eq (car f) '+)
       (list '+ (der (cadr f)) (der (caddr f)))]
      ...
```

Four macros will help in manipulating functions:

```
(defmacro opr (f) `(car ,f))        ;; extract the operator of f.
(defmacro opd1 (f) `(cadr ,f))      ;; extract the first operand of f.
(defmacro opd2 (f) `(caddr ,f))     ;; extract the second operand of f.
(defmacro binary? (f) `(cddr ,f))   ;; f = (op opd1 opd2)?
```

We also need a way of finding out whether a function is a constant. The auxiliary function `is-const` will do just that:

```
(defun is-const (f)  ;; -------------------------- is f a constant?
   (cond [(null f) nil]                 ;; f empty?
         [(atom (car f))                ;; head of f a atom?
          (and (neq (car f) 'x)         ;; head must not be x.
               (is-const (cdr f)))]     ;; and tail must be constant.
         [t (and (is-const (car f))     ;; head and
                 (is-const (cdr f)))])) ;; tail must be constants.
```

Note that a constant is not necessarily an atom (e.g., 1, a, c) but rather any expression which does not involve x. Using these definitions, and by translating each differentiation rule into LISP, we arrive at the following definition for `der`:

13.2 A differentiation program

```
(defun der (f)    ;; ---------------------------------- find derivative of f.
  (cond
    [(atom f) (cond [(eq f 'x) 1]                    ;; f=x? => der=1.
                    [t 0])]                          ;; f=const => der=0.
    [(is-const f) 0]                                 ;; f=const => der=0.
    [(eq (opr f) '+)                                 ;; f = g+h or +g?
     (cond [(binary? f)                              ;; binary +?
            (list '+ (der (opd1 f)) (der (opd2 f)))]
           [t (der (opd1 f))])]                      ;; unary +.
    [(eq (opr f) '-)                                 ;; f = g - h?
     (cond [(binary? f)                              ;; binary -?
            (list '- (der (opd1 f)) (der (opd2 f)))]
           [t (list '- (der (opd1 f)))])]            ;; unary -.
    [(eq (opr f) '*)                                 ;; f = g*h?
     (list '+ (list '* (der (opd1 f)) (opd2 f))
              (list '* (opd1 f) (der (opd2 f))))]
    [(eq (opr f) '/)                                 ;; f = g / h?
     (list '/ (list '- (list '* (der (opd1 f)) (opd2 f))
                       (list '* (opd1 f) (der (opd2 f))))
              (list '^ (opd2 f) 2))]
    [(eq (opr f) '^)                                 ;; f = g^h?
     (list '* (opd2 f)
              (list '* (der (opd1 f))
                       (list '^ (opd1 f) (list '- (opd2 f) 1))))]
    [(eq (opr f) 'exp)                               ;; f = exp g?
     (list '* (der (opd1 f)) f)]
    [(eq (opr f) 'log)                               ;; f = log g?
     (list '/ (der (opd1 f)) (opd1 f))]
    [(eq (opr f) 'sin)                               ;; f = sin g?
     (list '* (der (opd1 f)) (list 'cos (opd1 f)))]
    [(eq (opr f) 'cos)                               ;; f = cos g?
     (list '- (list '* (der (opd1 f)) (list 'sin (opd1 f))))]
    [(eq (opr f) 'arcsin)                            ;; f = arcsin g?
     (list '/ (der (opd1 f))
              (list '^ (list '- 1 (list '^ (opd1 f) 2)) 0.5))]
    [(eq (opr f) 'arccos)                            ;; f = arccos g?
     (list '- (list '/ (der (opd1 f))
                       (list '^ (list '- 1 (list '^ (opd1 f) 2))
                                0.5)))]
    [(eq (opr f) 'sinh)                              ;; f = sinh g?
     (list '* (der (opd1 f)) (list 'cosh (opd1 f)))]
    [(eq (opr f) 'cosh)                              ;; f = cosh g?
     (list '* (der (opd1 f)) (list 'sinh (opd1 f)))]))
```

Here are a few examples illustrating the use of `der`:

```
-> (der '(+ x c))
(+ 1 0)
-> (der '(+ (sin x) (^ x a)))
(+ (* 1 (cos x)) (* a (* 1 (^ x (- a 1)))))
-> (der '(* (log x) (sin (/ 1 x))))
(+ (* (/ 1 x) (sin (/ 1 x)))
   (* (log x) (* (/ (- (* 0 x) (* 1 1))
                    (^ x 2))
                 (cos (/ 1 x)))))
->
```

DESIGN NOTE

The structure of `der` closely resembles that of `match` (Section 11.3). Similar arguments therefore apply here: although the body of `der` consists of a large `cond`, breaking it down into further auxiliary functions will not help its structure. The only auxiliary functions which are justified here are `is-const` and the four macros described earlier. The reason for having the former is that it is best defined recursively, hence it should be a separate function. The reason for having the macros is that they make the program more readable and more flexible. For example, sometime in the future we might decide to use a *postfix* notation instead of a prefix one. (A postfix notation is one in which the operands appear first and the operator appears last; for instance, (2 5 +) is the postfix version of 2 + 5). In this case, all that we have to do is to modify the macros. The rest of the program will remain as before.

EXERCISE 13.1

A number of other differentiation rules are listed below:

$$d/dx[\tan(f(x))] = df/dx.\sec^2 x$$
$$d/dx[\cot(f(x))] = -df/dx.\text{cosec}^2 x$$
$$d/dx[\sec(f(x))] = df/dx.\sec x.\tan x$$
$$d/dx[\text{cosec}(f(x))] = -df/dx.\text{cosec} x.\cot x$$

Extend `der` by incorporating these rules.

EXERCISE 13.2

Modify the macros in the differentiation program above so that `der` will accept a postfix notation instead of a prefix one.

13.3 Notation conversion

A prefix notation is admittedly rather difficult to work with. A preferable notation is one in which operators appear between operands (as in mathematics) rather than before; this is

13.3 Notation conversion

called an *infix* notation. The following examples illustrate the correspondence between functions written in a prefix and an infix form:

PREFIX		INFIX
(+ (^ x 3) x)	↔	(x ^ 3 + x)
(* (sin x) (- x 1))	↔	(sin x * (x - 1))
(^ (* a x) (+ b c))	↔	(a * x ^ (b + c))

Infix notations can be ambiguous, in the sense that it may not be obvious which operator is to be applied first. For example,

(x ^ 3 * x)

may be interpreted as

((x ^ 3) * x)

or as

(x ^ (3 * x))

Such ambiguity is resolved by specifying *precedence rules* which decide which operator should be applied before others. We specify the precedence of our operators as follows.

```
exp, log, sin, cos, arcsin, arccos, sinh, cosh
^, *, /
+, -
```

where the operators in the first line have a higher precedence than the operators in the second line, which in turn have a higher precedence than the ones in the third line. All operators appearing in the same line have the same precedence. Ambiguity concerning operators in the same group is resolved by adopting a left to right precedence convention. For example,

(x ^ y / z)

is assumed to mean

((x ^ y) / z)

because ^ appears before /. Obviously the precedence rules can be overriden by the use of brackets when necessary.

Let us now concentrate on the problem of converting our notation from an infix form to a prefix form. A number of approaches are possible. One popular technique, commonly used in compilers and interpreters, is to formulate a syntax which implicitly reflects the intended precedence of the operators. This has the advantage that we will not have to worry about the problem of precedence any more. Using this technique we first formulate the syntax of our (infix) notation as shown in Figure 13.1.

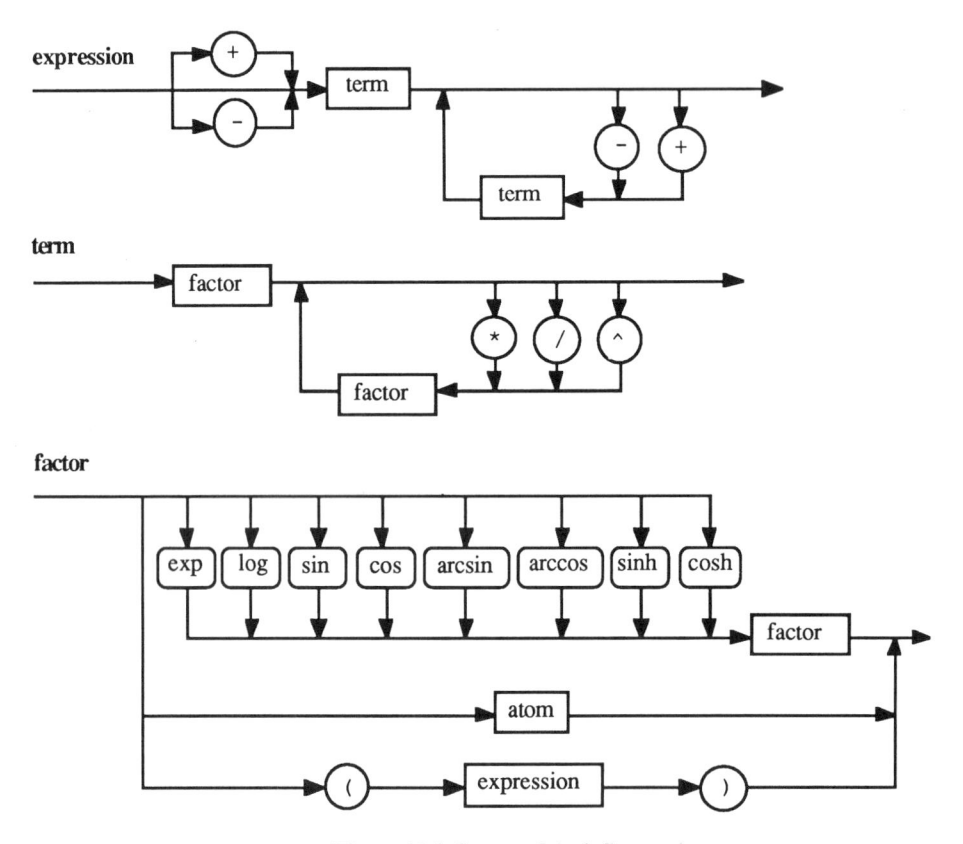

Figure 13.1 Syntax of the infix notation.

The diagrams in this figure are called *syntax diagrams* – a ubiquitous meta-notation for specifying the syntax of linear notations. A syntax diagram is specified in terms of *terminals* (represented by circles or round boxes) and *nonterminals* (represented by square boxes). Terminals depict the literal symbols of a notation (e.g., +). A nonterminal serves as an abstraction of an entire syntax diagram (e.g., expression). Directed lines in the diagrams depict the direction of travel. The idea is that if we start at the beginning of a diagram and follow the arrows in any permissible order and finally arrive at the end of the diagram, then the generated sequence of literal symbols is syntactically correct. During such a traversal, if we hit a terminal then we add its symbol to the list of generated symbols. If we hit a

13.3 Notation conversion

nonterminal then we move to the diagram that specifies that nonterminal, traverse it as before, and go back to the original diagram.

Figure 13.1 contains three diagrams, specifying three nonterminals: expression, term, and factor. Factor itself contains a further nonterminal, atom, which is assumed to denote an atomic constant (e.g., 10) or variable (e.g., x). The reader is urged to study these diagrams and be convinced that they precisely capture the precedence rules described earlier.

Using the specified syntax, it is now easy to write the conversion program. The program consists of four functions. The first function is the one that we will use for converting the notation:

```
(defun convert (f)      ;; ------------------------- infix => prefix.
    (cond [(atom f) f]                         ;; atoms need no conversion.
          [t (c-expression f)]))               ;; lists are converted.
```

The remaining functions are direct translations of the diagrams in Figure 13.1:

```
(defun c-expression (f)   ;; ------------------------- convert expression.
    (prog (op res)
          (cond [(memq (car f) '(+ -))              ;; unary + or -?
                 (setq op (car f)                   ;; operator.
                       f  (cdr f)                   ;; operand.
                       res (list op (c-term)))]     ;; signed term.
                [t (setq res (c-term))])            ;; unsigned term.
      loop
          (cond [(memq (car f) '(+ -))              ;; binary + or -?
                 (setq op (car f)                   ;; operator.
                       f  (cdr f)                   ;; operands.
                       res (list op res (c-term)))] ;; next term.
                [t (return res)])                   ;; final expression.
          (go loop)))

(defun c-term ()          ;; ------------------------- convert term.
    (prog (op res)
          (setq res (c-factor))                     ;; first factor.
      loop
          (cond [(memq (car f) '(* / ^))            ;; binary *, / or ^?
                 (setq op (car f)                   ;; operator.
                       f  (cdr f)                   ;; operands.
                       res (list op res (c-factor)))] ;; next factor.
                [t (return res)])                   ;; final term.
          (go loop)))
```

```
(defun c-factor ()       ;; -------------------------------- convert factor.
   (let [(fcar (car f))]                                     ;; head of f.
      (setq f (cdr f))                                       ;; tail of f.
      (cond [(dtpr fcar) (c-expression fcar)]                ;; (expression)?
            [(memq fcar                                      ;; unary operator?
                   '(exp log sin cos arcsin arccos sinh cosh))
             (list fcar (c-factor))]                         ;; operand is factor.
            [t fcar])))                                      ;; factor is atom.
```

Note that `f` is a bound variable with respect to `c-expression`, and a free variable with respect to `c-term` and `c-factor`. (Incidently, we have used a `c-` prefix for the last three function names to avoid confusion with a set of similar functions that we shall be describing in the next section.) `Convert` now faithfully converts a function from the infix form to the prefix form:

```
-> (convert '(x ^ a - b * x + c))
(+ (- (^ x a) (* b x)) c)
-> (convert '(sin (x + a) * cos (x / (x ^ 2 - x + b))))
(* (sin (+ x a)) (cos (/ x (+ (- (^ x 2) x) b))))
->
```

Using `convert`, we arrive at the following definition for our derivative function, which accepts a function in infix form:

```
(defun der1 (f)   ;; --------------------- f is expressed in infix form.
   (der (convert f)))                      ;; derivative will be in prefix form.
```

The following examples illustrate the use of `der1`:

```
-> (der1 '(exp x + x ^ a))
(+ (* 1 (exp x)) (* a (* 1 (^ x (- a 1)))))
-> (der1 '(a * x ^ b - c * sin x))
(- (* b (* (+ 0 x) (* a 1))) (^ (* a x) (- b 1))))
   (+ (* 0 (sin x)) (* c (* 1 (cos x)))))
-> (der1 '(a * x / log x))
(/ (- (* (+ (* 0 x) (* a 1)) (log x))
      (* (* a x) (/ 1 x)))
   (^ (log x) 2))
->
```

DESIGN NOTE

The development of `convert` illustrates how programs dealing with concrete notations should be constructed. In such cases, the first step in the design process should concentrate on specifying the syntax of the notation. Without a concrete syntax, writing transformation functions such as `convert`

13.4 Notation reversion

will be a laborious and error-prone task. The best structure for such programs is, in most cases, that suggested by the syntax itself. For example, in convert we simply captured each nonterminal by one LISP function. This one-to-one correspondence ensures elegance and simplicity. It also highlights a fairly intuitive fact: the structure of the program will, at best, be as good as the structure of the syntax. Care, therefore, should be taken to ensure that the syntax is simple, concise, and well-structured. Readers interested to know more about syntax specification and related topics are referred to the book by Rayward-Smith [1983].

EXERCISE 13.3
Modify the syntax diagrams of Figure 13.1 to include the extensions requested in Exercise 13.1. Similarly, modify the conversion program to incorporate these extensions.

13.4 Notation reversion

Ideally, we would like the result of der to appear in the infix form, too. This will require a program which converts our prefix notation back to its infix equivalent (i.e., the reverse of what we did above). This is done by following the same procedure as described in the previous section: first the syntax of the prefix notation is specified (this is simpler than the syntax of the infix notation and is left as an exercise for the readers to try); next, the program is designed, mirroring the formulated syntax. The end result is, as before, four functions:

```
(defun revert (f)   ;; ---------------------------- prefix => infix.
   (cond [(atom f) f]                               ;; atoms need no reversion.
         [t (r-expression f)]))                     ;; lists are reverted.

(defun r-expression (f)  ;; ---------------------- revert expression.
   (let [(op (opr f))                               ;; operator.
         term1 term2]
       (cond [(memq op '(+ -))                      ;; + or -?
                 (setq f (cdr f))                   ;; operand(s).
                       term1 (r-term))              ;; term 1.
                 (and f (setq term2 (r-term)))  ;;  term 2?
                 (and (atom term1)                  ;; atom => list.
                      (setq term1 (list term1)))
                 (cond [term2                       ;; was there a second term?
                           (and (or (atom term2)    ;; atom or signed term?
                                    (memq (car term2) '(+ -)))
                                (setq term2 (list term2)))
                           (nconc term1 (list op) term2)]  ;; make infix.
                       [t (cons op term1)])]        ;; unary.
             [t (r-term)])))                        ;; it's a term.
```

```
(defun r-term ()        ;; ---------------------------- revert term.
   (let [(op (opr f))]                     ;; operator.
        (cond [(memq op '(* / ^))          ;; *, /, or ^?
               (setq f (cdr f))            ;; operands.
               (list (r-factor) op (r-factor))]  ;; make infix.
              [t (r-factor)])))            ;; it's a factor.

(defun r-factor ()      ;; ---------------------------- revert factor.
   (let [(fcar (car f))]                   ;; head of f.
        (setq f (cdr f))                   ;; tail of f.
        (cond [(listp fcar) (r-expression fcar)] ;; head exprn?
              [(memq fcar                  ;; head unary operator?
                    '(exp log sin cos arcsin arccos sinh cosh))
               (list fcar (r-factor))]     ;; next factor.
              [t fcar])))                  ;; fcar is atom.
```

Using `revert`, we arrive at the next version of our derivative function which accepts a function in the infix form and produces its derivative, also in the infix form:

```
(defun der2 (f)   ;; -------------------- f is in infix form.
       (revert (der (convert f))))   ;; derivative will be in infix form.
```

The following examples illustrate:

```
-> (der2 '(x ^ a + b))
(a * (1 * (x ^ (a - 1))) + 0)
-> (der2 '(sin x / (cos x + 1)))
(((1 * (cos x)) * (cos x + 1) - (sin x) * (- 1 * sin x) + 0))
 / ((cos x + 1) ^ 2))
-> (der2 '(log log sin x))
(((1 * (cos x)) / (sin x)) / log (sin x)))
->
```

EXERCISE 13.4
   Modify the reversion program to include the extensions requested in Exercise 13.1.

13.5 Symbolic reduction

Careful examination of the results produced by `der` reveals a great deal of redundancy. For example, applying `der` to

```
(x ^ a + b)
```

13.5 Symbolic reduction

will produce

```
(a * (1 * (x ^ (a - 1))) + 0)
```

which may be written more compactly (and equivalently) as:

```
(a * (x ^ (a - 1)))
```

This form of transformation can be supported by a program which takes a function and looks for potential redundancies. It then simplifies the function by either removing redundant expressions (if possible) or replacing them by simpler forms.

The program will be guided by a number of simple *reduction rules*, as described below.

FORM	TRANSFORM TO
+f	f
-f	0 if f is 0
exp f	1 if f is 0
log f	0 if f is 1
sin f	0 if f is 0
cos f	1 if f is 0
arcsin f	0 if f is 0
arccos f	0 if f is 1
sinh f	0 if f is 0
cosh f	1 if f is 0
f + g	g if f is 0, f if g is 0
f - g	0 if f and g are 0, -g if f is 0, f if g is 0
f * g	0 if f or g is 0, g if f is 1, f if g is 1
f / g	0 if f is 0, infinity if g is 0, f if g is 1
f ^ g	0 if f is 0, 1 if g is 0, f if g is 1

The rules may be coded as a set of mutually recursive functions. The first function is the main reduction routine:

```
(defun reduce (f)   ;; ------------------------- f is in prefix form.
    (cond [(atom f) f]                      ;; atom reduces to itself.
          [(null (cdr f)) (reduce (car f))]  ;; reduce head.
          [(null (cddr f)) (reduce-unary f)] ;; reduce unary operator.
          [t (reduce-binary f)]))            ;; reduce binary operator.
```

Reduce-unary reduces a unary operator application of the form (op opd):

```
(defun reduce-unary (f)     ;; --------------------- f is in prefix form.
  (let [(op (opr f))                                 ;; unary operator.
        (opd (reduce (opd1 f)))]                     ;; its operand.
    (cond [(eq op '+)                          opd]
          [(and (eq op '-)    (zerop opd))     0]
          [(and (eq op 'exp)  (zerop opd))     1]
          [(and (eq op 'log)  (onep opd))      0]
          [(and (eq op 'sin)  (zerop opd))     0]
          [(and (eq op 'cos)  (zerop opd))     1]
          [(and (eq op 'arcsin) (zerop opd))   0]
          [(and (eq op 'arccos) (onep opd))    0]
          [(and (eq op 'sinh) (zerop opd))     0]
          [(and (eq op 'cosh) (zerop opd))     1]
          [t (list op opd)])))                       ;; any other unary operator.
```

Reduce-binary reduces a binary operator application of the form (op opd1 opd2):

```
(defun reduce-binary (f)    ;; ----------------------- f is in prefix form.
  (let [(op (opr f))                                 ;; binary operator.
        (opd1 (reduce (opd1 f)))                     ;; reduce first operand.
        (opd2 (reduce (opd2 f)))]                    ;; reduce second operand.
    (cond [(and (eq op '+)                           ;; op = +?
                (cond [(zerop opd1) opd2]
                      [(zerop opd2) opd1]))]
          [(and (eq op '-)                           ;; op = -?
                (cond [(zerop opd1)
                       (cond [(zerop opd2) 0]
                             [t (list '- opd2)])]
                      [(zerop opd2) opd1]))]
          [(and (eq op '*)                           ;; op = *?
                (cond [(or (zerop opd1) (zerop opd2)) 0]
                      [(onep opd1) opd2]
                      [(onep opd2) opd1]))]
          [(and (eq op '/)                           ;; op = /?
                (cond [(zerop opd1) 0]
                      [(zerop opd2) 'infinity]
                      [(onep opd2) opd1]))]
          [(and (eq op '^)                           ;; op = ^?
                (cond [(zerop opd1) 0]
                      [(or (zerop opd2) (onep opd1)) 1]
                      [(onep opd2) opd1]))]
          [t (list op opd1 opd2)])))                 ;; any other operator.
```

13.5 Symbolic reduction

The inclusion of reduce in our derivative function produces the final version of der, which we call deriv:

```
(defmacro deriv (f)   ;; ---------------------- f is in infix form.
   `(revert (reduce (der (convert ,(kwote f))))))
```

Deriv is defined as a macro so that its argument need not be quoted. Figure 13.2 illustrates the overall structure of deriv.

f in infix form

↓

convert to prefix form

↓

df/dx

↓

reduce the result

↓

revert to infix form

↓

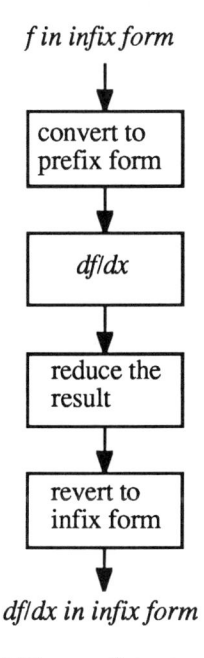

df/dx in infix form

Figure 13.2 The overall structure of deriv.

We now have a relatively sophisticated program for working out derivatives:

```
-> (deriv (sin x * cos x))
((cos x) * (cos x) + (sin x) * (- sin x))
-> (deriv (x ^ a + b * x - c))
(a * (x ^ (a - 1)) + b)
-> (deriv ((x + a) ^ b - sin ( x + c) / log x)))
(b * ((x + a) ^ (b - 1)) - ((cos (x + c)) * (log x) -
(sin (x + c)) * (1 / x)) / ((log x) ^ 2))
->
```

Obviously, a function like reduce can do a lot more by trying other, more complicated reduction rules. Project 13.1 at the end of this chapter invites you to use pattern matching to explore such extensions.

DESIGN NOTE
> The four programs developed in this chapter effectively illustrate the tool-oriented development approach (see Section 10.1). Each of `der`, `convert`, `revert`, and `reduce` is a simple filter tool which receives one input, transforms it, and produces one output. As argued earlier, this approach has two distinct advantages. Firstly, the use of each of the tools is not restricted to symbolic differentiation; for example, `convert` and `revert` may be useful in almost any other program that deals with algebraic manipulation (e.g., integration and solving differential equations). Secondly, the simplicity of the tools (especially their interfaces) facilitates their rapid integration. `Deriv`, for example, was constructed easily by placing the tools sequentially, one after the other.
>
> Needless to say, this is not a universal approach, and there are problems to which it cannot be comfortably applied. When applicable, however, it should be regarded as an attractive design alternative. In such cases, simplicity and flexibility often give the approach a winning edge.

EXERCISE 13.5
> Modify `reduce` to include the extensions requested in Exercise 13.1.

EXERCISE 13.6
> Extend `deriv` so that it takes an additional argument n which specifies the order of differentiation. For example, when n is 2, `deriv` should find the second derivative of a function.

13.6 Summary

In this chapter we have described symbolic differentiation as a case study. The main points of the chapter may be summarized as follows.

- Symbolic differentiation is easy in LISP.
- A symbolic differentiator simply follows the mathematical rules of differentiation.
- A *prefix* notation is one in which an operator appears before its operands.
- An *infix* notation is one in which an operator may appear between its operands.
- Ambiguity of an infix notation can be resolved by the use of *precedence rules*.
- Precedence rules of a notation may be implicitly incorporated by a careful formulation of the syntax of the notation.
- Conversion between prefix and infix notations is straightforward.
- Algebraic formulae may be simplified using *reduction rules*.
- Pattern matching facilitates the inclusion of complex reduction rules.

Projects

13.1 Use pattern matching to rewrite `der` and `reduce`. After you have done so, extend `reduce` by including the following reduction rules

FORM	TRANSFORM TO
sin(f(x))/cos(f(x))	tan(f(x))
cos(f(x))/sin(f(x))	cot(f(x))
1/sin(f(x))	cosec(f(x))
1/cos(f(x))	sec(f(x))

Now try adding some more difficult rules to `reduce`. Examples include cancellation and factorization rules which, for instance, reduce

```
        f(x) - f(x)      &     f(x) + f(x) + f(x)
to
        0                &     3 * f(x)
```

respectively.

13.2 Write `pder`, a function which works out the partial derivative of a function of two variables $f(x,y)$ with respect to x or y. `Pder` should take two arguments: f and a variable with respect to which f is to be differentiated.

13.3 Write a simple symbolic integration program which works out the indefinite integral of a single-variable function $f(x)$ with respect to x. You will find the rules of integration in any standard mathematical formulae book such as that by Barnett and Cronin [1979]. Integration is considerably more difficult than differentiation because certain functions do not have integrals. So, you are advised to initially restrict the scope of your program to a few general and simple function classes.

Chapter 14

Functional Extensions

The purpose of this chapter is to introduce a number of useful functional extensions to LISP. These include sets, sequences, mappings, relations, and logic. Each data type will be described briefly first and then implemented as a set of functions which allow the creation and manipulation of objects of that type. The logic operators of LISP will be extended by introducing two new binary operators, and facilities for quantification. We will also develop a simple pretty printer for pretty printing objects of the new data types.

The notation covered in this chapter increases the power of LISP as a functional programming language. The conciseness of the notation will be illustrated using a number of simple, purely functional programs.

14.1 Finite sets

A set is an unordered collection of objects with no repetitions. Typical examples are: the set of people in a city, the set of rooms in a building, and the set of telephone numbers in a telephone directory. Every object in a set is said to be a *member* of that set. One way of specifying a set is by enumerating its members. For example,

   {red, green, yellow, blue}

specifies a set of colors. This is called an *explicit* set enumeration.

To implement the set data type in LISP we need to adopt a suitable representation. We shall represent a set as a list from which repeated elements have been removed. Furthermore, we shall require the head of every such list to be a unique symbol, indicating that the list is a set representation. (This we shall refer to as a set flag.) For example, the above set will be represented as

14.1 Finite sets

```
(*s red green yellow blue)
```

where *s is the set flag.

Set operators

Sets are manipulated by set operators. We shall implement each set operator as a LISP function. The primary set operator is *membership*. It checks whether an object is a member of a set:[1]

```
(defun *member (item set)     ;; -------------------------- set membership.
   (cond [(null (setq set (cdr set))) nil]        ;; empty set?
         [(atom (car set))                        ;; if atomic,
          (and (member item set) t)]              ;; use member.
         [t (prog (eqf)
               (setq eqf (*equalf (car set)))     ;; equality fun.
            loop
               (cond [(funcall eqf item (car set)) ;; found?
                      (return t)]
                     [(null (setq set (cdr set))) ;; not there?
                      (return nil)])
               (go loop))]))
```

The function *member compares item against members of set until a match is found, or until set is exhausted. For efficiency reasons, *member uses member when set consists of atoms. Otherwise, it uses an equality function which is obtained by calling *equalf. This function will be defined later in this chapter. For the moment, we assume that (*equalf x) returns a function which can positively check for equality between objects of the same type as x.

When the equality function is known, we will use member1:

```
(defun *member1 (item set eqf)    ;; ------------ set membership.
   (prog ()
      loop                                  ;; check each member using eqf:
         (cond [(null (setq set (cdr set))) (return nil)]
               [(funcall eqf item (car set)) (return t)])
         (go loop)))
```

---

[1] The name of every function developed in this chapter is preceded by a *. This convention serves two purposes. Firstly, it avoids conflict with normal LISP functions and secondly, it indicates that the described functions are not a standard part of LISP but merely an extension.

Member1 is used by other operators to avoid the overhead of working out the equality function more than once.

The function *card returns the *cardinality* of a set. This is defined to be the number of members of a set:

```
(defun *card (set)    ;; ---------------------- set cardinality.
   (length (cdr set)))                          ;; card reduces to length.
```

A set set1 is a *subset* of a set set2 if every member of set1 is also a member of set2:

```
(defun *subset (set1 set2)   ;; -------------------- subset.
   (let [(eqf (*equalf (cadr set2)))]            ;; equality function.
      (apply 'and                                ;; every member of set1
             (mapcar '(lambda (item)             ;; must be in set2.
                         (*member1 item set2 eqf))
                     (cdr set1)))))              ;; members of set1.
```

The function *subset uses *member1 to ensure that every member of set1 is also a member of set2. A set set1 is a *proper subset* of a set set2 if set1 is a subset of set2 but not equal to set2:

```
(defun *psubset (set1 set2)  ;; -------------------- proper subset.
   (and (< (*card set1) (*card set2))            ;; card set1 < card set2?
        (*subset set1 set2)))                    ;; set1 is in set2?
```

The *union* of two sets set1 and set2 is the set containing all members of set1 and set2:

```
(defun *union (set1 set2)   ;; ---------------------- set union.
   (let [(eqf (*equalf (cadr set2)))]            ;; equality function.
      (cons '*s                                  ;; make a set by
            (nconc                               ;; collecting together:
               (mapcan                           ;; set of elements in
                  '(lambda (item)                ;; set1 but not set2, with
                     (cond [(*member1 item set2 eqf) nil]
                           [t (list item)]))
                  (cdr set1))
               (cdr set2)))))                    ;; members of set2.
```

The *intersection* of two sets set1 and set2 is the set of objects which are in both set1 and set2:

14.1 Finite sets

```
(defun *intsec (set1 set2)   ;; ---------------------- set intersection.
   (let [(eqf (*equalf (cadr set2)))]    ;; equality function.
      (cons '*s                          ;; make a set by
         (mapcan                         ;; finding the set of
            '(lambda (item)              ;; elements in both set2
               (cond [(*member1 item set2 eqf)
                      (list item)]))
            (cdr set1)))))               ;; and set1.
```

The *difference* of two sets set1 and set2 is the set of objects which are in set1 but not in set2:

```
(defun *differ (set1 set2)   ;; ------------------- set difference.
   (let [(eqf (*equalf (cadr set2)))]    ;; equality function.
      (cons '*s                          ;; make a set by
         (mapcan                         ;; finding those elements of
            '(lambda (item)              ;; set1 which are not in set2.
               (cond [(*member1 item set2 eqf) nil]
                     [t (list item)]))
            (cdr set1)))))               ;; members of set1.
```

The *power* set of a set is the set of all subsets of that set:

```
(defun *power (set)   ;; ---------------------------- power set.
   (cond
      [(null (cdr set)) '(*s (*s))]                  ;; trivial case.
      [(> (length set) 10)                           ;; set too big?
       (error "*power: set too big.")]               ;; report error.
      [t                                             ;; card set ≤ 10.
       (prog (pset pset1 len)                        ;; initialize power set:
             (setq pset (list (list '*s (cadr set)))
                   set (cdr set))                    ;; drop the *s.
         loop1                                       ;; set exhausted:
             (cond [(null (setq set (cdr set)))
                    (return (cons '*s                ;; return the result.
                               (cons '(*s) pset)))])
             (setq len (length pset) pset1 pset)
         loop2
             (cond [(zerop len)                      ;; all subsets considered?
                    (setq pset                       ;; add set itself.
                       (nconc pset
                          (list (list '*s (car set)))))])
```

```
                [t (nconc pset                      ;; next subset.
                       (list (append (car pset1)
                                     (list (car set))))))
                   (setq len (1- len) pset1 (cdr pset1))
                   (go loop2)])
             (go loop1))])))
```

Note that if a set s has cardinality n then (*power s) will have cardinality n!+1. So care should be taken not to apply *power to large sets. As a safeguard, *power checks that the cardinality of its argument is no greater than 10.

We shall use the following function for creating sets explicitly:

```
(defun *set macro (list)   ;; ----------------------- explicit set.
   (list '**set (cons 'list (cons ''*s (cdr list))))))

(defun **set (list)        ;; ----------------------- auxiliary.
   (prog (l eqf)
      (setq l list                        ;; l is used for iteration.
            eqf (*equalf (cadr l)))       ;; equality function.
    loop
      (cond [(null (cdr l)) (return list)]
            [(*member1 (cadr l) (cdr l) eqf)  ;; get rid of
             (rplacd l (cddr l))              ;; repetitions.
             (go loop)])
      (setq l (cdr l))                    ;; next element.
      (go loop)))
```

The following examples illustrate the use of set operators:

```
-> (setq s1 (*set 4 0 9 1 2))
(*s 4 0 9 1 2)
-> (setq s2 (*set 1 2 3))
(*s 1 2 3)
-> (*member 4 s1))
t
-> (*card s1)
5
-> (*subset s1 s2)
nil
-> (*subset s1 (*set 2 9 0 1 4 5))
t
-> (*psubset s2 (*set 1 2 3 4 5))
t
```

14.1 Finite sets

```
    -> (*union s1 s2)
    (*s 4 0 9 3 2 1)
    -> (*intsec s1 s2)
    (*s 1 2)
    -> (*differ s1 s2)
    (*s 4 0 9)
    -> (*power s2)
    (*s (*s) (*s 2) (*s 3 2) (*s 2) (*s 3 1) (*s 3 2 1)
    (*s 2 1) (*s 1))
    ->
```

Implicit sets

The explicit notation is rather tedious for specifying large and complicated sets. In such cases an *implicit* notation, which allows sets to be specified succinctly, is more appropriate. The mathematical form of an implicit set is

$$\{f(x) : p(x)\}$$

which specifies the set of values of $f(x)$ which satisfy the predicate $p(x)$. For example,

$$\{x^2 : \text{even}(x)\}$$

specifies the set of squares of all even numbers. This notation, however, is rather ambiguous since it is not obvious what the domain of x is. The extended form

$$\{x^2 : x \leftarrow s; \text{even}(x)\}$$

avoids this ambiguity and specifies the set of squares of all x taken from a set s such that x is even. This form consists of three parts: a *generator* (x^2), a *domain designator* ($x \leftarrow s$), and a *constraint* (even(x)). In general, there must be a domain designator per variable, and the constraint part is optional:

$$\{f(x1,...,xn) : x1 \leftarrow s1,...,xn \leftarrow sn; p(x1,...,xn)\}$$

The function *iset constructs sets implicitly:[2]

---

[2] The use of eval in **iset can lead to a name clash. As a precaution, all variables in **iset have been preceded by a $. This guarantees correct operation, provided variables used in an implicit set enumeration do not begin with a $.

```
(defun *iset macro (list)       ;; ---------------------- construct implicit set.
    `(**iset ,(kwote (cadr list))                         ;; generator.
             ,(kwote (caddr list))                        ;; domain designator.
             ,(kwote (cadddr list))))                     ;; constraint.

(defun **iset ($gen $dom $cons) ;; ---------------- auxiliary.
    (prog ($x $s $multi $set $y)
        (setq $x (car $dom)                              ;; domain variable.
              $s (eval (cadr $dom))                      ;; domain object.
              $multi (cddr $dom)                         ;; more designators?
              $set (list '*s))                           ;; initialize set.
        (and (null $cons) (setq $cons t))                ;; no constraint?
    loop
        (and (null (setq $s (cdr $s)))                   ;; domain exhausted?
             (return $set))                              ;; return constructed set.
        (set $x (car $s))                                ;; next domain element.
        (cond [$multi                                    ;; next designator.
                (setq $set
                    (*union $set
                        (**iset $gen (cddr $dom) $cons)))]
              [(eval $cons)                              ;; constraint holds?
               ;; add element to construction if not already there:
               (and (not (*member (setq $y (eval $gen)) $set))
                    (rplacd $set (cons $y (cdr $set))))])
        (go loop)))
```

The first and the last arguments to `*iset` specify the generator and the constraint, respectively. The second argument specifies the domain designators. This must be of the general form:

```
(var1 domain-1 var2 domain-2 ... varn domain-n)
```

For example, the set of squares of all even integers in a set s is obtained by:

```
(*iset (* x x) (x s) (evenp x))
```

Note that the generator, the domain designators, and the constraint may contain arbitrary expressions, even other implicit sets. The following examples illustrate:

```
-> (*iset (* x 2) (x (*set 1 2 3 4 5)))
(*s 10 8 6 4 2)
```

```
-> (*iset (* x y) (x (*set 1 2 3 4 5) y (*set 6 7 8 9 10)))
                  (oddp (+ x y)))
(*s 10 8 6 14 24 18 36 28 50 40 30)
-> (*iset (*iset x (x (*set 1 y))) (y (*set 1 2 3)))
(*s (*s 3 1) (*s 2 1) (*s 1))
->
```

EXERCISE 14.1
Define a more efficient version of `*psubset` which does not use `*card` or `*subset`.

EXERCISE 14.2
Define `*intsec` in terms of `*differ`.

EXERCISE 14.3
Write `*dunion`, a distributed union function which takes a set of sets `pset` and returns the union of all the sets in `pset`. Use examples like

```
(*equal (*dunion (*set s1 s2 ... sn))
        (*union s1 (*union s2 (*union ... sn) ... )))
```

to check `*dunion`.

EXERCISE 14.4
Write `*pick`, a function which takes a set and returns an arbitrary member of that set.

EXERCISE 14.5
Define `*intsec` and `*differ` as implicit sets.

14.2 Finite sequences

A *sequence* is a list of objects all of which have the same type. Options in a menu, prime numbers from 1 - 10, and a shopping list are examples. Like lists, and unlike sets, a sequence is always ordered. Every object in a sequence is said to be an *element* of that sequence. A sequence may be specified explicitly by enumerating its elements. For example,

«sparrow, fox, dog, elephant»

specifies a sequence of animals. Each element of a sequence is identified by its position within that sequence. If we call the above sequence x, then the following equalities will hold:

$x[1]$ = sparrow, $x[2]$ = fox, $x[3]$ = dog, $x[4]$ = elephant

Sequences are conveniently represented by lists in LISP. For instance, x is represented as

```
(*q sparrow fox dog elephant)
```

where `*q` is the sequence flag. We shall use the following function for building sequences:

```
(defun *seq macro (list)    ;; -------------------- explicit sequence.
   (cons 'list (cons ''*q (cdr list))))
```

Sequence operators

Sequences are manipulated by sequence operators. Most of the operators that we shall be implementing below are similar to list operators.

The function `*index` allows one to refer to an element of a sequence by specifying its position within that sequence:

```
(defmacro *index (seq idx)    ;; -------------------- index a sequence.
   `(nthelem ,idx (cdr ,seq)))
```

The functions `*head` and `*tail` return the head (i.e., the first element) and the tail (i.e., the rest) of a sequence:

```
(defmacro *head (seq)    ;; ----------------------- sequence head.
   `(cadr ,seq))

(defmacro *tail (seq)    ;; ----------------------- sequence tail.
   `(cons '*q (cddr ,seq)))
```

The function `*conc` concatenates two sequences `seq1` and `seq2` to produce a sequence which consists of the elements of `seq1` followed by the elements of `seq2`:

```
(defmacro *conc (seq1 seq2)    ;; ------------------ concatenate sequences.
   `(append ,seq1 (cdr ,seq2)))
```

The length of a sequence is obtained by `*len`:

```
(defmacro *len (seq)    ;; -------------------------- sequence length.
   `(length (cdr ,seq)))
```

The function `*inds` produces the set of all indices (i.e., positions of elements) of a

14.2 Finite sequences

sequence:

```
(defun *inds (seq)    ;; ---------------------------- sequence indices.
   (prog (inds indx)
        (setq indx 0)                             ;; initialize indx to 0.
     loop
        (and (null (setq seq (cdr seq)))          ;; seq exhausted?
             (return (cons '*s inds)))            ;; return set of indices.
        (setq inds (cons (setq indx (1+ indx))    ;; increment indx.
                         inds))                   ;; add indx to indices.
        (go loop)))
```

Finally, the set of all elements of a sequence is obtained by *elems. This function simply gets rid of the repeated elements of a sequence:

```
(defun *elems (seq)    ;; ---------------------------- sequence elements.
   (cond [(null (cdr seq)) (list '*s)]            ;; empty sequence?
         [t (setq seq (cdr seq))                  ;; drop the *q.
            (prog (set item seq1 eqf)
                 (setq eqf (*equalf (car seq)))   ;; equality function.
              loop1
                 (cond [(null (cdr seq))          ;; seq. exhausted?
                        (return                   ;; return set.
                           (cons '*s (cons (car seq) set)))])
                 (setq item (car seq)             ;; next seq. element.
                       seq1 (cdr seq))            ;; tail of subsequence.
              loop2
                 (cond [(null seq1)               ;; subseq exhausted?
                        (setq set (cons item set))]
                       [(not (funcall eqf item (car seq1)))
                        (setq seq1 (cdr seq1))    ;; next subseq elem.
                        (go loop2)])
                 (setq seq (cdr seq))             ;; next sequence element.
                 (go loop1))]))
```

The following examples illustrate the use of sequence operators:

```
-> (setq q1 (*seq 4 5 9 4)
         q2 (*seq 1 6 5))
(*q 1 6 5)
```

```
-> (*index q1 2)
5
-> (*head q1)
4
-> (*tail q1)
(*q 5 9 4)
-> (*conc q1 q2)
(*q 4 5 9 4 1 6 5)
-> (*len q1)
4
-> (*inds q1)
(*s 4 3 2 1)
-> (*elems q1)
(*s 4 5 9)
->
```

Implicit sequences

As with sets, an implicit notation simplifies the specification of long and complicated sequences. The general form of an implicit sequence is:

«$f(x1,...,xn) : x1 \leftarrow s1,...,xn \leftarrow sn; p(x1,...,xn)$»

For example, a sequence of squares of integers in a set s is specified as:

«$x^2 : x \leftarrow s; even(x)$»

It is worth noting that since x is extracted from a set, no order of extraction can be assumed. The order of elements in the resulting sequence is, in other words, unspecified. Such order may be forced by using a sequence q instead of a set s:

«$x^2 : x \leftarrow q; even(x)$»

Implicit sequences are constructed by *iseq:

```
(defun *iseq macro (list)    ;; ---------------------- implicit sequence.
   `(**iseq ,(kwote (cadr list))          ;; generator.
            ,(kwote (caddr list))         ;; domain designators.
            ,(kwote (cadddr list))))      ;; constraint.
```

14.3 Finite mappings

```
(defun **iseq ($gen $dom $cons)    ;; ----------------- auxiliary.
   (prog ($x $s $multi $seq)
         (setq $x (car $dom)                     ;; domain variable.
               $s (eval (cadr $dom))             ;; domain object.
               $multi (cddr $dom)                ;; more designators?
               $seq (list '*q))                  ;; initialize sequence.
         (and (null $cons) (setq $cons t))       ;; no constraint?
    loop
         (and (null (setq $s (cdr $s)))          ;; domain exhausted?
              (return $seq))                     ;; return constructed seq.
         (set $x (car $s))                       ;; next domain element.
         (cond [$multi                           ;; next designator.
                 (setq $seq
                       (*conc $seq
                              (**iseq $gen (cddr $dom) $cons)))]
               [(eval $cons)                     ;; constraint holds?
                (rplacd $seq                     ;; add element to seq.
                        (cons (eval $gen) (cdr $seq)))])
         (go loop)))
```

The syntax of the parameters of `*iseq` is identical to that of `*iset`:

```
-> (*iseq (* x 2) (x (*set 1 2 3 4 5)))
(*q 10 8 6 4 2)
-> (*iseq (* x y) (x (*seq 1 2 3 3 3) y (*seq 6 6 6 7 7))
                  (oddp (+ x y)))
(*q 6 6 6 14 14 18 18 18 18 18 18 18 18 18)
-> (*iseq (*iseq x (x (*seq 1 y))) (y (*seq 1 2 3)))
(*q (*q 3 1) (*q 2 1) (*q 1 1))
->
```

EXERCISE 14.6

Write `*dconc`, a distributed concatenation function which concatenates the sequences in a sequence of sequences. Use examples like

```
(*equal (*dconc (*seq q1 q2 ... qn))
        (*conc q1 (*conc q2 (*conc ... qn) ... )))
```

to check `*dconc`.

14.3 Finite mappings

A *mapping* (or map) is very similar to a function. It maps the members of a set, called its *domain*, to members of a set, called its *range*. Unlike normal functions, the domain and range of a mapping must be finite sets – hence the synonym *finite functions*. For instance, consider a mapping which maps each person in a group of people to his or her age. An example of such a mapping is shown below:

$$[\text{Peter} \to 20, \text{Leyla} \to 12, \text{John} \to 20]$$

Let us call this mapping *m*; it has the following domain and range:

domain m = {Peter, Leyla, John}
range m = {20, 12}

A mapping can be applied to the members of its domain in exactly the same way as a function can:

$$m(\text{Peter}) = 20, \ m(\text{Leyla}) = 12, \ m(\text{John}) = 20$$

We shall represent mappings as lists of pairs. For example, *m* will be represented as

```
(*m (Peter 20) (Leyla 12) (John 20))
```

where *m is the mapping flag. The following function allows us to construct mappings explicitly:

```
(defun *map macro (list)    ;; ---------------------- explicit mapping.
   (kwote (cons '*m
                (mapcar '(lambda (pair)        ;; make set of pairs.
                           (list (eval (car pair))
                                 (eval (cadr pair))))
                        (cdr list)))))         ;; list of pairs.
```

Mapping operators

Mappings are manipulated by mapping operators. Each operator will be defined below as a LISP function.

The function *apply applies a mapping to an element of its domain to produce the element in its range to which it is mapped:

14.3 Finite mappings

```
(defmacro *apply (map item)   ;; -------------------- apply mapping.
  `(cadr (*apply1 ,map ,item)))

(defun *apply1 (map item)     ;; --------------------- auxiliary.
   (prog (eqf)
        (setq map (cdr map)                    ;; drop the '*m.
              eqf (*equalf (caar map)))        ;; equality function.
    loop
        (cond [(null map) (return nil)]        ;; map exhausted?
              [(funcall eqf item (caar map))   ;; found it?
               (return (car map))])            ;; return it.
        (setq map (cdr map))                   ;; next pair.
        (go loop)))
```

The functions `*dom` and `*rng` extract the domain and the range of a mapping, respectively. Either of these returns a set:

```
(defmacro *dom (map)   ;; -------------------------- extract mapping domain.
  `(cons '*s (mapcar 'car (cdr ,map))))

(defmacro *rng (map)   ;; -------------------------- extract mapping range.
  `(*elems (cons '*q (mapcar 'cadr (cdr ,map)))))
```

The function `*merge` merges two mappings `map1` and `map2`, whose domains must be disjoint. The result is a mapping which maps the union of the domains of `map1` and `map2` to the union of the ranges of `map1` and `map2`:

```
(defmacro *merge (map1 map2)   ;; ------------------ merge two mappings.
  `(append ,map1 (cdr ,map2)))
```

The `*overwrite` function overwrites a mapping `map1` by another mapping `map2`; `map1` and `map2` need not be disjoint. However, when they are, the effect of `*overwrite` will be identical to `*merge`:

```
(defun *overwrite (map1 map2)   ;; ----------------- overwrite map1 by map2.
   (let [(dom2 (*dom map2))              ;; domain of map2.
         (eqf (*equalf (caadr map2)))]   ;; equality fun for domains.
     (cons '*m
           (nconc                        ;; construct a list of pairs in
             (mapcan                     ;; map1 and map2
               '(lambda (list)           ;; giving priority to
                   (cond [(*member1 (car list) dom2 eqf) nil]
                         [t (list list)]))
               (cdr map1))
             (cdr map2)))))              ;; the pairs in map2.
```

The *remove function removes the members of a given set set from the domain of a mapping map. If set and the domain of map are disjoint then *remove will return map itself. If the domain of map is a subset of set then *remove will return an empty map:

```
(defun *remove (map set)    ;; ---------------- remove set from domain of map.
   (let [(eqf (*equalf (cadr set)))]            ;; equality function.
       (cons '*m
            (mapcan                              ;; construct a list of pairs
                '(lambda (list)                  ;; in map, whose first
                    (cond [(*member1 (car list)
                                     set eqf) nil]
                          [t (list list)]))
                (cdr map)))))                    ;; elements are not in set.
```

The *restrict function restricts the domain of a mapping map to a set set. If set and the domain of map are disjoint then *restrict will return an empty map. If the domain of map is a subset of set then *restrict will return map itself:

```
(defun *restrict (map set)   ;; ---------------- restrict domain of map to set.
   (let [(eqf (*equalf (cadr set)))]            ;; equality function.
       (cons '*m
            (mapcan                              ;; construct a list of pairs in
                '(lambda (list)                  ;; map, whose first
                    (cond [(*member1 (car list) set eqf)
                           (list list)]))
                (cdr map)))))                    ;; elements are in set.
```

The *compos function composes two mappings map1 and map2, where the range of map2 must be a subset of the domain of map1. The result is a mapping m which maps the domain of map2 to the range of map1. If map2 maps x to y and map1 maps y to z, then m will map x to z:

```
(defun *compos (map1 map2)   ;; ------------------- compose two mappings.
   ;; range of map2 must be a subset of the domain of map1:
   (cond [(*subset (*rng map2) (*dom map1))
          (cons '*m
              (mapcar '(lambda (list)             ;; x -> y, and y -> z
                  (list (car list)                ;; gives x -> z.
                        (*apply map1 (cadr list))))
                  (cdr map2)))]
         [t '(*m)]))                              ;; cannot compose.
```

14.3 Finite mappings

The following examples illustrate the use of mapping operators:

```
-> (setq m1 (*map (1 10) (2 20) (3 30))
         m2 (*map (10 11) (20 21) (30 31)))
(*m (10 11) (20 21) (30 31))
-> (*apply m1 2)
20
-> (*dom m1)
(*s 1 2 3)
-> (*rng m1)
(*s 30 20 10)
-> (*merge m1 m2)
(*m (1 10) (2 20) (3 30) (10 11) (20 21) (30 31))
-> (*overwrite m1 (*map (2 200) (3 300)))
(*m (1 10) (2 200) (3 300))
-> (*remove m1 (*set 1 2))
(*m (3 30))
-> (*restrict m1 (*set 1 2))
(*m (1 10) (2 20))
-> (*compos m2 m1)
(*m (1 11) (2 21) (3 31))
->
```

Implicit mappings

A mapping is specified implicitly using a notation similar to that used for implicit sets and sequences. The general form an implicit mapping is

$$[f(x1,..,xn) \rightarrow g(x1,...,xn) : x1 \leftarrow s1,...,xn \leftarrow sn; p(x1,...,xn)]$$

which maps $f(x1,..,xn)$ to $g(x1,...,xn)$ for every value of $x1,...,xn$ in $s1,...,sn$ provided $p(x1,...,xn)$ holds. As before, f and g are generators, $xi \leftarrow si$ is a domain designator, and p is a constraint. For example, a mapping which maps each even number between 1 and 5 to its square may be specified implicitly as

$$[x \rightarrow x^2 : x \leftarrow \{1,2,3,4,5\}; even(x)]$$

where x and x^2 are the generators, $x \leftarrow \{1,2,3,4,5\}$ is the domain designator and $even(x)$ is the constraint.

Implicit mappings are defined by *imap:

```
(defun *imap macro (list)     ;; -------------------- implicit mapping.
    `(**imap ,(kwote (cadr list))              ;; generator 1.
             ,(kwote (caddr list))             ;; generator 2.
             ,(kwote (cadddr list))            ;; domain designators.
             ,(kwote (caddddr list))))         ;; constraint.

(defun **imap ($gen1 $gen2 $dom $cons)    ;; --------- auxiliary.
    (prog ($x $s $multi $map)
          (setq $x (car $dom)                  ;; domain variable.
                $s (eval (cadr $dom))          ;; domain object.
                $multi (cddr $dom)             ;; more designators?
                $map (list '*m))               ;; initialize map.
          (and (null $cons) (setq $cons t))    ;; no constraint?
     loop
          (and (null (setq $s (cdr $s)))       ;; domain exhausted?
               (return $map))                  ;; return constructed map.
          (set $x (car $s))                    ;; next domain element.
          (cond [$multi                        ;; next designator.
                   (setq $map (*merge $map
                                      (**imap $gen1
                                              $gen2
                                              (cddr $dom) $cons))]
                [(eval $cons)                  ;; constraint holds?
                 (setq $map                    ;; add pair to map.
                       (*overwrite $map
                                   (list '*m
                                         (list (eval $gen1)
                                               (eval $gen2)))))])
          (go loop)))
```

For example, the mapping specified above may be written as:

```
(*imap x (* x x) (x (*set 1 2 3 4 5)) (evenp x))
```

As before, an application of *imap may contain arbitrary expressions (including set, sequence, and mapping constructions) and there must be one domain designator per variable. The following examples illustrate the point:

```
-> (*imap x (* x x) (x (*set 1 2 3 4 5)) (evenp x))
(*m (2 4) (4 16))
```

```
-> ((imap (+ x y) y (x (*set 2 4 6) y (*set 20 40 60))))
(*m (22 20) (42 40) (62 60) (24 20) (44 40) (64 60) (26 20) (46 40)
(66 60))
->
```

EXERCISE 14.7

Write *assign, a function which changes an element of a sequence, or an object in the range of a mapping. For example,

```
(*assign obj idx newval)
```

should change the idxth element of obj to newval, if obj is a sequence. When obj is a mapping, it should change the object to which idx is mapped to newval.

EXERCISE 14.8

Define *merge, *remove, *restrict, and *compos as implicit mappings.

EXERCISE 14.9

Write *dmerge, a distributed merge function which merges the mappings in a set of mutually disjoint mappings. Use examples like

```
(*equal (*dmerge (*set m1 m2 ... mn))
        (*merge m1 (*merge m2 (*merge ... sn) ... )))
```

to check *dmerge.

14.4 Relations

The *cross-product* of an arbitrary set s is the set consisting of all pairs (x,y), where x and y are members of s. Formally,

$$s \times s = \{(x,y) : x \leftarrow s, y \leftarrow s\}$$

where $s \times s$ is read as 'the cross-product of s'. For example, given that

$$s = \{a, b, c\}$$

then

$$s \times s = \{(a,a), (a,b), (a,c), (b,a), (b,b), (b,c), (c,a), (c,b), (c,c)\}$$

Any subset of the cross-product of a set is said to specify a *relation*. For example,

$$r1 = s \times s$$

$r2 = \{(a,a), (a,c)\}$
$r3 = \{(b,c), (c,b), (a,c)\}$

are all relations. The existence of a pair (x,y) in a relation r is usually specified using the notation

$x\ (r)\ y$

which is read as 'x is related to y by r'.

Relations as such are conveniently represented in our notation as sets of pairs, where each pair is represented as a list of two elements. The relation $r2$ above, for example, is represented by:

```
(*s (a a) (a c))
```

The domain and range of a relation are defined similarly to those of mappings. The domain of a relation is the set of first elements of all pairs in a relation. The range of a relation is the set of second elements of all pairs in a relation. Formally,

domain $r = \{x : (x,y) \leftarrow r\}$
range $r = \{y : (x,y) \leftarrow r\}$

These two operators may be defined in LISP as:

```
(defmacro *domr (rel)    ;; ---------------------- relation domain.
  `(*elems (cons '*q (mapcar 'car (cdr ,rel)))))

(defmacro *rngr (rel) `(*rng ,rel))    ;; --------- relation range.
```

Given a relation `rel` and two objects `obj1` and `obj2`, `*rel?` returns t if and only if `obj1` is related to `obj2` by `rel`:

```
(defun *rel? (obj1 rel obj2)    ;; ---------------- obj1 related to obj2 by rel?
  (prog (eqf1 eqf2)
        (cond [(setq rel (cdr rel))                  ;; nonempty relation?
               (setq eqf1 (*equalf (get-obj1 rel))    ;; eqf for obj1.
                     eqf2 (*equalf (get-obj2 rel)))])  ;; eqf for obj2.
    loop
        (cond [(null rel) (return nil)]              ;; not found.
              [(and (funcall eqf1 obj1 (get-obj1 rel));; found?
                    (funcall eqf2 obj2 (get-obj2 rel)))
               (return t)])                          ;; return t.
        (setq rel (cdr rel))                         ;; next pair.
        (go loop)))
```

14.4 Relations

The function `*rel?` uses two macros, `get-obj1` and `get-obj2`, for extracting the first and second objects of a pair in a relation:

```
(defmacro get-obj1 (rel) `(caar ,rel))           ;; first object in a pair.
(defmacro get-obj2 (rel) `(cadar ,rel))          ;; second object in a pair.
```

Occasionally, we may want to know what object (if any) is related to a given object x by a relation r. We use the following notation to specify this:

$$? (r) x$$

which is read as 'an object related to x by r'. The notation applies in both directions; so

$$x (r) ?$$

specifies 'an object to which x is related by r'. For example, in $r1$ above

$$a (r1) ?$$

and

$$? (r1) a$$

may produce any of a, b, or c. This form of query is facilitated by `*rel1`:

```
(defun *rel1 (obj1 rel obj2)    ;; -------------------- find object in a relation.
   (cond [(eq obj1 '?)                                   ;; obj1 is unknown?
          (*rel1-aux rel obj2 'get-obj1 'get-obj2)]      ;; find obj1.
         [(eq obj2 '?)                                   ;; obj2 is unknown?
          (*rel1-aux rel obj1 'get-obj2 'get-obj1)]      ;; find obj2.
         [t (error "*rel1: one arg must be '?'")]))
```

In `*rel1` either `obj1` or `obj2` must be the question mark symbol to indicate which object is to be retrieved; `*rel1` uses `*rel1-aux` to perform the actual query. In this function, `rel` is the relation, `obj` is the known object, `this` is a macro for extracting the unknown object, and `that` is a macro for extracting `obj`:

```
(defun *rel1-aux (rel obj this that) ;; -------------- auxiliary.
   (prog (eqf)
         (and (setq rel (cdr rel))                    ;; nonempty relation?
              (setq eqf (*equalf (that rel))))        ;; equality function.
    loop
```

```
          (cond [(null rel) (return 'NIL)]          ;; all pairs considered?
                [(funcall eqf obj (that rel))       ;; matching pair found?
                 (return (this rel))])              ;; return object.
          (setq rel (cdr rel))                      ;; next pair.
          (go loop)))
```

Alternatively, we may want to know the set of all objects related to a given object by a relation. This is specified as

$x \, (r) \, \{?\}$

which reads 'the set of all objects to each of which x is related by r'. Similarly,

$\{?\} \, (r) \, x$

is 'the set of objects each of which is related to x by r'. For example, for relation $r1$ above, the following equalities hold:

$a \, (r1) \, \{?\} = \{a, b, c\}$
$\{?\} \, (r1) \, a = \{a, b, c\}$

This generalized form of query is supported by *reln:

```
(defun *reln (obj1 rel obj2)   ;; ------------------ find objects in a relation.
   (cond [(eq obj1 '?)                              ;; obj1 unknown?
          (*reln-aux rel obj2 'get-obj1 'get-obj2)] ;; find obj1's.
         [(eq obj2 '?)                              ;; obj2 unknown?
          (*reln-aux rel obj1 'get-obj2 'get-obj1)] ;; find obj2's.
         [t (error "*reln: one arg must be '?")]))
```

The function *reln uses *reln-aux; this is similar to rel1-aux:

```
(defun *reln-aux (rel obj this that) ;; -------------- auxiliary.
   (prog (eqf objs)
         (and (setq rel (cdr rel))                  ;; nonempty relation?
              (setq eqf (*equalf (that rel))))      ;; equality function.
    loop
         (cond [(null rel)                          ;; all pairs considered?
                (return (eval (cons '*set objs)))]  ;; return objs.
               [(funcall eqf obj (that rel))        ;; matching pair?
                (setq objs (cons (this rel) objs))]);; update objs.
         (setq rel (cdr rel))                       ;; next pair.
         (go loop)))
```

14.5 Equality operators

As with *rel1, in *reln either obj1 or obj2 must be the question mark symbol, indicating what object set is to be retrieved. The following examples illustrate the use of our relation operators:

```
-> (setq ? '?)            ;; first bind ? to itself.
?
-> (setq r1 (*set '(1 10) '(10 1) '(1 1) '(2 20) '(2 3)))
(*s (1 10) (10 1) (1 1) (2 20) (2 3))
-> (*rel? 2 r1 20)
t
-> (*rel? 20 r1 30)
nil
-> (*rel1 ? r1 10)
1
-> (*rel1 2 r1 ?)
20
-> (*reln 2 r1 ?)
(*s 3 20)
->
```

EXERCISE 14.10
    Define *merger, *remover, and *restrictr, three functions which do for relations what *merge, *remove, and *restrict do for mappings, respectively. Note that the result returned by these functions must be a set of pairs.

14.5 Equality operators

Having defined our new data types, we now need to extend the equality operators of LISP to cope with objects of such types. We first define an equality operator for each type, and then integrate these to produce a generalized equality operator that will work for any object. Each operator will be defined as a function of two arguments.

    Two sets are equal if they have exactly the same members, that is, if they have the same cardinality and one is a subset of the other:

```
(defun *sequal (set1 set2)    ;; ------------------- set equality.
    (and (= (length set1) (length st2))        ;; card set1 = card set2?
         (*subset set1 set2)))                 ;; set1 a subset of set2?
```

Two sequences are equal if they have the same length and consist of identical objects arranged in the same order:

```
(defun *qequal (seq1 seq2)     ;; ------------------ sequence equality.
   (and (= (length seq1) (length seq2))       ;; len seq1 = len seq2?
        (cond
           [(atom (cadr seq1))                ;; atomic elements?
            (equal (cdr seq1) (cdr seq2))]    ;; use equal.
           [t (let [(eqf (*equalf (cadr seq1)))]  ;; equality function.
               (prog ()
                  loop
                    (setq seq1 (cdr seq1)     ;; next element of seq1.
                          seq2 (cdr seq2))    ;; next element of seq2.
                    (cond [(null seq1) (return t)]  ;; matched.
                          [(funcall eqf (car seq1) (car seq2))
                           (go loop)])
                    (return nil)))])))        ;; do not match.
```

Two mappings are equal if they contain the same number of pairs and the set of pairs in one is a subset of the pairs in the other:

```
(defun *mequal (map1 map2)    ;; ------------------ map equality.
   (and (= (length map1) (length map2))    ;; len map1 = len map2?
        (*subset (cons '*s (cdr map1))     ;; set of pairs in map1
                 (cons '*s (cdr map2)))))  ;; a subset of map2 pairs?
```

We also require a function for testing equality between lists. Equal is no longer adequate for this purpose since a list's elements can be objects for which equal does not necessarily work (e.g., sets). The *lequal function tests for equality between two arbitrary lists:

```
(defun *lequal (list1 list2)    ;; ------------------ list equality.
   (and (= (length list1) (length list2))    ;; len list1 = len list2?
        (prog ()
           loop
             (cond [(null list1) (return t)]    ;; matched.
                   [(or (equal (car list1)      ;; if equal works
                               (car list2))     ;; then use it.
                        (funcall (*equalf (car list1))  ;; else,
                                 (car list1)    ;; use an equality fun.
                                 (car list2)))
                    (setq list1 (cdr list1)     ;; next element of list1.
                          list2 (cdr list2))    ;; next element of list2.
                    (go loop)])
             (return nil))))                    ;; do not match.
```

14.6 Logic

We are now in a position to define `*equal`, a function which can test for equality between any two objects:

```
(defun *equal (obj1 obj2)   ;; ---------------------- general equality.
   (cond [(and (listp obj1) (listp obj2))        ;; composite objects?
          (cond [(eq (car obj1) '*s) (*sequal obj1 obj2)]   ;; sets.
                [(eq (car obj1) '*q) (*qequal obj1 obj2)]   ;; seqs.
                [(eq (car obj1) '*m) (*mequal obj1 obj2)]   ;; maps.
                [t                   (*lequal obj1 obj2)])] ;; lists.
         [t (equal obj1 obj2)]))                            ;; use equal.
```

We also define `*equalf`, a function which was used earlier by various operators. This function takes one argument and returns an equality function which can positively test for equality between objects of the same type as that of the argument:

```
(defun *equalf (obj)   ;; ------------------------- equality function.
   (cond [(atom obj) 'equal]              ;; normal equality.
         [(eq (car obj) '*s) '*sequal]    ;; set equality.
         [(eq (car obj) '*q) '*qequal]    ;; seq quality.
         [(eq (car obj) '*m) '*mequal]    ;; map equality.
         [t                  '*lequal]))  ;; list equality.
```

14.6 Logic

LISP provides only three logic operators, namely `and`, `or` and `not`. Two additional useful operators are *implication* and *equivalence*, represented by the symbols $\Rightarrow$ and $\Leftrightarrow$ respectively

$$p1 \Rightarrow p2$$
$$p1 \Leftrightarrow p2$$

where *p1* and *p2* are both predicates. The former is false if *p1* is false and *p2* is true; otherwise, it is true. The latter is true if both *p1* and *p2* are either false or true; otherwise, it is false. Using `nil` and `nonnil` for representing false and true, we arrive at the following definitions for $\Rightarrow$ and $\Leftrightarrow$:

```
(defmacro *imply (p1 p2)   ;; ---------------------- p1 ⇒ p2.
   `(or (not ,p1) ,p2))                     ;; (not p1) or p2.
```

```
(defmacro *equiv (p1 p2)    ;; -------------------- p1 ⇔ p2.
  `(or (and ,p1 ,p2)                                ;; both true.
       (and (not ,p1) (not ,p2))))                  ;; both false.
```

More complicated assertions in logic involve the use of *quantifiers*. There are two quantifiers in logic. The first, the *universal* quantifier, represented by the symbol ∀, asserts that some predicate holds for all members of one or more sets:

$$(\forall\ x1 \leftarrow s1,...,xn \leftarrow sn : p(x1,...,xn))$$

For example,

$$(\forall\ x \leftarrow \{2,4,6,8\} : even(x))$$

asserts that for all x taken from the set $\{2,4,6,8\}$, x is an even number. A quantifier consists of three parts: a quantifier symbol (e.g., ∀), one or more domain designators (e.g., $x \leftarrow s$), and a predicate (e.g., $even(x)$). The predicate may, in general, be any logical expression (even another quantifier).

A universal quantifier is specified by the *all function. This is defined as follows:

```
(defmacro *all (dom pred)   ;; -------------------- universal quantifier.
  `(**all ,(kwote dom) ,(kwote pred)))              ;; designators and pred.

(defun **all ($dom $pred)   ;; -------------------- auxiliary.
  (prog ($x $s $multi)
        (setq $x (car $dom)                         ;; domain variable.
              $s (eval (cadr $dom))                 ;; domain object.
              $multi (cddr $dom))                   ;; more designators?
    loop
        (and (null (setq $s (cdr $s)))              ;; domain exhausted?
             (return t))                            ;; return t.
        (set $x (car $s))                           ;; next domain element.
        (and (cond [$multi (**all (cddr $dom) $pred)] ;; next des.
                   [(eval $pred)])                  ;; predicate holds?
             (go loop))
        (return nil)))                              ;; predicate did not hold.
```

The first argument to *all specifies the domain designators and must be of the same general form and the designators of implicit sets, sequences and mappings. The second argument may be any valid s-expression. The above quantifier, for example, is specified as:

14.6 Logic

```
(*all (x (*set 2 4 6 8)) (evenp x))
```

The *existential* quantifier, represented by the symbol $\exists$, asserts that a predicate holds for one or more members of one or more sets:

$$(\exists\ x1{\leftarrow}s1,...,xn{\leftarrow}sn: p(x1,\ ...,\ xn))$$

For example,

$$(\exists\ x{\leftarrow}\{2,3,5\} : x^2 < 9)$$

asserts that there is at least one x in $\{2,3,5\}$ such that the square of x is less than 9. Existential quantifiers are specified by the *exist function:

```
(defmacro *exist (dom pred)      ;; ------------------ existential quantifier.
   `(**exist ,(kwote dom) ,(kwote pred)))   ;; designators and pred.

(defun **exist ($dom $pred)      ;; ------------------ auxiliary.
   (prog ($x $s $multi)
         (setq $x (car $dom)                 ;; domain variable.
               $s (eval (cadr $dom))         ;; domain object.
               $multi (cddr $dom))           ;; more designators?
      loop
         (and (null (setq $s (cdr $s)))      ;; domain exhausted?
              (return nil))                  ;; return nil.
         (set $x (car $s))                   ;; next domain element.
         (and (cond [$multi (**exist (cddr $dom) $pred)]
                    [(eval $pred)])          ;; predicate holds?
              (return t))                    ;; return t.
         (go loop)))
```

For example, the above quantifier is specified as:

```
(*exist (x (*set 2 3 5)) (< (sqr x) 9))
```

A special form of the existential quantifier is the *unique existential* quantifier, represented by the symbol $\exists!$. It asserts that a predicate holds for a unique (set of) member(s) of one or more sets:

$$(\exists!\ x1{\leftarrow}s1,...,xn{\leftarrow}sn : p(x1,...,xn))$$

For example,

$$(\exists! \, x \leftarrow \{2,3,5\} : x^2 = 9)$$

asserts that there is a unique x in $\{2,3,5\}$ such that the square of x is equal to 9. The function `*exist!` defines quantifiers of this form:

```
(defmacro *exist! (dom pred)     ;; ----------------- unique existential quant.
   `(**exist! ,(kwote dom) ,(kwote pred)))    ;; designators and pred.

(defun **exist! ($dom $pred)     ;; ----------------- auxiliary.
   (prog ($x $s $multi $total)
      (setq $x (car $dom)                ;; domain variable.
            $s (eval (cadr $dom))        ;; domain object.
            $multi (cddr $dom)           ;; more designators?
            $total 0)                    ;; no. of successes.
    loop
      (and (null (setq $s (cdr $s)))     ;; domain exhausted?
           (return (eq $total 1)))       ;; there must be 1 success.
      (set $x (car $s))                  ;; next domain element.
      (and (cond [$multi (**exist! (cddr $dom) $pred)]
                 [(eval $pred)]          ;; predicate holds?
                 [t (go loop)])
           (and (eq (setq $total (1+ $total)) 1)  ;; inc. total.
                (go loop)))              ;; loop if total is 1.
      (return nil)))                     ;; more than 1 success.
```

For example, the above quantifier is specified as:

```
(*exist! (x (*set 2 3 5)) (= x 9))
```

It is worth noting that, because of the way `*all`, `*exist`, and `*exist!` have been defined (and similarly `*iset`, `*iseq`, and `*imap`), the objects in the domain designators need not necessarily be sets: sequences, mappings and lists may also be used. The designator simply iterates over the objects in the given domain. The only requirement is that the predicate on the right hand side of the construct must be meaningful with respect to the objects in the given domain(s).

The following examples illustrate the use of quantifiers:

```
-> (*all (x (*set 1 5 7) y (*set 8 4 12)) (< (+ x y) 21))
t
-> (*exist (s (*set (*set 2) (*set 4 6))))
```

```
                    (*exist! (x s) (> (* x x) 20)))
t
-> (*iset x (x (*set 3 6 9 12)
            (*all (y (*set (1- x) (- x 2)))
                 (not (= (remainder x y) 0)))))
(*s 12 9 6)
->
```

EXERCISE 14.11
Write *one and *one!, two functions with the following call forms:

```
(*one (x s) (p x))
(*one! (x s) (p x))
```

The former returns an x in s that satisfies the predicate p, if any, and nil otherwise. The latter returns an x in s that satisfies p, if any and if x is unique, and nil otherwise.

14.7 Pretty printing objects

Although our representation of the various data types described above is adequate as far as LISP is concerned, it is rather cumbersome from the point of view of a human reader. Ideally, we would like objects to be represented in their actual mathematical notation. For example, a set would be much more readable and suggestive if it were printed using curly brackets with all its members separated by commas. A further improvement concerns the layout of large and complicated objects. For example, a large mapping which maps sequences of integers to sets of strings looks very cryptic when it is printed as a series of lines of characters. Preferably, it should be formatted on the screen, with each part properly indented to suggest the structure of the object.

Both these requirements can be met by a simple pretty printer. Below we shall describe a program which takes an s-expression, evaluates it, and pretty prints the result to the screen. The pretty printer keeps track of objects using the object flags *s, *q, and *m. It consists of a number of function. The main function *pp; it pretty prints f using *pp-aux and then prints a new line:

```
(defun *pp (f)   ;; ------------------------------- pretty print f.
    (*pp-aux f 0 0)                       ;; margins initially 0.
    (terpri))
```

*pp-aux takes three arguments: an expression which is to be printed, and two numbers, specifying the left- and right-hand margins:

```
(defun *pp-aux (f lmar rmar)   ;; ----------------- auxiliary.
   (prog (kind)
         (tab lmar)                              ;; put left margin.
         (cond
            [(not (dtpr f)) (print f)]           ;; f is nonnil atom.
            [t (setq kind (car f)                ;; kind of f.
                     f (cdr f))
               (cond [(eq kind '*s)              ;; f is a set?
                      (patom "{") (and f (*body)) (patom "}")]
                     [(eq kind '*q)              ;; f is a sequence?
                      (patom "«") (and f (*body)) (patom "»")]
                     [(eq kind '*m) (*pp-map)]   ;; f is a mapping?
                     [t (*pp-list kind)])])))    ;; f is a list.
```

The left and right margins (i.e., `lmar` and `rmar`) are initially zero; `lmar` is increased appropriately by `*pp-aux` to enable the indentation of subparts. The function `*pp-aux` uses `*pp-map` and `*pp-list` to pretty print mappings and lists:

```
(defun *pp-map ()  ;; -------------------------- pretty print a mapping.
   (patom "[")
   (and f                                        ;; f nonempty?
        (cond [(< (*pr-len f) GAP)               ;; enough room here?
               (prog ()                          ;; yes, pretty print pairs
                  loop                           ;; in f using *pp-aux:
                     (*pp-aux (caar f) (nwritn) rmar)
                     (patom " -> ")
                     (*pp-aux (cadar f) (nwritn) rmar)
                     (cond [(setq f (cdr f))    ;; next pair.
                            (patom ", ")
                            (go loop)]))]
              [t (prog (c)                       ;; not enough room.
                    (setq c (nwritn))            ;; freeze left margin.
                    loop                         ;; print a pair .
                       (*pp-aux (caar f) c rmar)
                       (patom " -> ")
                       (*pp-aux (cadar f) (nwritn) rmar)
                       (cond [(setq f (cdr f))  ;; next pair.
                              (patom ",")       ;; print a comma.
                              (terpri)          ;; new line.
                              (go loop)])]))
   (patom "]"))
```

14.7 Pretty printing objects

```
(defun *pp-list (kind)      ;; ---------------------- pretty print a list.
   (patom "(")
   (setq f (cons kind f))                        ;; lists have no flag.
   (cond [(< (*pr-len f) GAP)                    ;; enough room here?
          (prog ()                               ;; yes, use *pp-aux to
             loop                                ;; print each object.
                (*pp-aux (car f) (nwritn) rmar)
                (cond [(setq f (cdr f))          ;; next object.
                       (patom " ")
                       (go loop)]))]
         [t (prog (c)                            ;; not enough room.
               (setq c (nwritn))                 ;; freeze left margin.
             loop
                (*pp-aux1 f c)                   ;; print object.
                (cond [(setq f (cdr f))          ;; next object.
                       (terpri)                  ;; new line.
                       (go loop)]))])
   (patom ")"))
```

The above functions use `*pr-len` to decide whether there is enough room on the current line for printing all objects in a composite object. This function is defined as follows:

```
(defmacro *pr-len (obj)     ;; ---------------------- object print-length.
   `(+ rmar (flatc ,obj (setq GAP (- COLS (nwritn))))))
```

The free variables GAP and COLS specify the right-hand gap and the maximum number of columns. COLS should be set to the width of the screen:

```
(setq COLS 80)
```

The function `*pp-aux` also uses `*body` for printing the body of sets and sequences:

```
(defun *body ()             ;; ---------------------- pretty print a set or sequence body.
   (cond
      [(< (*pr-len f) GAP)                          ;; enough room here?
       (cond [(atom (car f)) (*body-atomic t)]      ;; objects are atomic.
             [t (*body-other t)])]                  ;; objects are composite.
      [(atom (car f)) (*body-atomic nil)]           ;; objects are atomic.
      [t (*body-other nil)]))                       ;; objects are composite.
```

Bodies consisting of atomic elements are pretty printed using `*body-atomic`:

```
(defun *body-atomic (short)   ;; ------------------ pretty print atomic body.
   (prog ()
      loop
         (print (car f))                              ;; print object.
         (cond [(null (setq f (cdr f))) (return)];; body exhausted.
               [short (patom ", ")]                   ;; short object.
               [t (patom ", ")                        ;; long object.
                  (cond [(> (*pr-len (car f)) GAP)
                         (terpri)                     ;; new line.
                         (tab (1+ lmar))])])
         (go loop)))
```

Other bodies are pretty printed using `*body-other`:

```
(defun *body-other (short)   ;; -------------------- pretty print other body.
   (prog (c)
         (setq c (nwritn))                            ;; freeze left margin.
      loop                                            ;; print individual objects.
         (cond [short (*pp-aux (car f) (nwritn) rmar] ;; short obj.
               [t (*pp-aux1 f c)])                    ;; long object.
         (cond [(null (setq f (cdr f))) (return)]
               [short (patom " , ")]                  ;; short object.
               [t (patom ",")])
         (go loop)))
```

Some of the functions above use `*pp-aux1` instead of `*pp-aux`. This function increases the right margin by one character to accommodate the ending symbol (e.g., }), when all the elements of an object have already been printed:

```
(defun *pp-aux1 (f n)   ;; ------------------------ auxiliary.
   (*pp-aux (car f)                                  ;; print the head of f.
            n                                        ;; left margin.
            (cond [(null (setq f (cdr f))) (1+ rmar)]
                  [t rmar])))                        ;; right margin.
```

Using `*pp`, now we can pretty print any object. To make life easier we redefine the LISP top level so that everything is pretty printed automatically:

```
(defun top-level ()   ;; -------------------------- new top level.
   (prog ()
      loop
         (patom "=> ")                               ;; print prompt =>.
         (*pp (eval (read)))                         ;; read-eval-print
         (go loop)))
```

The following examples illustrate what the pretty printer can do:

```
=> (*power (*set 'green 'red 'blue))
{{},
 {green},
 {green, red},
 {red},
 {green, blue},
 {green, red, blue},
 {red, blue},
 {blue}}
=> (*union (*set (*set 2 4 2) (*set 3 5 3) (*set 4 6 4))
           (*set (*set 1 10 1) (*set 1 100 1) (*set 1 0)))
{{4, 2} , {5, 3} , {6, 4} , {10, 1} , {100, 1} , {1, 0}}
=> (*imap s (*power s) (s (*power (*set 'red 'blue))))
[{} -> {{}},
 {red} -> {{} , {red}},
 {red, blue} -> {{} , {red} , {red, blue} , {blue}},
 {blue} -> {{} , {blue}}]
=>
```

14.8 Summary of notation

The following table summarizes the LISP-based operators developed in this chapter, together with their proper mathematical notation. The operators also include the ones that were described in the exercises.

MATHEMATICAL FORM	LISP FORM
SETS	
$\{x, y, \ldots, z\}$	`(*set x y z)`
$\{f(x1, \ldots, xn) : x1 \leftarrow s1, \ldots, xn \leftarrow sn;\ p(x1, \ldots, xn)\}$	`(*iset (f x1 ... xn) (x1 s1 ... xn sn) (p x1 ... xn))`
$(\iota\, x \leftarrow s)$	`(*pick x s)`
$(\iota\, x \leftarrow s : p(x))$	`(*one (x s) (p x))`
$(\iota!\, x \leftarrow s : p(x))$	`(*one! (x s) (p x))`
$s1 \in s2$	`(*member s1 s2)`
card s	`(*card s)`
$s1 \subseteq s2$	`(*subset s1 s2)`

$s1 \subset s2$	`(*psubset s1 s2)`
$s1 \cup s2$	`(*union s1 s2)`
$s1 \cap s2$	`(*intsec s1 s2)`
$s1 - s2$	`(*differ s1 s2)`
power s	`(*power s)`
union ps	`(*dunion ps)`

SEQUENCES

«x,y,...z»	`(*seq x y ... z)`
«$f(x1,...,xn) : x1 \leftarrow s1,...,xn \leftarrow sn;$ $p(x1,...,xn)$»	`(*iseq (f x1 ... xn)` `   (x1 s1 ... xn sn) (p x1... xn))`
$q[i]$	`(*index q i)`
hd q	`(*head q)`
tl q	`(*tail q)`
$q1 \parallel q2$	`(*conc q1 q2)`
len q	`(*len q)`
inds q	`(*inds q)`
elems q	`(*elems q)`
conc pq	`(*dconc pq)`

MAPPINGS

$[x1 \rightarrow x2, y1 \rightarrow y2, ..., z1 \rightarrow z2]$	`(*map (x1 x2) (y1 y2) ... (z1 z2))`
$[f(x1,...,xn) \rightarrow g(x1,...,xn) :$ $x1 \leftarrow s1,...,xn \leftarrow sn; p(x1,...,xn)]$	`(*imap (f x1 ... xn) (g x1 ... xn)` `   (x1 s1 ... xn sn) (p x1 ... xn))`
$m(x)$	`(*apply m x)`
dom m	`(*dom m)`
rng m	`(*rng m)`
$m1 + m2$	`(*merge m1 m2)`
$m1 \oplus m2$	`(*overwrite m1 m2)`
$m \rceil s$	`(*remove m s)`
$m \lceil s$	`(*restrict m s)`
$m1 \circ m2$	`(*compos m1 m2)`
merge ms	`(*dmerge ms)`

RELATIONS

$s \times s$	`(*iset (list x y) (x s y s))`
dom r	`(*domr r)`
rng r	`(*rngr r)`
$r1 + r2$	`(*merger r1 r2)`
$r \rceil s$	`(*remover r s)`
$r \lceil s$	`(*restrictr r s)`
$x \, (r) \, y$	`(*rel? x r y)`
$? \, (r) \, y$	`(*rel1 ? r y)`

$x\ (r)$?	`(*rel1 x r ?)`
$\{?\}\ (r)\ y$	`(*reln ? r y)`
$x\ (r)\ \{?\}$	`(*reln x r ?)`
LOGIC	
$p1 \land p2$	`(and p1 p2)`
$p1 \lor p2$	`(or p1 p2)`
$\sim p$	`(not p)`
$p1 \Rightarrow p2$	`(*imply p1 p2)`
$p1 \Leftrightarrow p2$	`(*equiv p1 p2)`
$(\forall\ x1 \leftarrow s1,...,xn \leftarrow sn;\ p(x1,...,xn))$	`(*all (x1 s1...xn sn) (p x1...xn))`
$(\exists\ x1 \leftarrow s1,...,xn \leftarrow sn;\ p(x1,...,xn)))$	`(*exist (x1 s1...xn sn) (p x1...xn))`
$(\exists!\ x1 \leftarrow s1,...,xn \leftarrow sn;\ p(x1,...,xn))$	`(*exist! (x1 s1...xn sn) (p x1...xn))`

All operators described above are pure, in the sense that none of them causes any side-effects. The addition of these facilities to a pure subset of LISP provides us with a powerful, purely functional notation which achieves a remarkable level of conciseness and abstraction. The use of the notation is illustrated in the next section using a few simple functional programs.

14.9 Examples of functional programs

This section describes three simple functional programs which collectively illustrate the power of the functional extensions developed in this chapter. Each program is first formulated in our notation and then implemented as one or more LISP functions. In addition to our operators, we will use three constructs in our formulations:

CONSTRUCT	LISP FORM

let var1 = expr1,
    var2 = expr2,
    ...
    varn = exprn **in**
expression
	`(let [(var1 expr1)`
	`     (var2 expr2)`
	`        :`
	`     (varn exprn)]`
	`  expression)`

if pred **then** expression1 **else** expression2	`(cond [pred expression1]` `      [t expression2])`
$f(x1,...,xn)$ == expression	`(defun f (x1 ... xn)` `  expression)`

Quick sort

In Section 10.3 we quoted a functional Miranda program which implements the quick sort algorithm. Using our notation, we can specify the same program in a similar style:

qsort(q) == **if** q = «» **then** «»
  else qsort «x: $x \leftarrow q$; $x \leq$ hd q» ‖ «hd q» ‖ qsort «x: $x \leftarrow q$; $x >$ hd q»

The function 'qsort' takes a sequence of numbers q and sorts it by recursively partitioning the sequence into two subsequences. The subsequences are constructed using implicit sequences. All elements of the first subsequence are less than or equal to the head of q. All elements of the second subsequence are greater than the head of q. The sequence is reconstructed by concatenating the two subsequences and putting the head of q in the middle. Translating 'qsort' into our LISP notation produces the following recursive function:

```
(defun qsort (q)
   (cond [(*equal q (*seq)) (*seq)]
         [t (let [(h (*head q))]
               (*conc (*conc (qsort (*iseq x (x q) (<= x h)))
                             (*seq h))
                      (qsort (*iseq x (x q) (> x h)))))]))
```

Testing qsort reveals that it works as expected:

```
=> (qsort (*seq 8 3 2 1 8 5 9 2))
«1, 2, 2, 3, 5, 8, 8, 9»
=>
```


Relation types

A relation r is *reflexive* if for every object x in the domain or range of r, the pair (x,x) is in r. Formally, this may be defined as the following predicate

reflexive(r) == ($\forall\ x \leftarrow$ (dom $r\ \cup$ rng r) : $x\ (r)\ x$)

which translates to the following LISP function:

```
(defun reflexive (r)
   (*all (x (*union (*domr r) (*rngr r))) (*rel? x r x)))
```

14.9 Examples of functional programs

A relation r is *symmetric* if for every pair (x,y) in r, the pair (y,x) is also in r:

$$\text{symmetric}(r) == (\forall\ (x,y) \leftarrow r : (y,x) \in r)$$

Equivalently in LISP:

```
(defun symmetric (r)
   (*all (pair r) (*member (reverse pair) r)))
```

Finally, a relation r is *transitive* if for every two pairs (x,y) and (y,z) in r, there is also a third pair (x,z) in r:

$$\text{transitive}(r) == (\forall\ (x,y) \leftarrow r, (y,z) \leftarrow r : x\ (r)\ z)$$

```
(defun transitive (r)
   (*all (pair1 r pair2 r)
         (*imply (*equal (cadr pair1) (car pair2))
                 (*rel? (car pair1) r (cadr pair2)))))
```

If a relation has all the above properties (i.e., reflexive, symmetric, and transitive) then it is said to be an *equivalence* relation:

$$\text{equivalence}(r) == \text{reflexive}(r) \wedge \text{symmetric}(r) \wedge \text{transitive}(r)$$

```
(defun equivalence (r)
   (and (reflexive r) (symmetric r) (transitive r)))
```

An example of an equivalence relation is *equality*:

```
=> (setq r (*set '(1 1) '(2 2) '(3 3)))
{(1 1) , (2 2) , (3 3)}
=> (reflexive r)
t
=> (symmetric r)
t
=> (transitive r)
t
=> (equivalence r)
t
=>
```

A cross-usage program

Consider a LISP program which consists of a set of function f1, f2, ..., fn. The relationship between these functions is represented by a reference diagram, which illustrates to what functions each function refers (see Section 10.1). An example is shown in Figure 14.1. It shows a program which consists of four function f1, f2, f3, and f4, where f1 refers to f2 and f3, f3 refers to itself and f4, and f4 refers to f3.

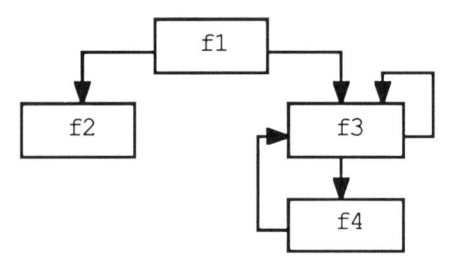

Figure 14.1 A simple reference diagram.

Our task is to write a program which manages a small database that records such relationships. The program should allow us to do the following.

- Add a new function to the database.
- Remove a function from the database.
- List what functions a given function refers to.
- List what functions refer to a given function.
- List the set of all recursive functions.

Each of these will be specified as a function.

Let us call the database d; it will be represented by a mapping which maps each function to the set of functions that it refers to. For example, the diagram in Figure 14.1 will be represented by the following mapping:

$$[f1 \rightarrow \{f2, f3\}, f2 \rightarrow \{\}, f3 \rightarrow \{f3, f4\}, f4 \rightarrow \{f3\}]$$

The database d is initially an empty mapping (i.e., $d = []$):

```
(setq d (*map))
```

We now define 'add-fun', a function which adds a function f together with fs – the set of functions that it refers to – to the database:

add-fun(f, fs) == $d = (d + [x \rightarrow \{\} : x \leftarrow (fs - \text{dom } d)]) \oplus [f \rightarrow fs]$

14.9 Examples of functional programs

For example, add-fun(f1,{f2,f3}) will produce:

$$d = [f1 \rightarrow \{f2,f3\}, f2 \rightarrow \{\}, f3 \rightarrow \{\}]$$

Direct translation of 'add-fun' to LISP will produce the following function:

```
(defun add-fun (f fs)
   (setq d (*overwrite
                    (*merge d (*imap x (*set)
                                       (x (*differ fs (*dom d)))))
                 (*map (f fs)))))
```

The function 'del-fun' deletes a function from the database

$$\text{del-fun}(f) == d = [x \rightarrow d(x) - \{f\} : x \leftarrow (\text{dom } d - \{f\})]$$

which translates to:

```
(defun del-fun (f)
   (setq d (*imap x (*differ (*apply d x) (*set f))
               (x (*differ (*dom d) (*set f))))))
```

The function 'uses' returns the set of functions that a given function refers to:

$$\text{uses}(f) == d(f)$$

```
(defmacro uses (f) `(*apply d ,f))
```

The function 'used-by' returns the set of functions that refer to a given function:

$$\text{used-by}(f) == \{x : x \leftarrow \text{dom } d; f \in d(x)\}$$

```
(defun used-by (f)
   (*iset x (x (*dom d)) (*member f (*apply d x))))
```

Finally, the function 'recursives' returns the set of all recursive functions in the database:

$$\text{recursives}() == \{x : x \leftarrow \text{dom } d; x \in \text{reach}(x)\}$$

This is read as: the set of functions x in the domain of d such that x reaches itself. The function 'reach' returns the set of functions a given function can reach through one or more calls:

reach(f) == **let** $fs = d(f)$ **in**
$\qquad fs \cup$ union $\{\text{reach}(y) : y \leftarrow (fs - \{f\})\}$

Direct translation of these into LISP produces:

```
(defun recursives ()
   (*iset x (x (*dom d)) (*member x (reach x))))

(defun reach (f)
   (let [(fs (*apply d f))]
        (*union fs
                (*dunion (*iset (reach y)
                                (y (*differ fs (*set f)))))))))
```

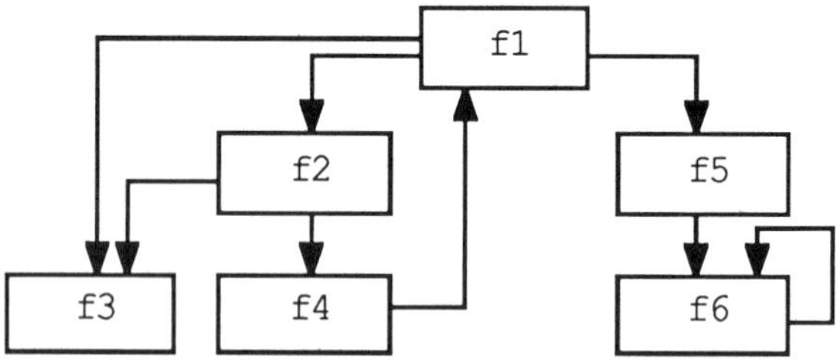

Figure 14.2 A more complicated reference diagram.

We now have a complete program for manipulating our database. The following examples illustrate the use of the program by setting up the reference diagram shown in Figure 14.2, and experimenting with the functions:

```
=> (add-fun 'f1 (*set 'f2 'f3 'f5))
[f2 -> {}, f3 -> {}, f5 -> {}, f1 -> {f2, f3, f5}]
=> (add-fun 'f2 (*set 'f3 'f4))
[f3 -> {},
 f5 -> {},
 f1 -> {f2, f3, f5},
 f4 -> {},
 f2 -> {f3, f4}]
=> (add-fun 'f4 (*set 'f1))
[f3 -> {},
 f5 -> {},
 f1 -> {f2, f3, f5},
 f2 -> {f3, f4},
 f4 -> {f1}]
```

14.9 Examples of functional programs

```
=> (add-fun 'f5 (*set 'f6))
[f3 -> {},
 f1 -> {f2, f3, f5},
 f2 -> {f3, f4},
 f4 -> {f1},
 f6 -> {},
 f5 -> {f6}]
=> (add-fun 'f6 (*set 'f6))
[f3 -> {},
 f1 -> {f2, f3, f5},
 f2 -> {f3, f4},
 f4 -> {f1},
 f5 -> {f6},
 f6 -> {f6}]
=> (uses 'f1)
{f2, f3, f5}
=> (uses 'f6)
{f6}
=> (used-by 'f3)
{f2, f1}
=> (used-by 'f6)
{f6, f5}
=> (recursives)
{f1, f2, f6, f4}
=> (del-fun 'f2)
[f3 -> {},
 f1 -> {f3, f5},
 f4 -> {f1},
 f5 -> {f6},
 f6 -> {f6}]
=> (recursives)
{f6}
=>
```

EXERCISE 14.12
A relation r is *antisymmetric* if the existence of any two pairs (x,y) and (y,x) in r implies that $x=y$. Furthermore, a relation is *partial order* if it is reflexive, antisymmetric, and transitive. Define these properties as two functions.

EXERCISE 14.13
Define is-mapping, a function which takes a relation as argument and returns t if and only if the relation can be equivalently represented by a mapping.

EXERCISE 14.14
> Define `recursives1`, a function which returns the set of functions in a reference diagram which directly refer to themselves. For example, given the diagram in Figure 14.2, `recursives1` should return `{f6}`.

14.10 Summary

In this chapter we have described a number of extensions to LISP which support a functional programming style. Here is a summary of the main points.

- A *set* is an unordered collection of objects with no repetitions.
- A *sequence* is a list whose elements are all of the same type.
- A *mapping* is a finite function.
- A *relation* is a subset of the *cross-product* of a set (i.e., a set of pairs).
- Sets, sequences, mappings, and relations are manipulated by a set of predefined pure operators.
- Composite objects (e.g., sets) may be constructed *explicitly* (by enumerating all their elements) or *implicitly* (by specifying a general element of the object).
- *Quantifiers* make assertions about a whole class of objects rather than one.
- LISP is easily extended to support composite objects and quantifiers.
- Such facilities support a concise, purely functional style in LISP.
- Pretty printing composite objects is relatively easy.
- Purely functional programs are concise and elegant but usually less efficient.

Projects

14.1 Relations are suitable for representing reference diagrams. For example, the reference diagram of Figure 14.1 is represented by the following relation:

```
{(f1,f2),(f1,f3),(f3,f3),(f3,f4),(f4,f3)}
```

Use the relation notation to redefine the cross-usage program of Section 14.9.

14.2 Rewrite the programs described in Section 14.9 without the use of the operators described in this chapter. Which version is more elegant? Which version is more efficient?

14.3 Rewrite the graph optimization programs of Section 12.3 using the notation introduced in this chapter. Compare your programs in terms of length, elegance and efficiency with those developed in Section 12.3.

14.4 Design and implement a simple language processor which converts the mathematical notation described in this chapter to its equivalent LISP form. If you need assistance on compilation techniques, you will find the book by Bornat [1979] useful.

Appendix 1

Summary of LISP Functions

This appendix summarizes the LISP functions used in this book. The specification of the functions follows closely those of the Franz LISP dialect. Each function description begins with a specification of a general call to that function and is then followed by a verbal description of its effect. A number of conventions have been used to achieve brevity and to indicate to what extent the functions can be used in other LISP dialects as well. The conventions are as follows.

- Function names appearing in **bold** are most likely to be available in other LISP systems under the same name. Other functions might not be available, or may have slightly different mnemonics.
- Function arguments have been given mnemonic names, depicting their role.
- Function arguments appearing in *italics* are always evaluated. Plain arguments are not evaluated by default, but may be evaluated explicitly by the function itself.
- Function arguments enclosed in square brackets are optional and may be omitted in a call.
- A * superscript specifies that an argument may appear zero or more times.
- A + superscript specifies that an argument may appear one or more times.

The functions are also classified into four categories. This is depicted by a keyword appearing at the top right-hand corner of each function description. The categories are given below.

- *Pure*. Represents functions which do not cause any side-effects.
- *Impure*. Represents functions which cause side-effects, but do not modify list structures.
- *Destructive*. Represents functions which cause side-effects by destructively modifying list structures.
- *Other*. Represents functions which are not really pure, but do not comfortably fit into the last two categories.

(+ *fixnum**) *pure*
> Returns the sum of arguments, if any, and zero otherwise. In some systems this function works on float numbers as well.

(- *fixnum**) *pure*
> Returns the result of subtracting the arguments in the order they occur, if any, and zero otherwise. In some systems this function works on float numbers as well.

(* *fixnum**) *pure*
> Returns the product of the arguments, if any, and one otherwise. In some systems this function works on float numbers as well.

(/ *fixnum**) *pure*
> Returns the integral part of the result of dividing the arguments in the order they occur, if any, and 1 otherwise. In some systems this function works on float numbers as well.

(1+ *fixnum*) *pure*
> Returns `fixnum + 1`.

(1- *fixnum*) *pure*
> Returns `fixnum - 1`.

(< *num1 num2*) *pure*
> Returns `t` if `num1` is less than `num2`, and `nil` otherwise.

(> *num1 num2*) *pure*
> Returns `t` if `num1` is greater than `num2`, and `nil` otherwise.

(= *num1 num2*) *pure*
> Returns `t` if `num1` is equal to `num2`, and `nil` otherwise.

(**abs** *num*) *pure*
> Returns the absolute value of `num`.

(add1 *num*) *pure*
> Returns `num + 1`.

(alphalessp *exp1 exp2*) *pure*
> Returns `t` if `exp1` alphabetically precedes `exp2`. Either of `exp1` and `exp2` must evaluate to a string or to a symbol (in which case the print name of the symbol will be used).

Summary of LISP functions 253

(**and** *exps**) *pure*
    Evaluates the expressions from left to right. If an expression evaluates to nil then evaluation will cease and nil will be returned, otherwise the value of the last expression will be returned. And returns t when given no arguments.

(**append** *list1 list2*+) *pure*
    Returns a list containing the elements of list1 followed by the elements of list2, etc. New cons-cells will be used in this list for elements of all arguments except the last.

(**apply** *fun arglist*) *pure*
    Returns the result of applying function fun to the argument list arglist.

(**arg** [*argnum*]) *pure*
    Returns the argument to the immediately enclosing lexpr specified by argnum, if present, and the number of arguments to the lexpr otherwise.

(**array** *name type dim*+) *other*
    Returns an array of the specified type and dimensions. When name is nonnil the function definition of name is set to the created array structure. Note that none of the arguments are evaluated.

(arraydims *array*) *pure*
    Returns a list whose head is the type of array and whose tail is a list of the dimensions of array.

(**arrayp** *exp*) *pure*
    Returns t if exp evaluates to an array structure, and nil otherwise.

(**assoc** *key alist*) *pure*
    Returns the first element of alist whose car is equal to key, if any, and nil otherwise.

(**assq** *key alist*) *pure*
    Same as assoc except that eq is used instead of equal for testing equality.

(**atom** *exp*) *pure*
    Returns t if exp evaluates to an atom and nil otherwise. Note that nil is itself an atom so (atom ()) will return t.

(boundp *symbol*)   *pure*
    Returns t if symbol is currently bound, and nil otherwise.

(**car** *list*)   *pure*
    Returns the head (i.e., the first element) of list. The case when list is nil is system dependent: in some system nil will be returned, in others an error message will be generated.

(**catch** exp [tag])   *other*
    Evaluates exp and returns its value if no throw occurs. If a value is thrown during the evaluation of exp then catch will return this value provided the tag of throw matches the tag of catch. A tagless catch will catch anything; tag may be a symbol or a list of symbols.

(**cdr** *list*)   *pure*
    Returns the tail of list (i.e., that part of list consisting of the second through to the last element of list). The case when list is nil is system dependent: in some systems nil will be returned, in others an error message will be generated.

(cfasl *obj-file foreign-fun lisp-fun category*)   *other*
    Opens foreign object file obj-file, and sets up a LISP function lisp-fun to represent the foreign function foreign-fun, having the category category (see Section 9.3).

(close *port*)   *other*
    Flushes the buffer of port and then closes port; close returns t.

(concat *exp**)   *pure*
    Returns a symbol with a print name identical to that obtained by concatenating the print names of the expressions in the order they occur. Note that each of exp must be a symbol, string or number. When no arguments are given concat will return a symbol with a nil print name.

(**cond** [clause]*)   *pure*
    Each clause is a list. The head of each clause is evaluated, starting with the first clause. If it does not evaluate to nil then the rest of the clause is evaluated and the last value is returned as the result. Otherwise, the same procedure is applied to the next clause. If there are no clauses or no clause is satisfied then nil will be returned.

(**cons** *exp1 exp2*)   *pure*
    Returns a new cons-cell whose head is exp1 and whose tail is exp2. Note that if

Summary of LISP functions 255

      `exp2` is not a list then the result will be a dotted pair.

(cos *angle*)   *pure*
      Returns the cosine of `angle`.

(cxr *index hunk*)   *pure*
      Returns the element of `hunk` indexed by `index`. The latter starts at 0 and must be within the size bound of `hunk`.

(debug)   *other*
      Invokes the *fixit* debugger.

(declare *declaration*[+])   *other*
      Specifies one or more compiler-specific declarations (see Section 9.2). Such declarations are altogether ignored by the interpreter.

(**def** *name* (*type arglist exp*[+]))   *other*
      Defines a function with the specified name where `type` must be one of `lambda`, `nlambda`, `lexpr` or `macro`. If `type` is `nlambda` or `macro` then `arglist` must contain exactly one nonnil symbol. The expressions `exp` form the body of the function. `Def` returns `name` as its result.

(defmacro *name arglist exp*[+])   *other*
      Defines a macro with the specified name. `Arglist` and `exp` are similar to those in `defun`.

(**defun** *name* [*type*] *arglist exp*[+])   *other*
      Defines a function with the specified name and type where `type` may be one of `expr` (for lambda), `fexpr` (for nlambda), `macro` (for macro), or `args` (for lexpr). When `arglist` is a nonnil symbol the function will be assumed to be of type lexpr and `arglist` will be bound to the number of arguments when the function is called. `Defun` returns `name` as its result. `Defun` is usually implemented as a macro which expands into a `def` form.

(delete *elem list*)   *destructive*
      Destructively deletes all elements of `list` which are `equal` to `elem`, and returns the modified list.

(delq *elem list*)   *destructive*
      Same as `delete` except that `eq` is used for comparing `elem` to elements of `list` rather than `equal`.

(**difference** *num**)   *pure*
    Same as – but works for float as well as fixed numbers.

(**do** ((var [init [repeat]])*) clause exp⁺)   *impure*
    Each `var` is first bound to `init` (if any). `Clause` is a list whose head is evaluated during each iteration. If it evaluates to `nonnil` then the rest of `clause` is evaluated, iteration is terminated, and the last value is returned. This happens provided the tail of clause is `nonnil`, otherwise `nil` will be returned. However, if the head of clause evaluates to `nil` then the `exps` will be evaluated. The `exps` take the form of a `prog` body and may contain labels, `gos`, and `returns`. Following this, the next iteration step commences whereby each `var` is bound to its `repeat` value (if any) and the whole process is repeated.

(**drain** [port])   *other*
    Flushes the buffer corresponding to `port`. If `port` is not given then the default output will be assumed.

(**dreverse** list)   *destructive*
    Returns `list` with its elements arranged in the reverse order. `List` itself will be modified as a result of the reversal.

(**dsubst** this that list)   *destructive*
    Returns a list obtained by substituting `this` for every occurrence of `that` at all levels of `list`. Substitution is done destructively by modifying `list`.

(**dtpr** exp)   *pure*
    Returns `t` if `exp` is a cons-cell. Note that `nil` is not a cons cell, so `(dtpr ())` will return `nil`.

(**eq** exp1 exp2)   *pure*
    Returns `t` if `exp1` and `exp2` are identical, and `nil` otherwise. Note that if `exp1` and `exp2` have the same appearance it does not guarantee that `eq` will return `t`.

(**equal** exp1 exp2)   *pure*
    Returns `t` if `exp1` and `exp2` are equal, and `nil` otherwise. Note, for example, that if `x` and `y` are equal lists but made of different cons-cells then `(equal x y)` will return `t`, whereas `(eq x y)` will return `nil`. Similar principles apply to strings, real numbers and to large integers.

(**error** [message1 [message2]])   *other*
    This function prints the given error messages (if any) and then enters a debug loop.

Summary of LISP functions 257

(errset exp [flag]) *other*
    Evaluates `exp` and returns a list of one element which is the result of evaluation, provided no error occurs during the evaluation of `exp`. If an error does occur then `errset` will print the error message (provided `flag` is not present or that it evaluates to a `nonnil` object) or ignore the message (if `flag` evaluates to `nil`) and then return `nil`. `Errset` avoids the transfer of control to a debug loop.

(**eval** exp) *pure*
    Causes extra evaluation of `exp`. `Exp` in fact will be evaluated twice: once during the call and once by `eval` itself. The final value will be returned as the result.

(evenp *fixnum*) *pure*
    Returns `t` if `fixnum` is even, and `nil` otherwise.

(exit) *other*
    Terminates the LISP system.

(**exp** num) *pure*
    Returns the number *e* raised to the power of `num`.

(**explode** exp) *pure*
    Returns a list of characters in the same order as they would occur if `exp` was printed using `print`.

(exploden exp) *pure*
    Same as `explode` except that a list of integer equivalents of characters is returned.

(**expt** num1 num2) *pure*
    Returns `num1` raised to the power of `num2`.

(fasl *name*) *other*
    Opens the object file with the specified name (if it exists and is readable), and reads the forms in the file. `Name` must evaluate to a symbol.

(fix *num*) *pure*
    Returns a fixed number as close as possible to `num`.

(fixp exp) *pure*
    Returns `t` if `exp` evaluates to a fixed number, and `nil` otherwise.

(flatc exp [max])   pure
    Returns the number of characters required if exp was to be printed using patom. Max is optional and specifies an upper bound to this number.

(float num)   pure
    Returns a float number as close as possible to num.

(floatp exp)   pure
    Returns t if exp evaluates to a float number, and nil otherwise.

(**funcall** fun arg*)   pure
    Returns the result of calling the function fun with the specified arguments. If fun is a macro then the result will receive an extra evaluation.

(**function** fun)   pure
    Returns the function binding of fun when fun is a symbol with a function binding, and fun itself otherwise.

(**gensym** [symbol])   pure
    Returns a new symbol whose print name starts with the first character of the print name of symbol (the default for which is g).

(**get** symbol property)   pure
    Returns the value in property list of symbol stored under property, if any, and nil otherwise.

(getaddress foreign-fun lisp-fun category)   other
    Sets up LISP definition for a foreign function where foreign-fun is the name of the foreign function, lisp-fun is the name of the LISP function, and category is the category of the foreign function. The object file in which the foreign function is stored must have already been opened by cfasl (see Section 9.3).

(getd symbol)   pure
    Returns the function binding of symbol (if any), and nil otherwise.

(get_pname symbol)   pure
    Returns the print name of symbol. The result is always a string.

(getlength array)   pure
    Returns the length of array. This will be simply the product of the dimensions of array.

Summary of LISP functions 259

(**go** label) *other*
    Transfers control to an expression just after the point specified by label (which must be an atom). This function may only be used in a prog or do body.

(**greaterp** num*) *pure*
    Returns t if each argument is successively greater than the previous one, and nil otherwise. When there are no arguments or only one argument greaterp will return t.

(hunk exp+) *other*
    Creates and returns a hunk structure, whose size is greater or equal to the number of arguments supplied to the function. (The size of a hunk is always a power of 2, i.e., 1, 2, 4, 8, ..., 128.) The elements of the hunk are initially bound to the values of the arguments, in the order given.

(hunkp exp) *pure*
    Returns t if exp evaluates to a hunk structure, and nil otherwise.

(hunksize exp) *pure*
    Returns the size of a hunk structure. Exp must evaluate to a hunk structure.

(**implode** list) *pure*
    Returns a symbol with a print name identical to that obtained by concatenating the first characters of the print names of the elements of list. Note that each element of list must be a symbol, string or small positive integer (which will be converted to its character representation).

(infile name) *other*
    Opens a file with the given name (if it exists and is readable) for reading, and returns a port for it; otherwise, it will produce an error message. Name must evaluate to a symbol.

(kwote exp) *pure*
    Returns the quoted value of exp (after it is evaluated). This is equivalent to (list (quote quote) exp).

(**lambda** arglist exp+) *pure*
    Returns an anonymous function, the type of which is lambda. The body of the function is treated similarly to that of defun.

(last *list*) *pure*
> Returns the sublist of list, consisting of its last element. When list is nil, nil will be returned.

(**length** *list*) *pure*
> Returns the length (i.e., the number of elements) of list.

(**lessp** *num**) *pure*
> Returns t if each argument is successively less than the previous one, and nil otherwise. When there are no arguments or only one argument lessp will return t.

(**let** ((var [init])*) exp+) *pure*
> Each var is first bound to the value of its associated init, if any. Otherwise it will be bound to nil. The exps are then evaluated within this binding context and the value of the last exp is returned. Note that the binding of vars is done in parallel and will last for the duration of the call to let only.

(let* ((var [init])*) exp+) *impure*
> Same as let except that the binding of vars is done sequentially from left to right.

(**list** *exps**) *pure*
> Returns a new list whose elements are the values of the arguments in the order they occur. List will return nil when given no arguments.

(**listp** *exp*) *pure*
> Returns t if exp is a list object, and nil otherwise. Note that (listp nil) returns t.

(load *name*) *other*
> Opens the file with the specified name (if it exists and is readable), and reads and evaluates the s-expressions in this file. Name must evaluate to a symbol.

(log *num*) *pure*
> Returns the natural logarithm of num.

(make-equivalent *symbol1 symbol2*) *other*
> Makes symbol1 equivalent to symbol2. Following this call, symbol1 will have the same value binding, function binding, and property list as symbol2.

(makhunk *list*) *other*
> Creates and returns a hunk structure, whose size is greater or equal to the length of

Summary of LISP functions

list. (The size of a hunk is always a power of 2, i.e., 1, 2, 4, 8, ..., 128.) The elements of the hunk are initially bound to the elements of list, in that order.

(**mapc** *fun arglist$^+$*)   *pure*
Applies the function fun to successive elements of arglists. All arglists must have the same length. mapc returns the first arglist as its result.

(**mapcan** *fun arglist$^+$*)   *destructive*
Same as mapcar except that nconc is applied to the result. This function is, in other words, equivalent to (apply 'nconc (mapcar fun arglist$^+$)).

(**mapcar** *fun arglist$^+$*)   *pure*
Same as mapc except that it returns a list of values produced as a result of successive applications of fun (in the same order).

(max *num$^+$*)   *pure*
Returns the largest number in the list of arguments.

(**member** *exp list*)   *pure*
Returns (starting from left) the first sublist of list having a head equal to exp, if any, and nil otherwise.

(memq *exp list*)   *pure*
Same as member except that eq is used for testing equality rather than equal.

(min *num$^+$*)   *pure*
Returns the smallest number in the list of arguments.

(**minus** *num*)   *pure*
Returns 0 - num.

(**minusp** *num*)   *pure*
Returns t if num is less than zero, and nil otherwise.

(**nconc** *list1 listi$^+$*)   *destructive*
Returns a list which is the result of concatenating list1, list2, etc. The returned list, in other words, will consist of the elements of list1, followed by the elements of list2, etc. All lists will be modified except the last.

(neq *exp1 exp2*)   *pure*
Is equivalent to (not (eq exp1 exp2)).

(nequal *exp1 exp2*) *pure*
    Is equivalent to `(not (equal exp1 exp2))`.

(**not** *exp*) *pure*
    Returns `t` if `exp` evaluates to `nil`, and `nil` otherwise.

(nreverse *list*) *destructive*
    Same as `dreverse`.

(nthcdr *n list*) *pure*
    Returns the result of `n` successive application of `cdr` to `list`. When `n` is zero or less than zero, `list` itself will be returned.

(nthelem *n list*) *pure*
    Returns the nth element of `list`. When `n` is zero or less than zero, or when `n` is larger than the length of `list`, `nil` will be returned.

(**null** *exp*) *pure*
    Is equivalent to `(not exp)`.

(numberp *exp*) *pure*
    Returns `t` if `exp` evaluates to a number, and `nil` otherwise.

(nwritn [*port*]) *pure*
    Returns the number of pending characters in the specified port. When `port` is not given the default output port is assumed.

(oddp *fixnum*) *pure*
    Returns `t` if `fixnum` is an odd number, and `nil` otherwise.

(onep *exp*) *pure*
    Returns `t` if `exp` evaluates to one, and `nil` otherwise.

(**or** *exp**) *pure*
    Evaluates the expressions from left to right. If an expression evaluates to nonnil then evaluation will cease and that value will be returned. Otherwise, `nil` will be returned. `Or` returns `nil` when given no arguments.

(outfile *name*) *other*
    Opens a file with the given name, for output, and returns a port for it. `Name` must evaluate to a symbol.

Summary of LISP functions 263

(patom *exp* [*port*]) *other*
> Prints the value of *exp* to the specified port (or the default output if port is not specified). The value of *exp* is returned as the result.

(plist *symbol*) *pure*
> Returns the property list of symbol. This is initially an empty list.

(**plus** *num**) *pure*
> Returns the sum of the arguments, if any, and zero otherwise.

(**plusp** *num*) *pure*
> Returns t if num is greater than zero, and nil otherwise.

(pp [(F *file*)] *fun*[+]) *other*
> Pretty prints the specified functions. Here (F file) is optional and specifies a file to which the output will be sent instead of the default output.

(pp-form *exp* [*port*]) *other*
> Pretty prints exp. When port is not given the default output will be assumed.

(**princ** *exp* [*port*]) *other*
> Same as patom.

(**print** *exp* [*port*]) *other*
> Similar to patom except that it always returns nil and uses escape characters around special characters in the print name symbols. It also prints strings with their double quotes.

(**prog** *varlist* *exp*[+]) *impure*
> Varlist is a list of symbols which are all initially bound to nil. Each exp is then evaluated, provided it is not a symbol, in which case it is treated as a label. Prog returns the value explicitly specified by a return expression or just nil if no return or go is encountered by the time the last exp gets evaluated.

(**prog1** *exp*[+]) *other*
> Evaluates exps from left to right and returns the value of the first exp.

(**prog2** *exp1* *exp*[+]) *other*
> Same as prog1 except that it returns the value of the second exp.

(**progn** exp⁺)   other
    Same as prog1 except that it returns the value of the last exp.

(**putprop** symbol exp property)   destructive
    Stores the value of exp under property in the property list of symbol and returns
    the value of exp.

(**quote** exp)   pure
    Returns exp. Note that quote does not evaluate its argument.

(**quotient** num*)   pure
    Same as / except that it works for float as well as fixed numbers.

(**read** [port])   other
    Reads and returns the next s-expression from the given port (or the default input if
    no port is given). At the end of the file read will return nil.

(readc [port])   other
    Reads and returns the next character from the specified port (or the default input if
    no port is given).

(remainder fixnum1 fixnum2)   pure
    Returns the remainder of integer division: fixnum1 over fixnum2.

(**remprop** symbol property)   destructive
    Removes property from the property list of symbol. Both the property name and
    the associated value will be removed. Remprop returns the sublist of the property list
    of symbol starting with property, if any, and nil otherwise.

(remove elem list)   pure
    Same as delete except that list is not modified and instead a new list is returned.

(remq elem list)   pure
    Same as delq except that list is not modified and instead a new list is returned.

(reset)   other
    Clears the LISP stack and restarts at the top level.

(**return** [exp])   other
    Is only valid within a prog or do body and returns the value of exp (or nil if exp is
    not present), thereby terminating the enclosing prog or do.

Summary of LISP functions 265

(**reverse** *list*) *pure*
    Same as dreverse except that a new list is returned instead of modifying list.

(**rplaca** *list newhead*) *destructive*
    Modifies list by replacing its head by newhead, and returns the modified list. An empty list will generate an error.

(**rplacd** *list newtail*) *destructive*
    Modifies list by replacing its tail by newtail, and returns the modified list. An empty list will generate an error.

(rplacx *index hunk exp*) *impure*
    Changes the value of the element of hunk depicted by index, to the value of exp. Index must be within the size bound of hunk.

(**set** *symbol exp*) *impure*
    The value of symbol is set to the value of exp which is itself returned as the result.

(setarg *argnum exp*) *impure*
    Must be used only within the body of an lexpr. It sets the argnum-th argument of the enclosing lexpr to the value of exp and returns this value as the result.

(setplist *symbol plist*) *impure*
    The property list of symbol is set to the value of plist, which is itself returned as the result.

(**setq** *symbol1 exp1* [*symboli expi*]*) *impure*
    The value of symboli is set to the value of expi. Note that setq does not evaluate any of symboli. Setq returns the value of the last expi.

(showstack [*fixnum*]) *other*
    Displays the contents of the top fixnum stack frames on the run-time stack. When fixnum is not specified, all stack frames will be displayed.

(sine *angle*) *pure*
    Returns the sine of angle.

(sload *file*) *other*
    Opens file and reads, prints, and evaluates each form. For forms which are function definitions only the function name is printed. Sload is similar to load but prints additional information which may be useful for locating errors (e.g., unbalanced brackets).

(**sqrt** *num*) *pure*
    Returns the square root of num.

(**store** *arrayelem exp*) *impure*
    Stores the value of exp in the array location specified by arrayelem and returns the value of exp.

(stringp *exp*) *pure*
    Returns t if exp evaluates to a string, and nil otherwise.

(sub1 *num*) *pure*
    Returns num - 1.

(**subst** *this that list*) *pure*
    Same as dsubst except that list is not modified and instead a new list is returned.

(**symbolp** *exp*) *pure*
    Returns t if exp evaluates to a symbol, and nil otherwise.

(tab *column* [*port*]) *other*
    Prints enough spaces to port (or the standard output if port is not specified) to position the cursor on column. If the cursor is already positioned after column then printing will be done on a new line.

(**terpri** [*port*]) *other*
    Terminates the current line by flushing the contents of the buffer and resumes printing on the next line of the file depicted by port. When port is not specified the standard output will be assumed.

(**throw** *exp* [*tag*]) *other*
    Returns the value of exp to the first enclosing catch with the same tag or no tag at all. If tag is not present it will be assumed to be nil.

(**times** *num**) *pure*
    Same as * except that it works for float as well as fixed numbers.

(top-level) *other*
    This corresponds to the top level read-eval-print loop of LISP. It can be redefined by the user and brought into operation by doing (reset).

Summary of LISP functions 267

(trace funs⁺) *other*
    Marks `funs` for tracing. The tracer will display details of calls to marked functions in subsequent evaluations.

(untrace funs⁺) *other*
    Unmarks `funs`. Subsequent calls to `funs` will not be traced any longer.

(**zerop** *exp*) *pure*
    Returns `t` if `exp` evaluates to zero, and `nil` otherwise.

Appendix 2
Answers to Exercises

1.1

10	is an atom
(10 20)	is a list
(5 ()	is not an s-expression
plus (2 5)	is not an s-expression
'plus	is an atom
'(list of atoms)	is a list
Jack	is an atom
atom	is an atom
list	is an atom
10-20*6	is an atom
*s*t*a*r*	is an atom
$%s=k	is an atom
5=10	is an atom
-+-+	is an atom

1.2

```
(times 10 (plus 9 (difference 61 20)))
(times (difference 52 (quotient 16.0 3))
       (plus 2 (expt 8 5)))
(quotient (difference 99 (sqrt 18))
          (difference (sqrt 99) 18))
(difference (plus (quotient (times 1 2 3 4 5) 55.0)
                  (times 81 81))
            (expt 17 3))
```

1.3, 1.4, 1.5
Use the LISP interpreter to find the answers.

2.1

```
(car '(LISP is fun))                    ;; extracts: LISP
(cadr '(LISP is fun))                   ;; extracts: is
```

Answers to Exercises 269

```
(caddr '(LISP is fun))                          ;; extracts: fun
(car '(lists (have) brackets))                  ;; extracts: lists
(caadr '(lists (have) brackets))                ;; extracts: have
(caddr '(lists (have) brackets))                ;; extracts: brackets
(car '(like ((this)) or (even (this))))         ;; extracts: like
(caaadr '(like ((this)) or (even (this))))      ;; extracts: this
(caddr '(like ((this)) or (even (this))))       ;; extracts: or
(caadddr '(like ((this)) or (even (this))))     ;; extracts: even
(caadadddr '(like ((this)) or (even (this))))   ;; extracts: this
(caaaar '((((trapped)))))                       ;; extracts: trapped
```

2.2
```
(cons 'one (cons 'two (cons 'three nil)))
(cons 'two
      (cons 'and
            (cons (cons 'four (cons 'times (cons 'two nil)))
                  (cons 'is (cons (cons 'ten nil) nil)))))
;; etc.
(list 'one 'two 'three)
(list 'two 'and (list 'four 'times 'two) 'is (list 'ten))
;; etc.
```

2.3, 2.4, 2.5
Use the LISP interpreter to find the answers.

3.1
```
(defun head (list) (car list))

(defun tail (list) (cdr list))
```

3.2
```
(defun last-elem (list) (car (last list)))
```

3.3
```
(defun circumference (radius)
       (times 2 radius 3.14))                   ;; 2πr.

(defun area (radius)
       (times (times radius radius) 3.14))      ;; πr^2.
```

3.4
```
(defun head (list)
       (cond [(null list) nil]        ;; head is nil when list is nil.
             [t (car list)]))         ;; head of list.
(defun tail (list)
       (cond [(null list) nil]        ;; tail is nil when list is nil.
             [t (cdr list)]))         ;; tail of list.
```

3.5
```
(defun divisible (m n)                ;; m divisible by n?
       (cond [(or (floatp m) (floatp n) (zerop n)) nil]
             [t (zerop (remainder m n))]))
```

3.6
```
(cond [(member x y) (list x)]
      [t (last y)])

(cond [(is-employee name)
         (cond [(does-overtime name) (extra-earning name))
               [t (normal-earning name)])]
      [(is-retired name) (pension name)]
      [t (report-unknown name)])

(let [(token (get-token)) (context (get-context))]
     (cond [(is-variable token context)
              (add-table token 'var)]
           [(is-function token context)
              (add-table token 'fun)]
           [t (error token 'unknown)]))
```

3.7
```
(and (plusp n) (sqrt n))

(or (and (plusp n) (sqrt n))
    (sqrt (abs n)))

(or (and (atom x) x)
    (car x))

(or (and (null x) 'empty)
    (and (atom x) 'atom)
    'list)
```

3.8

```
(defun pronoun (subject)
   ((lambda (sex)
       (cond [(eq sex 'female)  'she]
             [(eq sex 'male)    'he]
             [(eq sex 'neutral) 'it]
             [t                 '??]))
    (sex-of subject)))
```

3.9

```
(defun quad-equation (a b c)
   ((lambda (delta)
       (cond [(plusp delta)                                ;; Δ>0?
              (setq left (quotient b (times 2 a))
                    right (quotient (sqrt delta) (times 2 a)))
              (list (plus left right) (difference left right))]
             [(minusp delta) 'no-solution]                 ;; Δ<0?
             [t (list (minus (quotient b (times 2 a))))])) ;; Δ=0?
    (difference (times b b) (times 4 a c))))              ;; Δ=b^2-4ac.

(defun quad-equation (a b c)
   (let [(delta (difference (times b b)                   ;; Δ=b^2-4ac.
                            (times 4 a c)))]
      (cond [(plusp delta)                                 ;; Δ>0?
             (setq left (quotient b (times 2 a))
                   right (quotient (sqrt delta) (times 2 a)))
             (list (plus left right) (difference left right))]
            [(minusp delta) 'no-solution]                  ;; Δ<0?
            [t (list (minus (quotient b                    ;; Δ=0?
                                      (times 2 a))))])))
```

3.10

```
(defun error-ratio (err-fun ave-fun measure1 measure2)
   (quotient (funcall err-fun measure1 measure2)
             (funcall ave-fun measure1 measure2)))

(defun ave-fun (measure1 measure2)                         ;; average function.
   (quotient (plus measure1 measure2) 2))
```

3.11
```
(defun error-ratio (err-fun measures)
   (cond [(null (cdr measures)) 0]                    ;; 0 or 1 measure?
         [t (quotient (funcall err-fun (car measures)
                                      (car (last measures)))
                      (quotient (apply 'plus measures)  ;; average.
                                (length measures)))]))
```

4.1, 4.2
Similar to the trees in Section 4.1.

4.3
```
(defun append-cost (list)
   (prog (cost)
         (setq cost 0)                                ;; initialize cost to 0.
      loop
         (and (null (cdr list)) (return cost))        ;; all sublists done?
         (setq cost (+ cost (length (car list))))     ;; cost of this sublist
               list (cdr list))                        ;; next sublist.
         (go loop)))
```

4.4
Use the LISP interpreter to find the answers.

4.5
```
(defun copy (list) (append list nil))
```

4.6
Use the LISP interpreter to find the answers.

4.7
```
(rplaca '(birds can fly) 'BIRDS)              ;; birds -> BIRDS.
(rplaca (cdr '(birds can fly)) 'CAN)          ;; can -> CAN.
(rplaca (cddr '(birds can fly)) 'FLY)         ;; fly -> FLY.
(rplaca '(pigs ((cannot))) 'PIGS)             ;; pigs -> PIGS.
(rplacd '(pigs ((cannot))) '(((CANNOT))))     ;; cannot -> CANNOT.
;; etc.
```

4.8
Use the LISP interpreter to find the answers.

Answers to Exercises

5.1

```
(defun member (item list)                      ;; item a member of list?
   (cond [(null list) nil]                     ;; empty list?
         [(equal item (car list)) list]        ;; match?
         [t (member item (cdr list))]))        ;; recursive step.

(defun length (list)                           ;; length of list.
   (cond [(null list) 0]                       ;; empty list?
         [t (1+ (length (cdr list)))]))        ;; recursive step.

(defun subst (this that list)        ;; substitute this for that in list.
   (cond [(null list) list]                    ;; empty list?
         [(equal that (car list))              ;; match?
          (cons this (subst this that (cdr list)))]    ;; recurse.
         [t
          (cons (cond [(atom (car list)) (car list)]   ;; atomic head?
                      [t (subst this that (car list))]) ;; recurse.
                (subst this that (cdr list)))]))       ;; recurse.
```

5.2

```
(defun nth-tail (n list)                       ;; nth tail of list.
   (cond [(zerop n) list]                      ;; n=0?
         [t (nth-tail (1- n) (cdr list))]))    ;; recurse.
```

5.3

```
(defun is-in (list1 list2)           ;; no. of occurrences of list1 in list2.
   (is-in-aux list1 list2 0))                  ;; start with 0.

(defun is-in-aux (list1 list2 count)           ;; auxiliary.
   (cond [(null list2) count]                  ;; termination condition.
         [(equal list1 (car list2))            ;; match?
          (is-in-aux list1 (cdr list2) (1+ count))];; inc. count.
         [(listp (car list2))                  ;; head is a list?
          (+ count                             ;; count +
             (is-in list1 (car list2))         ;; occurrences in head +
             (is-in list1 (cdr list2)))]       ;; occurrences in tail.
         [t (is-in-aux list1 (cdr list2) count)])) ;; recurse on tail.
```

5.4

```
(defun member (item list)                        ;; item a member of list?
   (prog ()
      loop
         (cond [(null list) (return)]            ;; termination condition.
               [(equal item (car list)) (return list)]) ;; match.
         (setq list (cdr list))                  ;; next element.
         (go loop)))

(defun length (list)                             ;; length of list.
   (prog (len)
         (setq len 0)                            ;; initialize len to 0.
      loop
         (and (null list) (return len))          ;; termination condition.
         (setq list (cdr list)                   ;; next tail.
               len (1+ len))                     ;; increment len.
         (go loop)))

(defun subst (this that list)        ;; substitute this for that in list.
   (prog (res)
      loop
         (and (null list)                        ;; termination condition.
              (return (nreverse res)))
         (setq res (cons (cond [(equal that (car list)) this]
                               [(atom (car list)) (car list)]
                               [t (subst this that
                                         (car list))])
                         res))
         (setq list (cdr list))                  ;; next tail.
         (go loop)))
```

5.5

```
(defun nth-tail (n list)                         ;; nth tail of list.
   (prog ()
      loop
         (and (zerop n) (return list))           ;; n=0?
         (setq n (1- n)                          ;; decrement n.
               list (cdr list))                  ;; next tail.
         (go loop)))
```

Answers to Exercises   275

```
(defun nth-element (n list)                      ;; nth element of list.
   (prog ()
      loop
         (and (onep n) (return (car list)))      ;; n=1?
         (setq n (1- n)                          ;; decrement n.
               list (cdr list))                  ;; next element.
         (go loop)))
```

5.6
```
(defun nth-element (n list)                      ;; nth element of list.
   (prog ()
         (and (< n 1) (return nil))              ;; n<1 => return nil.
      loop
         (and (onep n) (return (car list)))      ;; n=1?
         (setq n (1- n)                          ;; decrement n.
               list (cdr list))                  ;; next element.
         (go loop)))

(defun nth-tail (n list)                         ;; nth tail of list.
   (prog ()
         (and (minusp n) (return nil))           ;; n<0 => return nil.
      loop
         (and (zerop n) (return list))           ;; n=0?
         (setq n (1- n)                          ;; decrement n.
               list (cdr list))                  ;; next tail.
         (go loop)))
```

5.7
```
(defun is-in (atom list)                         ;; is atom in list?
   (prog ()
      loop
         (cond [(null list) (return nil)]        ;; termination condition.
               [(atom (car list))                ;; head is atom?
                 (and (eq atom (car list))       ;; match?
                      (return t))]               ;; return t.
               [(is-in atom (car list)) (return t)]) ;;recurse on tail.
         (setq list (cdr list))                  ;; next element.
         (go loop)))
```

```
(defun reduce (pred)                              ;; reduce predicate.
   (prog (op res)
         (and (or (atom pred)                     ;; atomic predicate or
                  (not (memq (car pred) '(and or))));; not and/or?
              (return pred))                      ;; return predicate.
         (setq op (car pred))                     ;; extract operator.
    loop
         (cond [(null (setq pred (cdr pred)))     ;; exhausted?
                (return (cons op (reverse res)))] ;; return result.
               [(and (listp (car pred))           ;; head is a list?
                     (eq (caar pred) op))         ;; operator op?
                (setq res                         ;; reduce head.
                      (append (reverse (cdr (reduce (car pred))))
                              res))]
               [t (setq res                       ;; reduce tail.
                        (cons (reduce (car pred)) res))])
         (go loop)))
```

5.8
```
(defun union (set1 set2)                          ;; set union.
   (nconc (mapcan                                 ;; set of elements in
           '(lambda (item)                        ;; set1 but not set2, with
              (cond [(memq item set2) nil]
                    [t (list item)]))
           set1)
          set2))                                  ;; members of set2.
```

5.9
```
(defun intersection (set1 set2)                   ;; set intersection.
   (mapcan '(lambda (item)                        ;; elements in both set2
              (cond [(memq item set2) (list item)]))
           set1))                                 ;; and set1.
```

6.1
Use the LISP interpreter to find the answers.

6.2
```
(defun calc ()                                 ;; simple calculator.
       (prog (opd1 op opd2)
          loop
             (patom "calc> ")                  ;; prompt.
             (and (eq (setq opd1 (read)) 'stop) ;; stop?
                  (return))
             (setq opd1 (eval opd1)            ;; evaluate operand1.
                   op (read)                   ;; operator.
                   opd2 (eval (read)))         ;; evaluate operand2.
             (print (cond [(eq op '+) (plus opd1 opd2)]
                          [(eq op '-) (difference opd1 opd2)]
                          [(eq op '*) (times opd1 opd2)]
                          [(eq op '/) (quotient opd1 opd2)]
                          [t 'error]))
             (terpri)
             (go loop)))
```

6.3
```
(defun verbose-load (file)                     ;; verbose LISP loader.
       (prog (fun port)
             (setq port (infile file))         ;; open input file.
          loop
             (cond [(null (setq fun (read port)))
                    (close port)               ;; close input file.
                    (return)])
             (print (eval fun))                ;; eval & print fun. name.
             (terpri)
             (go loop)))
```

6.4
```
(defun pp-file (from to)                       ;; pretty print file.
       (prog (fun)
             (setq from (infile from))         ;; open input file.
             (and (neq to 'VDU)                ;; output to VDU?
                  (setq to (outfile to)))      ;; open output file.
          loop
             (cond [(null (setq fun (read from)))
                    (close from)
                    (and (neq to 'VDU) (close to))
                    (return)])
              (pp-form fun to)    ;; to=nil => output goes to VDU.
             (terpri to)
             (go loop)))
```

6.5
```
(defun start-log (log)                              ;; start logging.
       (setq logf (outfile log)))                    ;; open log file.

(defun stop-log ()                                   ;; stop logging.
       (close logf)                                  ;; close log file.
       (setq logf nil))                              ;; reset log flag.

(defun top-level ()                                  ;; top level.
       (prog (x y)
          loop
             (patom "=> ")                           ;; prompt.
             (print (setq y (eval (setq x (read))))) ;; read-eval-print.
             (terpri)
             (cond [logf (patom "=> " logf)          ;; log everything:
                         (print x logf)
                         (terpri logf)
                         (print y logf)
                         (terpri logf)])
             (go loop)))
```

7.1
```
(defun if fexpr (exp)                                ;; if conditional.
   (cond [(cdddr exp)                                ;; has else part?
          (cond [(eval (car exp)) (eval (caddr exp))] ;; then.
                [t (eval (caddddr exp))])]           ;; else.
         [(eval (car exp)) (eval (caddr exp))]))     ;; then.
```

7.2
```
(defmacro head (list)                                ;; head macro
        `(car ,list))

(defmacro tail (list)                                ;; tail macro.
         `(cdr ,list))

(defmacro change-head (list head)                    ;; change head macro.
         `(rplaca ,list ,head))

(defmacro change-tail (list tail)                    ;; change tail macro.
          `(rplacd ,list ,tail))
```

7.3
```
(defun if macro (exp)                               ;; if conditional.
        (cond [(cddddr exp)                         ;; has else part?
                `(cond (,(cadr exp) ,(cadddr exp))  ;; then.
                       (t ,(caddddr exp)))]         ;; else.
              [t
                `(and ,(cadr exp) ,(cadddr exp))])) ;; then.
```

7.4
```
(defun if macro (exp)                               ;; extended if macro.
   (prog (res)
        (setq res `((,(cadr exp) ,(cadddr exp)) cond)
              exp (cddddr exp))                     ;; drop 'if .. then ..'
    loop
        (cond [(null exp) (return (nreverse res))]
              [(eq (car exp) 'elseif)               ;; elseif .. then ..
                (setq res (cons `(,(cadr exp) ,(cadddr exp)) res)
                      exp (cddddr exp))]
              [t                                    ;; else ..
                (setq res (cons `(t ,(cadr exp)) res)
                      exp (cddr exp))])
        (go loop)))
```

7.5
```
(defun case macro (exp)                             ;; case macro.
   (prog (switch body)
        (setq switch (cadr exp)                     ;; case switch.
              exp (cdddr exp)                       ;; case body.
              body exp)
    loop
        (and (null exp)                             ;; body exhausted?
             (return (cons 'cond body)))            ;; return code.
        (rplaca exp (cons (list 'equal switch (caar exp))
                          (cdar exp)))              ;; next condition.
        (setq exp (cdr exp))
        (go loop)))
```

7.6
```
(defun while macro (exp)                            ;; while-do macro.
   (let [(label (gensym))]                          ;; prog label.
     `(prog ()
        ,label
            (cond ,(cons (cadr exp) (cdddr exp))    ;; loop body.
                  (t (return)))
            (go ,label))))
```

```
(defun repeat macro (exp)                           ;; repeat-until macro.
   (let [(label (gensym))                           ;; prog label.
         (pred (car (last exp)))]                   ;; predicate.
      (cons 'prog
          (cons ()
              (cons label
                  (nconc
                      (nreverse (cddr (nreverse (cdr exp))))
                      `((and (null ,pred)           ;; loop back?
                          (go ,label)))))))))

(defun for macro (exp)                              ;; for-in-do macro.
   (let [(label (gensym))                           ;; prog label.
         (list (gensym))                            ;; iteration list.
         (var (cadr exp))]                          ;; iteration variable.
      `(prog ()
          (setq ,list ,(cadddr exp))                ;; iteration list.
         ,label
          (cond ((null ,list) (return))             ;; termination condn.
               ,(cons t
                   (cons (list 'setq var
                               (list 'car list))
                       (cdddddr exp))));; loop body.
          (setq ,list (cdr ,list))                  ;; next list element.
          (go ,label))))
```

7.7

```
(defun do-1 macro (list)                            ;; simplified do macro.
   (let [(label (gensym))                           ;; prog label.
         (part1 (cadr list))                        ;; head of do-1.
         (part2 (caddr list))                       ;; clause of do-1.
         (part3 (cdddr list))]                      ;; body of do-1.
      `(prog (,(car part1))                         ;; variable.
          (setq ,(car part1) ,(cadr part1))         ;; initialize var.
         ,label
          ,(list 'cond (append part2 '((return)))   ;; clause.
               (cons t part3))                      ;; body.
          (setq ,(car part1)                        ;; next value for var.
               ,(caddr part1))
          (go ,label))))
```

Do-n is a generalization of do-1, and will not be described here.

7.8
```
(defun printf num                              ;; formatted print.
   (prog (n)
         (setq n 1)                            ;; initialize n to 0.
      loop
         (and (> n num) (return))              ;; no more args?
         (tab (arg (1+ n)))                    ;; put tab.
         (print (arg n))                       ;; print arg.
         (setq n (+ 2 n))                      ;; next arg & tab position.
         (go loop)))
```

8.1
Trivial!

8.2
```
(defun uses comp                               ;; uses lexpr.
   (prog (n res comps)
         (setq n 1)                            ;; initialize n to 1.
      loop
         (and (> n comp)                       ;; all args considered?
              (return (apply 'append res)))    ;; append the result.
         (cond [(setq comps (get (arg n) 'uses)) ;; get used comps.
                (setq res (cons comps          ;; used subcomponents.
                          (cons (apply 'uses comps)
                                res)))])
         (setq n (1+ n))                       ;; next arg.
         (go loop)))
```

8.3
```
(defun new-book (book)                         ;; add new book to
books.
   (cond [(member book books)                  ;; book already in books?
          (patom "already stored")
          (terpri)]
         [t (setq books (cons book books))]))  ;; add book.

(defun list-all (attr)                         ;; list attribute.
   (prog (bks res)
         (setq bks books)                      ;; books.
      loop
         (and (null bks) (return res))         ;; all books considered?
         (and (setq value (assoc attr (car bks))) ;; has attribute?
              (setq res (cons (cdr value) res))) ;; add it to list.
         (setq bks (cdr bks))                  ;; next book.
         (go loop)))
```

8.4
```
(defun maximum (nums)                           ;; find maximum number.
   (prog (size max)
         (cond [(cddr (arraydims (getd nums)))  ;; multi-dimensional?
                (return nil)]
               [(zerop (setq size               ;; empty array?
                             (getlength (getd nums))))
                (return nil)])
         (setq max                              ;; initialize size.
               (funcall nums (setq size (1- size))))
    loop
         (cond [(minusp (setq size (1- size)))  ;; all elems searched?
                (return max)]
               [(greaterp (funcall nums size) max) ;; new max?
                (setq max (funcall nums size))]) ;; record it.
         (go loop)))
```

8.5
```
(defun sort (hunk)                              ;; sort a hunk of lists.
   (prog (size)
         (setq size (1- (hunksize hunk)))       ;; size - 1.
    loop
         (and (sorted hunk size) (return hunk)) ;; sorted?
         (go loop)))

(defun sorted (hunk size)                       ;; hunk sorted?
   (prog (n swapped)
         (setq n 0)                             ;; initialize index n.
    loop
         (cond [(>= n size)                     ;; all elems. considered?
                (return (not swapped))]
               [(> (length (cxr n hunk))        ;; element n should go
                   (length (cxr (1+ n) hunk))) ;; before element n+1?
                (swap hunk n (1+ n))            ;; swap them.
                (setq swapped t)])              ;; set swapped flag.
         (setq n (1+ n))                        ;; next element.
         (go loop)))

(defun swap (hunk n m)                          ;; swap elements n & m.
   (let [(temp (cxr n hunk))]                   ;; n -> temp.
        (rplacx n hunk (cxr m hunk))            ;; m -> n.
        (rplacx m hunk temp)))                  ;; temp -> m.
```

Answers to Exercises   283

8.6
This is similar to Exercise 8.5. All that needs to be changed is the definition of sorted:
```
(defun sort-names (hunk)                      ;; sort a hunk of strings.
   (prog (size)
        (setq size (1- (hunksize hunk)))      ;; size - 1.
     loop
        (and (sorted hunk size) (return hunk)) ;; sorted?
        (go loop)))

(defun sorted (hunk size)                     ;; hunk sorted?
   (prog (n swapped)
        (setq n 0)                            ;; initialize index n.
     loop
        (cond [(>= n size)
                 (return (not swapped))]      ;; all elems. considered?
              [(alphalessp (cxr (1+ n) hunk)  ;; element n+1 should
                           (cxr n hunk))      ;; go after element n+1?
                 (swap hunk n (1+ n))         ;; swap them.
                 (setq swapped t)])           ;; set swapped flag.
        (setq n (1+ n))                       ;; next element.
        (go loop)))
```

8.7
```
(defun subpattern (sym1 sym2)                 ;; chars of sym1 in sym2?
   (prog ()
        (setq sym1 (explode sym1)             ;; chars of sym1.
              sym2 (explode sym2))            ;; chars of sym2.
     loop
        (cond [(null sym1) (return t)]        ;; all chars considered?
              [(not (memq (car sym1) sym2))   ;; char not in sym2?
                 (return nil)])
        (setq sym1 (cdr sym1))                ;; next char in sym1.
        (go loop)))
```

8.8
```
(defun sort-names (hunk)                      ;; sort a hunk of strings.
   (prog (size)
        (and (not (hunkp hunk))               ;; not a hunk?
             (error "sort-names: arg must be a hunk."))
        (setq size (1- (hunksize hunk)))      ;; size - 1.
     loop
        (and (sorted hunk size) (return hunk)) ;; sorted?
        (go loop)))
```

```
(defun subpattern (sym1 sym2)              ;; chars of sym1 in sym2?
   (prog ()
       (and (or (not (symbolp sym1))        ;; sym1 or
                (not (symbolp sym2)))       ;; sym2 not a symbol?
            (error "subpattern: both args must be symbols."))
       (setq sym1 (explode sym1)            ;; chars of sym1.
             sym2 (explode sym2))           ;; chars of sym2.
     loop
       (cond [(null sym1) (return t)]       ;; all chars considered?
             [(not (memq (car sym1) sym2))  ;; char not in sym2?
              (return nil)])
       (setq sym1 (cdr sym1))               ;; next char in sym1.
       (go loop)))
```

8.9

```
(defun top-level ()                         ;; top level.
   (prog (x)
     loop
       (patom "=> ")                        ;; prompt.
       (cond [(setq x (errset (eval (read))))  ;; read-eval.
              (print (car x)) (terpri)])    ;; print if no error.
       (go loop)))
```

11.1

Change the fourth clause in the cond of match to the following:

```
[(listp (car pat))                          ;; head of pat a list?
 (cond [(eq (caar pat) '^) (match^ pat expr)]  ;; match ^ pattern.
       [(listp (car expr))                  ;; expr must be a list.
        (and (match (car pat) (car expr))   ;; heads and
             (match (cdr pat) (cdr expr)))])]

(defun match^ (pat expr)                    ;; match ^ pattern.
   (prog (args)
       (setq args (car pat)                 ;; args to ^.
             pat (cdr pat))                 ;; rest of pattern.
         loop
           (cond [(null (setq args (cdr args)))  ;; no more args?
                  (return nil)]             ;; does not match.
                 [(match                    ;; arg matches?
                    (cons (car args) pat) expr)
                  (return t)])
           (go loop)))
```

11.2
Change the fourth clause in the `cond` of `match` to the following:
```
[(listp (car pat))                          ;; head of pat a list?
 (cond [(eq (caar pat) '^) (match^ pat expr)]     ;; match ^ pattern.
       [(eq (caar pat) '^^) (match^^ pat expr)]   ;; match ^^ pattern.
       [(listp (car expr))                  ;; expr must be a list.
        (and (match (car pat) (car expr))   ;; heads and
             (match (cdr pat) (cdr expr)))])]     ;; tails must match.

(defun match^^ (pat expr)                   ;; match ^^ pattern.
   (prog (args var)
         (setq args (cdar pat)              ;; args of ^^.
               var (car args)               ;; pattern variable.
               pat (cdr pat))               ;; rest of pattern.
      loop
         (cond [(null (setq args (cdr args)))   ;; no more args?
                (return nil)]               ;; does not match.
               [(match                      ;; arg matches?
                  (cons (car args) pat) expr)
                (set var (car expr))        ;; bind pattern var.
                (return t)])
         (go loop)))
```

12.1
First define SHOW as follows:
```
(defun SHOW (what item)         ;; instrumentation function.
   (patom "** ") (patom what) (patom " ** ")
   (patom item) (terpri))

(defun depth (tree item)        ;; instrumented depth-first search.
  (SHOW 'node (car tree))
     (cond [(atom tree) nil]                 ;; empty tree?
           [(equal (car tree) item) tree]    ;; item=root node?
           [(depth (car tree) item)]         ;; search 1st subtree.
           [(depth (cdr tree) item)]))       ;; search other subtrees.

(defun breadth (tree item)      ;; instrumented breadth-first search.
     (cond [(eq (car tree) item) tree]       ;; item=root node?
           [t (prog (queue nodes)            ;; root is level 1.
                 (setq queue (cdr tree)      ;; queue for level 2.
                       nodes queue)          ;; nodes in level 2.
              loop
      (and nodes (SHOW 'node (caar nodes)))
```

```
              (cond [(null nodes)                  ;; nodes exhausted?
                     ;; if last level then item is not there, return nil:
                     (and (null queue) (return nil))
                     ;; update queue and nodes for the next level:
                     (setq queue (apply 'append
                                          (mapcar 'cdr queue))
                           nodes queue)
                     (go loop)]                    ;; try next level.
                    [(eq (caar nodes) item)        ;; found item,
                     (return (car nodes))])        ;; return its tree.
              (setq nodes (cdr nodes))             ;; move to next node.
              (go loop))])))

(defun search (tree item)              ;; instrumented binary tree search.
  (and (car tree) (SHOW 'node (caar tree)))
  (cond [(null (car tree)) nil]                    ;; exhausted?
        [(eq item (caar tree)) (car tree)]         ;; found it?
        [(alphalessp item (caar tree))             ;; left node.
         (search (cdar tree) item)]
        [t (search (cddar tree) item)]))           ;; right node.
```

12.2

```
(defun remove (tree item)              ;; remove item from binary tree.
  (cond [(null (car tree)) nil]                    ;; trivial case.
        [(eq item (caar tree))                     ;; found item?
         (cond [(null (cadar tree))                ;; no left child?
                (rplaca tree (caddar tree))]       ;; keep right.
               [(null (caddar tree))               ;; no right child?
                (rplaca tree (cadar tree))]        ;; keep left.
               [t ;; insert left subtree into right subtree:
                  (rplaca tree
                          (car (insert-tree (cddar tree)
                                             (cadar tree))))])]
        [(alphalessp item (caar tree))             ;; left node.
         (remove (cdar tree) item)]
        [t (remove (cddar tree) item)]))           ;; right node.

;; insert one subtree into another in a binary tree.
(defun insert-tree (tree subtree)
  (cond [(null (car tree))                         ;; exhausted?
         (rplaca tree subtree)]
        [(eq (car subtree) (caar tree)) nil]       ;; already there?
        [(alphalessp (car subtree) (caar tree))    ;; left node.
         (insert-tree (cdar tree) subtree)]
        [t (insert-tree (cddar tree) subtree)]))   ;; right node.
```

12.3
```
(defun slot (name)                          ;; find slot for name in a HAL table.
   (cdr (cxr (hash name) table)))           ;; tail of slot entries.
```

12.4
```
(defun remove (name)                        ;; remove an entry from a HAL table.
   (prog (entries)
         (setq entries (cxr (hash name) table))    ;; slot entries.
      loop
         (cond [(or (null (cdr entries))
                    (alphalessp name (caadr entries)))
                (return nil)]                      ;; not in table.
               [(equal name (caadr entries))       ;; found it.
                (return (rplacd entries            ;; remove it.
                                (cddr entries)))])
         (setq entries (cdr entries))              ;; next entry.
         (go loop)))

(defun size ()                              ;; find the size of a HAL table.
   (prog (size idx)
         (setq size 0 idx 0)                ;; initialize.
      loop
         (cond [(< idx table-size)          ;; more slots?
                (setq size (+ size
                              (length (cdr (cxr idx table))))
                      idx (1+ idx))         ;; next slot.
                (go loop)])
         (return size)))
```

12.5
```
(defun optimize (node bound)                ;; find optimal route in a graph.
   (prog (subnodes subbound route op-route cost)
         (and (null (setq subnodes (eval node)))   ;; no children?
              (return (list 0 node)))              ;; return node with cost 0.
      loop
  (and subnodes (SHOW 1 (car subnodes)))
         (cond
            [(null subnodes)                ;; no more children?
             (return (cond [op-route        ;; had an optimal route?
                            (cons (car op-route)   ;; return it.
                                  (cons node (cdr op-route)))]
                           [t (list bound)]))]     ;; return dummy.
```

```
                     [(plusp (setq subbound              ;; edge cost below bound?
                                   (- bound (setq cost
                                                 (node-cost subnodes)))))
                      (setq route                        ;; find optimal subroute.
                            (optimize (node subnodes) subbound))
(SHOW 2 route)
                      (cond [(< (car route) subbound)    ;; cost within bound?
                             ;; update bound and optimal subroute:
                             (setq bound (+ (car route) cost)
                                   op-route (cons bound (cdr route)))])])
                     (setq subnodes (cdr subnodes))      ;; next child.
                     (go loop)))

(defun optimize (node bound visited)                     ;; optimize and-or graph.
  (prog (subnodes subbound route op-route cost)
        (and (or (null (setq subnodes (eval node)))      ;; no children?
                 (is-in node visited))                   ;; or node already visited?
             (return (list 0 node)))                     ;; return node with cost 0.
     loop
(and subnodes (SHOW 1 (car subnodes)))
        (cond
          [(null subnodes)                               ;; no more children?
           (return (cond [op-route                       ;; had optimal route?
                          (cons (car op-route)           ;; return it.
                                (cons node (cdr op-route)))]
                         [t (list bound)]))]             ;; return dummy.
          [(plusp (setq subbound                         ;; edge cost within bound?
                        (- bound (setq cost
                                       (node-cost subnodes)))))
           (setq route                                   ;; find optimal subroute.
                 (optimize-aux (car subnodes) subbound
                               (cons node visited)))
(SHOW 2 route)
           (cond [(< (car route) subbound)               ;; cost within bound.
                  ;; update bound and optimal route:
                  (setq bound (+ (car route) cost)
                        op-route (cons bound (cdr route)))])])
        (setq subnodes (cdr subnodes))                   ;; next child.
        (go loop)))
```

12.6
```
(defun search (node item visited)           ;; search a graph for an item.
   (prog (subnodes found)
         (cond [(eq item node) (return node)]    ;; found it?
               [(or (null (setq subnodes         ;; no children?
                                (eval node)))
                    (is-in node visited))        ;; already visited this?
                (return nil)])                   ;; is not there.
     loop
         (cond
               [(null subnodes) (return nil)]    ;; is not there.
               [(setq found (search (caar subnodes)
                                    item
                                    (cons node visited)))
                (return found)])                 ;; found it.
         (setq subnodes (cdr subnodes))          ;; next child.
         (go loop)))
```

13.1
```
;; add the following to the cond in der.
[(eq (car f) 'tan)                              ;; f = tan g?
 (lisy '* (der (cadr f))
          (list '^ (list 'sec (cadr f)) 2))]
[(eq (car f) 'cot)                              ;; f = cot g?
 (list '- (list '* (der (cadr f))
                   (list '^ (list 'cosec (cadr f)) 2)))]
[(eq (car f) 'sec)                              ;; f = sec g?
 (list '* (der (cadr f))
          (list 'sec (cadr f))
          (list 'tan (cadr f)))]
[(eq (car f) 'cosec)                            ;; f = cosec g?
 (list '- (list '* (der (cadr f))
                   (list 'cosec (cadr f))
                   (list 'cot (cadr f))))]
```

13.2
```
(defmacro opr (f) `(caddr ,f))                  ;; extract the operator of f.
(defmacro opd1 (f) `(car ,f))                   ;; extract the first operand of f.
(defmacro opd2 (f) `(cadr ,f))                  ;; extract the second operand of f.
(defmacro binary? (f) `(cddr ,f))               ;; f = (opd1 opd2 op)?
```

13.3
Only the factor diagram needs to be modifies. The modification will include `tan`, `cot`, `sec`, and `cosec` next to other unary operators (e.g., `sin`) in exactly the same manner. The clause starting with `memq` in the `cond` of `c-factor` should be changed to:

```
[(memq fcar                                   ;; unary operator?
       '(exp log sin cos arcsin arccos
             sinh cosh tan cot sec cosec))
 (list fcar (c-factor))]                      ;; operand is factor.
```

13.4
The clause starting with `memq` in the `cond` of `r-factor` should be changed to:

```
[(memq fcar                                   ;; head unary operator?
       '(exp log sin cos arcsin arccos
             sinh cosh tan cot sec cosec))
 (list fcar (r-factor))]                      ;; next factor.
```

13.5
Include the following in the `cond` in `reduce-unary`:

```
[(and (eq op 'tan) (zerop opd))    0]
[(and (eq op 'cot) (zerop opd))    'infinity]
[(and (eq op 'sec) (zerop opd))    1]
[(and (eq op 'cosec) (onep opd))   'ambiguous]
```

13.6
```
(defun deriv (n f)                            ;; nth derivate of f.
    (revert (deriv-aux n (convert ,(kwote f)))))

(defun deriv-aux (n f)                        ;; auxiliary.
    (prog (res)
          (setq res f)                        ;; initialize result.
       loop
          (and (zerop n) (return res))        ;; n=0?
          (setq res (reduce (der res))        ;; differentiate & reduce.
                n (1- n))                     ;; decrement n.
          (go loop)))
```

14.1
```
(defun *psubset (set1 set2)                    ;; proper subset.
   (and (< (length set1) (length set2))        ;; card set1 < card set2?
        (let [(eqf (*equalf (cadr set2)))]     ;; equality function.
           (apply 'and                         ;; every member of set1
                  (mapcar '(lambda (item)      ;; must be in set2.
                              (*member1 item set2 eqf))
                          (cdr set1))))))      ;; members of set1 .
```

14.2
```
;; set1 ∩ set2 = set1 - (set1 - set2).
(defun *intsec (set1 set2)                     ;; set intersection.
   (*differ set1 (*differ set1 set2)))
```

14.3
```
(defun *dunion (pset)                          ;; distributed union.
   (prog (du)
         (setq pset (cdr pset))                ;; drop the *s.
               du   (car pset))                ;; initialize du.
         (and (null pset) (return (list '*s))) ;; trivial case.
     loop
         (and (null (setq pset (cdr pset)))    ;; no more sets?
              (return du))                     ;; return du.
         (setq du (*union du (car pset)))      ;; include set in du.
         (go loop)))
```

14.4
```
(defun *pick (set)                             ;; pick one element from set.
   (cond [(cdr set) (cadr set)]                ;; nonempty set.
         [t 'NIL]))                            ;; return NIL when empty.
```

14.5
```
;; set1 ∩ set2 = {x : x←set1; x ∈ set2}.
(defun *intsec (set1 set2)                     ;; set intersection.
   (*iset x (x set1) (*member x set2)))

;; set1 - set2 = {x : x←set1; ~(x ∈ set2)}.
(defun *differ (set1 set2)                     ;; set difference.
   (*iset x (x set1) (not (*member x set2))))
```

14.6
```
(defun *dconc (pseq)                         ;; distributed seq. concatenation.
   (cons '*q
         (apply 'append
                (mapcar '(lambda (seq)
                                 (cdr seq))
                        (cdr pseq)))))
```

14.7
```
(defun *assign (obj idx newval)              ;; assign seq. or mapping.
   (cond [(eq (car obj) '*q)
          (rplaca (nthcdr idx obj) newval)]
         [(eq (car obj) '*m)
          (rplaca (cdr (*apply1 obj idx)) newval)]))
```

14.8
```
;;  map1 + map2 = [x → (if x ∈ dom map1 then map1(x)
;;                      else map2(x)):
;;                      x ← (dom map1 ∪ dom map2)].
(defun *merge (map1 map2)                    ;; merge two maps.
   (*imap x (or (*apply map1 x)
                (*apply map2 x))
            (x (*union (*dom map1) (*dom map2)))))

;;  map ⌉ set = [x → map(x) : x←(dom map - set)].
(defun *remove (map set)                     ;; remove set from map.
   (*imap x (*apply map x) (x (*differ (*dom map) set))))

;;  map⌈ set = [x → map(x) : x ← (dom map ∩ set)].
(defun *restrict (map set)                   ;; restrict map to set.
   (*imap x (*apply map x) (x (*intsec (*dom map) set))))

;;  map1 o map2 = [x → map1(map2(x)) : x ← dom map2].
(defun *compos (map1 map2)                   ;; compose maps.
   (*imap x (*apply map1 (*apply map2 x))
            (x (*dom map2))))
```

14.9
```
(defun *dmerge (mapset)                      ;; distributed map merge.
   (cons '*m
         (apply 'append
                (mapcar '(lambda (map)
                                 (cdr map))
                        (cdr mapset)))))
```

14.10
```
(defmacro *merger (rel1 rel2)                      ;; merge relations.
  `(*merge ,rel1 ,rel2))

(defmacro *remover (rel set)                       ;; remove set from relation.
  `(cons '*s (cdr (*remove ,rel ,set))))

(defmacro *restrictr (rel set)                     ;; restrict relation to set.
  `(cons '*s (cdr (*restrict ,rel ,set))))
```

14.11
```
(defmacro *one (dom pred)                          ;; extract one element.
  `(**one ,(kwote dom) ,(kwote pred)))             ;; designators and pred.

(defun **one ($dom $pred)                          ;; auxiliary.
   (prog ($x $s)
        (and (cddr $dom) (return nil))             ;; only 1 desig. allowed.
        (setq $x (car $dom)                        ;; domain variable.
              $s (eval (cadr $dom)))               ;; domain object.
    loop
        (and (null (setq $s (cdr $s)))             ;; domain exhausted?
             (return nil))                         ;; return NIL.
        (set $x (car $s))                          ;; next domain element.
        (and (eval $pred)                          ;; predicate holds?
             (return (eval $x)))                   ;; return element.
        (go loop)))

(defmacro *one! (dom pred)                         ;; extract unique element.
  `(**one! ,(kwote dom) ,(kwote pred)))            ;; designators and pred.

(defun **one! ($dom $pred)                         ;; auxiliary.
   (prog ($x $s $single $obj)
        (and (cddr $dom) (return))                 ;; only 1 desig. allowed.
        (setq $x (car $dom)                        ;; domain variable.
              $s (eval (cadr $dom)))               ;; domain object.
    loop
        (and (null (setq $s (cdr $s)))             ;; domain exhausted?
             (return (and $single $obj)))          ;; return unique element.
        (set $x (car $s))                          ;; next domain element.
        (and (eval $pred)                          ;; predicate holds?
             (cond [$single (return nil)]          ;; not unique.
                   [t (setq $obj (eval $x)         ;; record object.
                            $single t)]))          ;; 1 object found.
        (go loop)))
```

14.12

```
;; anti-sym(r) == (∀ (x,y)←r : (y,x) ∈ r ⇒ x=y)
(defun anti-sym (r)                                    ;; antisymmetric relation?
   (*all (pair r) (*imply (*member (reverse pair) r)
                          (*equal (car pair) (cadr pair)))))

;; part-order(r) == reflexive(r) ∧ anti-sym(r) ∧ transitive(r)
(defun part-order (r)
   (and (reflexive r) (anti-sym r) (transitive r)))
```

14.13

```
;; is-mapping(r) == (∀ (x,y)←dom r : card(x (r) {?}) = 1)
(defun is-mapping (r)                                  ;; relation is mapping?
   (*all (pair (*domr r)) (= (*card (*reln (car pair) r ?)) 1)))
```

14.14

```
;; recursives1() == {x : x←dom d; x ∈ d(x)}
(defun recursives1 ()                                  ;; self-recursive functions.
   (*iset x (x (*dom d)) (*member x (*apply d x))))
```

Bibliography

Abelson, H., and Sussman, G. J., 1985, *The Structure and Interpretation of Computer Programs*, MIT Press, Cambridge, MA.

ACM, 1986, Object-oriented programming workshop, *ACM SIGPLAN Notices*, Vol. **21**(10), pp. 1-192.

Aron, J. D., 1983, *The Program Development Process, Part II*, Addison Wesley, Reading, MA.

Banerji, R. B., 1980, *Artificial Intelligence: A Theoretical Approach*, North Holland, New York.

Barnett, S., and Cronin, T. M., 1979, *Mathematical Formulae*, Bradford University Press, Bradford.

Basili, V. R., and Baker, F. T. (eds), 1981, *Tutorials on Structured Programming: Integrated Practices*, IEEE EHO 178-4.

Bornat, R., 1979, *Understanding and Writing Compilers*, Macmillan, London.

Booch, G., 1986, Object-oriented development, *IEEE Transactions on Software Engineering*, Vol. **12**(2), pp. 211-221.

Burstall, R. M., MacQueen, D. B., and Sannella, D. T., 1980, HOPE: an experimental applicative language, *Conf. Rec. 1980 LISP Conference*, Stanford University, CA, pp. 136-143.

Comer, D., 1979, The ubiquitous B-tree, *ACM Computing Surveys*, Vol. **11**(2), pp. 121-137.

Cox, B. J., 1986, *Object Oriented Programming: An Evolutionary Approach*, Addison Wesley, Reading, MA.

ExperTelligence, 1986, *ExperLISP*, Expertelligence Inc.

Even, S., 1979, *Graph Algorithms*, Pitman, London.

Foderaro, J. K., Skowler, K. L., and Layer, K., 1983, *The Franz LISP Manual*, University of California, Berkeley, CA.

Genesereth, M. R., and Ginsberg, M. L., 1985, Logic programming, *Communications of the ACM*, Vol. **28**(9), pp. 933-841.

Harper, R., 1986, Introduction to standard ML, *Technical Report ECS-LFCS-86-14*, University of Edinburgh.

Henderson, P., 1980, *Functional Programming: Application and Implementation*, Prentice Hall, Hemel Hempstead (1980).

Hurley, W. D., 1985, An enhanced flavors environment for prototyping and knowledge aquisition, *Technical Report GWU-IIST-85-24*, George Washington University, WA.

Kernighan, B. W., and Plauger, P. J., 1978, *The Elements of Programming Style*, 2nd. edition, McGraw Hill, New York.

Kernighan, B. W., and Plauger, P. J., 1981, *Software Tools in Pascal*, Addison Wesley, New York.

Knuth, D. E., 1974, *The Art of Computer Programming*, Vol. 1, Addison Wesley, Reading, MA.

Kronfeld, W. A., 1979, Pattern-directed invocation languages, *Byte*, Vol. **4**(8), pp. 46-55.

Kowalski, R., 1979, Algorithm = Logic + Control, *Communications of the ACM*, Vol. **22**(7), pp.424-436.

McCarthy, J., Abrahams, P. W., Edwards, D. J., Hart, T. P., and Levin, M. I., 1962, *LISP 1.5 Programmer's Manual*, MIT Press, Cambridge, MA.

Meyer, G. J., 1978, *The Art of Software Testing*, Wiley, New York.

Meyer, B., 1982, Principles of package design, *Communications of the ACM*, Vol. **25**(7) pp. 419-428.

Moon, D., 1974, *MacLISP Reference Manual*, Massachusetts Institute of Technology, Cambridge, MA.

Parnas, D. L., 1972, On the criteria to be used in decoposing systems into modules, *Communications of the ACM*, Vol. **15**(12), pp. 1053-1058.

Parnas, D. L., 1979, Designing software for ease of extension and contraction, *IEEE Transactions on Software Engineering*, Vol. **5**(2), pp. 128-138.

Peterson, J. L., 1977, Petri nets, *ACM Computing Surveys*, Vol. **9**(3), pp. 223-252.

Rayward-Smith, V. J., 1983, *A First Course in Formal Language Theory*, Blackwell, Oxford.

Sedgewick, R., 1983, *Algorithms*, Addison Wesley, Reading, MA.

Shooman, M. L., 1982, *Software Engineering: Design, Reliability, and Management*, McGraw Hill, New York.

Sommerville, I., 1982, *Software Engineering*, Addison Wesley, London.

Steele, G. L., 1984, *Common LISP Reference Manual*, Digital Press, Bedford, MA.

Teitelman, W., 1974, *InterLISP Reference Manual*, Xerox PARC, Palo Alto, CA.

Temperley, H. N. V., 1981, *Graph Theory and Applications*, Ellis Horwood, Chichester.

Turner, D. 1982, Recursion equations as a programming language, *Functional Programming and its Applications*, edited by J. Darlington *et al.*, Cambridge University Press, pp. 1-28.

Turner, D. 1986, An overview of Miranda, *ACM SIGPLAN Notices*, Vol. **21**(12), pp. 158-166.

Varadharajan, V., and Baker, K. D., 1987, Directed graph based representation for software system design, *Software Engineering Journal*, Vol. **2**(1), pp. 21-28.

Winston, P. H., 1979, *Artificial Intelligence*, Addison Wesley, Reading, MA.

Winston, P. H., and Horn, B. K. P., 1984, *LISP*, 2nd. edition, Addison Wesley, Reading, MA.

Wirth, N., 1971, Program development by stepwise refinement, *Communications of the ACM*, Vol. **14**(4), pp. 221-227.

Wirth, N., 1976, *Algorithms + Data Structures = Programs*, Prentice Hall, Englewood Cliffs, NJ.

Xerox PARC, 1981, The Smalltalk-80 System, *Byte*, Vol. **6**(8), pp. 36-48.

Yau, S. S., and Tsai, J. J., 1986, A survey of software design techniques, *IEEE Transactions on Software Engineering*, Vo. **12**(6), pp. 713-721.

Index

', 12-13
`, 102
", 89-90, 118-120
,, 102
+, 13, 252
-, 13, 252
*, 13, 252
/, 13, 252
1+, 13, 252
1-, 13, 252
<, 32, 252
>, 32, 252
=, 32, 252

abs, 8, 252
abstract data type, 155
add1, 13, 252
alphalessp, 119, 252
and, 29, 43-44, 253
and-or graph, 184-188
anonymous function, 46-47
antisymmetric, 247
append, 23, 253
apply, 50, 253
arc, 167
arg, 107, 253
argument, 7, 37
array, 115, 253
arraydims, 116, 253
arrayp, 116, 253
assoc, 114, 253
association list, 114
assq, 253

atom, 5, 71-72
atom, 43, 253
autorun, 141
&aux, 108

backquote, 102
binary search, 173-175
binary tree, 171
binding, 9-11, 55-56
bottom-up design, 148
boundp, 120, 254
bound variable, 11
branch-and-bound, 184
breadth-first search, 169-170

car, 19, 254
car pointer, 56
catch, 124, 254
cdr, 19, 254
cdr pointer, 56
cfasl, 140, 254
children, 167
circular list, 63
clause, 40
clause predicate, 40
close, 91, 254
comment, 14, 151-152
Common LISP, 40
compilation, 135
compiler declaration, 137-139
compiler option, 136-137
concat, 120, 254
cond, 40, 254

conditional, 40-42
`cons`, 21-22, 254
cons-cell, 56
constraint, 213, 223
`cos`, 13, 255
critical route, 180
cross-product, 225
`cxr`, 117, 255

data structure, 167
data type, 208
`debug`, 129, 255
debugging, 127-132
declarative, 154
`declare`, 137, 255
decomposition, 148-151
`def`, 109, 255
default clause, 42
`defmacro`, 101, 255
`defun`, 34, 255
`delete`, 61, 255
`delq`, 255
depth-first search, 168-169
derivative, 192
design, 148
design criteria, 149-151
design iteration, 146-148
destructive, 60
`difference`, 7, 256
differentiation, 192
`do`, 79, 256
documentation, 151-152
domain designator, 213, 223
dotted pair, 67
`drain`, 256
`dreverse`, 256
`dsubst`, 60, 256
`dtpr`, 256
dynamic scoping, 39

edge, 167
element, 5, 215

empty list, 5
`eq`, 30, 256
`equal`, 28, 256
equality, 229
equivalence relation, 243
`error`, 121, 256
error handling, 121-123
`errset`, 122, 257
`eval`, 12, 257
evaluation, 7
`evenp`, 27, 257
existential quantifier, 232
`exit`, 16, 257
`exp`, 257
ExperLISP, 40
explicit, 208
`explode`, 120, 257
`exploden`, 257
expr, 97
`expt`, 8, 257

`fasl`, 257
fexpr, 97
file, 91
filter, 148
`fix`, 12, 257
`fixp`, 27, 257
`flatc`, 258
`float`, 12, 258
`floatp`, 27, 258
flow of control, 124
foreign function, 139-141
FORTRAN, 2
Franz LISP, 4, 87
free variable, 39
`funcall`, 49, 258
function, 7
`function`, 258
functional abstraction, 34
functional programming, 153, 241
function binding, 11, 55
function call, 7

Index

garbage collection, 66-67
generator, 213, 223
gensym, 258
get, 112, 258
getaddress, 141, 258
getd, 258
getlength, 116, 258
get_pname, 118, 258
go, 77, 259
graph structure, 178
graph theory, 179
greaterp, 27, 259

hash-and-link structure, 175
head, 18
HOPE, 154
hunk, 117, 259
hunkp, 259
hunksize, 259

identity, 30-31, 59
implementation, 146
implicit, 213, 218, 223
implode, 120, 259
impure, 66
indentation, 14, 152
infile, 92, 259
infix, 197
information hiding, 150
inheritance, 155
input, 87
instrumentation, 133-134
invalid data, 121
iteration, 76
I/O, 87

KRC, 154
kwote, 259

lambda, 47
lambda calculus, 153
last, 24, 260

leaves, 167
length, 24, 260
lessp, 27, 260
let, 47, 260
let*, 48, 260
lexical scoping, 39
lexpr, 107
LISP interpreter, 4
list, 5
list, 22, 260
listp, 27, 260
liszt, 135
load, 93, 260
localf, 138
local variable, 77
log, 260
logic programming, 154

macro, 99
macro expansion, 100
make-equivalent, 260
makhunk, 117, 261
mapc, 83, 261
mapcan, 84, 261
mapcar, 81, 261
mapping, 220
mapping function, 81-84
mark, 66
max, 12, 261
member, 25, 261
memq, 31, 261
min, 13, 261
minus, 8, 261
minusp, 261
Miranda, 154
ML, 154
mutual recursion, 74-77

name clash, 104
nested application, 8
nconc, 60, 261
neq, 31, 262

`nequal`, 28, 262
`nil`, 14
node, 167
`not`, 28, 262
`nreverse`, 262
`nthcdr`, 262
`nthelem`, 262
`null`, 27, 262
`numberp`, 27, 262
numbers, 6
`nwritn`, 262

object code, 135
object-oriented programming, 155
`oddp`, 27, 262
`onep`, 32, 262
optimal route, 180
`&optional`, 108
`or`, 29, 262
`outfile`, 91, 263
output, 87

parameter, 37
parent, 167
partial order relation, 247
Pascal, 2
path, 179
`patom`, 89, 263
pattern, 158
pattern symbol, 158-160
pattern variable, 162-163
Petri net, 190
`plist`, 112, 263
`plus`, 7, 263
`plusp`, 263
port, 91
`pp`, 92, 263
`pp-form`, 92, 263
precedence rule, 197
predicate, 14, 26
prefix, 194
pretty printing, 92, 235-239

primitive, 18
`princ`, 89, 263
`print`, 87, 263
procedural programming, 153
`prog`, 77, 263
`prog1`, 79, 263
`prog2`, 79, 264
`progn`, 79, 264
PROLOG, 154
property, 111-112
proprty list, 111
`putprop`, 111, 264

quantifier, 232
`quote`, 11, 264
`quotient`, 7, 264

`read`, 88, 264
`readc`, 264
read-eval-print, 94
recursion, 69-76
reduction rule, 203
refinement, 147
reflexive, 242
relation, 154, 225
`remainder`, 8, 264
`remprop`, 264
`remove`, 23, 60, 113, 264
`remq`, 31, 264
requirements, 146
`reset`, 15, 264
`&rest`, 108
`return`, 77, 265
`reverse`, 24, 265
root, 168
route, 179
`rplaca`, 62, 265
`rplacd`, 62, 265
`rplacx`, 118, 265

Scheme, 40

scope, 39
search strategy, 168, 174, 189
sequence, 215
`set`, 26, 265
`setarg`, 265
`setplist`, 113, 265
`setq`, 9, 265
s-expression, 5
`showstack`, 128, 265
side-effect, 10
`sine`, 13, 265
`sload`, 266
snapshot, 141
software engineering, 146
software tool, 147-148
`special`, 137
special symbol, 30
`sqrt`, 266
static scoping, 39
stepwise refinement, 146
storage, 65
`store`, 116, 266
strange atom, 89
`stringp`, 119, 266
structured design, 148
structure diagram, 148-149
structured loop, 79
`sub1`, 9, 266
`subst`, 24, 266
super bracket, 42-43
sweep, 66
symbol, 6
symbolic reduction, 202-203
symbol manipulation, 3

`symbolp`, 119, 266
symbol table, 177
symmetric, 243
syntax, 198-199

`t`, 14
`tab`, 266
table structure, 173
tail, 18
tail recursion, 71-72
termination, 15
termination condition, 70
`terpri`, 88, 266
`throw`, 124, 266
`times`, 7, 266
top-down design, 146-147
top level, 94
`top-level`, 94, 267
`trace`, 133, 267
tracing, 132-133
transitive, 243
tree, 167

unbound symbol, 11
universal quantifier, 232
UNIX, 4
`unspecial`, 137
`untrace`, 133, 267

value binding, 11, 55
valid data, 121
variable, 11

`zerop`, 32, 267